Marion Toolsey

JULIO

The Unsung Story

JULIO

The Unsung Story

Daphne Lockyer

A BIRCH LANE PRESS BOOK
Published by Carol Publishing Group

First Carol Publishing Group Edition, 1997

A Birch Lane Press Book
Published by Carol Publishing Group
Birch Lane Press is a registered trademark of Carol
Communications, Inc.

Editorial, sales and distribution, rights and permissions inquiries
should be addressed to Carol Publishing Group, 120 Enterprise
Avenue, Secaucus, N.J. 07094

Carol Publishing Group books may be purchased in bulk at special
discounts for sales promotion, fund-raising, or educational
purposes. Special editions can be created to specifications. For
details, contact Special Sales Department, 120 Enterprise Avenue,
Secaucus, N.J. 07094.

First published in Great Britain by Simon & Schuster Ltd

Manufactured in the United States of America
10 9 8 7 6 5 4 3 2 1

Library of Congress Cataloging-in-Publication Data

Lockyer, Daphne.
    Julio : the unsung story / Daphne Lockyer.
        p.   cm.
    "A Birch Lane Press Book."
    ISBN 1-55972-394-7
    1. Iglesias, Julio, 1943–   . 2. Singers—Spain—Biography.
I. Title.
ML420.I35L63   1997
782.42164'092—dc21
    [B]   96-50934
                                                        CIP
                                                        MN

Acknowledgements

Julio Iglesias is a man who has given countless interviews. Nevertheless, very little is known about the more private side of his life and his nature. Perhaps because of his intent to keep this side – the left-hand side, shall we say – shrouded from view, he has always refused offers to participate in biographies written about him.

Since, however, on another contradictory level, he also loves publicity and notoriety, he made it plain when approached to give an interview for this book that, though he did not want to be involved personally, he would not oppose the project either. Nor, he said, would he advise others not to speak with me. It was, he said, entirely up to each individual that I approached to decide for themselves.

'It is better,' he concluded, 'for people to write about you than to ignore you.' For this sentiment and for the fact that, because of it, avenues of inquiry remained consistently open to me, I am extremely grateful.

I am grateful too, for those who agreed, on this basis, to share their knowledge of Julio Iglesias with me. In particular, Dr

Iglesias Puga whose candour, humour and honesty on the subject of his son were at times rather startling. Thanks, too, must go to Isabel Preysler, who guided me past the Spanish paparazzo camped outside her magnificent Madrid home, welcoming me not just into her living room, but into the world of vivid memories which she retains of her marriage to Julio – none of which she has ever shared with another interviewer.

Alfredo Fraile's testament was to prove equally important. His insights and understanding of Julio gleaned after fifteen years of turbulent and intense friendship were to form an indispensable part of this book.

Equally indispensable were interviews given to me by Gabi Fominaya, who continues to live at Benito Gutierrez, and who spoke to me of Julio's childhood in that place as though it had occurred yesterday. Likewise, Enrique Bassat's vivid recollections of Julio during his Cambridge days were an unexpected and very much appreciated bonus.

For other contributions, great and small, thanks also go to Fernandez Cecilia Fernando Valls, Gerry Davis, Alvaro Rodriguez, and Jesus Hernandez (who proved to be a font of Julio-useful telephone numbers). I am likewise indebted to Feliciano Fidalgo and Gabriel Gonzalez, who both took time away from their busy careers to meet with me, and to Fernan Martinez, for his wealth of outrageous Julio anecdotes which added light and laughter where sometimes it seemed that Julio might become all sadness and shadows.

Given the difficulties of often having to work in what was for me a second language, I am eternally grateful to Concha Montalban, who was on hand during interviews to find words that I could not and to interpret the subtleties of the Spanish language. She was both a first-rate interpreter and tireless and brilliant researcher.

Translation advice and help was also received from my Spanish mother, Julia, who – for love rather than lucre – spent hours at my side wading through recorded interviews, as did my brother, Peter. His knowledge of Spanish was invaluable as was that of Marbella-based English journalist Nigel Bowden, who tracked down and interviewed Maria Edite Santos on my behalf. In this same vein thanks are also due to Graham Terse in Paris for his attempts to track down both Gwendoline Bollore and Sydne Rome.

The task of writing this book would have been infinitely more difficult had it not been for the excellent efficiency of the IPC magazines cuttings library and the National Sound Archive, who answered endlessly obscure Julio questions with good grace and humour. In Madrid, the news agency EFE gave me access to their mountainous supply of Spanish newspaper cuttings as did the *Hemeroteca National*, while in New York Dudley Freeman's excellent cuttings service also came to my aid.

Thanks are also due to Titi Alvarez for allowing me to quote extensively from her interviews with Virginia Sipl, to José Antonio Olivar for his permission to quote from his interview with Isabel Preysler and to R.L. Torrente Legazpi for permission to reproduce material from his interview with Priscilla Presley.

There were times when it seemed to me – and to those close to me – that this book would never reach completion. But, kindly, my dearest friends – Sue, Wyn, Steve, Tara, Jim, Lisa, Louisa, Richard, Helen, Steve B, Andy, Deb, Wayne, Sarah and Shannon, constantly avoided questions of the 'Is It Finished Yet' variety and uttered only words of encouragement. For this, many thanks are due, just as they are to journalist and biographer Garry Jenkins, whose faith sparked my involvement in the project in the first place and whose unswerving friendship, support and advice saw me through many a dark hour.

It was Garry who first introduced me to his own editor, Helen Gummer, who was to become guardian of this biography. Her understanding of when to apply pressure and when to leave well alone seemed at times almost psychic. Her support, humour and confidence in the project were utterly invaluable.

Lastly my heartfelt thanks and love must go to my children, Jessica and Frankie, and to my partner Martyn Palmer. The latter soothed, believed and, ultimately, sub-edited into the wee small hours on my behalf. All three of these characters, who are central to my own life story, saw both the right and left-hand side of my nature during the writing of this biography – and stuck with me all the same. For this no thanks can ever be enough.

For Martyn, Jessica and Frankie

*Behind the success of every human being there is always
a profound bitterness. A profound loneliness. If I wasn't
completely conscious that this bitterness, this loneliness and
angst is the fuel that makes me creative then I would be a
complete* desgraciado. *A ruined man.'*

(Julio Iglesias, 1984)

Prologue

South of France, 31 November 1981

In the glass and marble lobby of the Meridian Hotel in Nice, the hyenas are waiting. Members of the international press – the latter-day posse – prepare for a lynching. Tape recorders are being loaded. Pencils sharpened to dagger points. Lenses are being snapped onto cameras like a magazine of bullets is snapped onto a machine gun.

He is here. They know it. After all, three 'members of his entourage' – tall blondes, cheekbones like shoulder blades, eyes Côte d'Azur blue, bellies tighter than tarpaulin – have just clack-clacked across the veined marble on long, stilettoed, unveined legs. Wherever there is smoke there is fire. Wherever there is Julio there are blondes. You can guarantee it.

Behind them, incongruously carrying a pink leather vanity case – belonging either to one of the blondes or to a Barbie-Goes-to-the-South-of-France-on-Holiday doll – comes one of Julio's bodyguards. Reputedly, he has twenty-two of them – so, hey, he can spare one for the girls. This one is hand picked for his ability to look as though he has crunched on human bones for breakfast. He smiles malignantly at the shuffling corduroy-and-leather-clad photographers. Is that human flesh between his broken teeth?

No time to ponder, here comes Julio's manager, Señor Alfredo Fraile, to announce that Julio will receive them all on the rooftop terrace overlooking the Mediterranean. He is now departing his sixth-floor suite and will meet them up there. The hyenas head for the lifts, cram themselves inside and ride to the top with shoulders hunched to ears. The doors open with a ding and they spill onto the terrace where they spy Julio in the far corner, gazing wistfully out to sea as though recalling a moment of tender intimacy with a love now far away in a distant land. With Julio, who knows which one of the many she could be?

He is awoken from his reverie by the general caffuffle and his teeth – the bright white of the meringue clouds that hang suspended above the still-blue November ocean – flash a welcome. Despite the time of year, he is bronzed. He is a Spaniard dressed with the casual ease of an expensive Italian: butter-soft leather bomber jacket, slacks, white shirt and cashmere scarf. He does not wear cologne, preferring, he says, the animal smell of both himself and of women. He is a Latin icon made flesh.

His arms open to the newly arrived press in the gesture of a Mafia godfather preparing to embrace an errant member of the 'family' now and have him garrotted later – which is, no doubt, what will also happen to any photographer failing to stick to the rules that govern such encounters with Julio. No one, but no one, must take a picture of his left profile. Or else.

This is why he has placed himself on the far flung corner of the terrace. Let anyone attempt a left-hand shot of his face and they will fall directly into the ocean. The French photographers, who know the code of old and have been charting his meteoric progress since the mid seventies, assume their correct positions on the terrace like Pavlov's pre-programmed pups. The British snappers, on the other hand, who know nothing more about their subject than the fact that their wives are going ga-ga over some Cole Porter song – 'Begin the Beguine' – that Julio has recently warbled into the British charts, are not impressed. 'Aye?' grunts one. 'What's he going on about? Why can't we take his left-hand profile?'

And the answer is both terrifyingly simple and complex all in one go. 'Because,' says Julio, 'I do not want those who have their illusions about me to lose them.'

Illusion, of course, was to form a large part of Julio's success, as it does with all legends (which is precisely what Julio became for millions of fans worldwide). Julio the Latin Lover; Julio the Tragic Hero; Julio the Superman flying constantly around the globe conquering new territories.

But what did the left and the right sides of his face have to do with any of this? And what possible illusion might be shattered if some rogue photographer caught him unawares and showed his 'wrong' side to the world?

Julio himself would talk vaguely about the differences between one side and the other. The left eye was too weak, the nose on the left a little bent, perhaps. He would reiterate one of the many ritualistic mantras that make up his conversations in interviews. 'If a man does not know his good side from his bad side then he knows nothing about himself.'

His own towering self knowledge on this front could make him, as one publicist puts it, 'difficult.' On a tour of Australia in the mid eighties, for example, he turned up for the Ray Martin chat show insisting that the host's own desk be shifted to face the other way so that he, Julio, could give his good side to the camera. At a White House dinner in which he was to sit between Ronald and Nancy Reagan, he deliberated endlessly about which of the duo should sit on his right and which on his left, finally engineering it so that Ronald – the most important of the two – should sit on his left side. This way, whenever Julio turned to talk to the President he would get the right-hand side of his face in sharper focus. There are tales, too, of photographers attempting left profile shots being manhandled by burly security chaps and beefy bodyguards and there is the classic story about a 1994 reunion of Julio's old Real Madrid team-mates at Maxim's of Paris.

'Julio seemed okay. Very important and famous, of course, but not that different from the guy we had known all those years ago,' says footballer Fernandez Cecilia. 'There was one odd thing, though – he had this complex about what side of his face the camera could shoot him from and we all had to move around the table so that he was always in the right place for the photographers. And it was the same when we did the group pictures. We thought it was funny, you know. We thought it was a joke. But Julio was dead serious about it.'

Obviously, for Julio it was not a laughing matter. Nor was it an attempt to appear eccentric or showbizzy. There were many madnesses conjured up for him by marketing people over the years to make him appear more interesting than the average normal human being. But this was not one of them. It was real. He had a genuine paranoia about exposing the left side of his face.

It was all the more bizarre because to the average person – and even to photographers who look at such things with an expert eye – the left side of Julio's face was pretty much like, well, the right side. But what the hell did they know? For to Julio, regardless of the physical reality, the left side had come to represent everything that he felt was weak and bad, or small and wrong about his personality and the right side was all that was strong and noble, heroic and loyal, and good. The left and the right became the perfect metaphor for the extremes of his personality and of his life. He took the obsession to extremes. Even when fans approached with their Kodaks, Julio would allow himself to be pecked on both cheeks but would offer only his right profile to the camera.

'He would pose for a fan, showing only his good side as though the picture were for the cover of *Time* magazine,' says Julio's former press chief, Fernan Martinez. 'And why? Precisely because you never know where any picture might end up.'

'Julio has this idea that if a photographer took a picture of the left-hand side of his face and duplicated it, then put it together to form a whole, the world would see the image of a monster,' says Fernan Martinez. This says a lot about Julio's view of himself and his dark side, but nothing about the way that those who have known him actually perceive him. To them he is not a monster – or even a potential one – he is a human being with superhuman strengths and superhuman failings. They all end up loving him just the same.

'Julio is the best person in the world . . . and also the worst,' observes Gabriel Gonzalez, who has known the singer for the last twenty-six years. 'You want human qualities then Julio has the biggest in the world. But you want failings then Julio has these as large as mountains too. This is the way he is.'

Julio's personality became one of shadows and light. So much so that, somewhere along the line, he began to split the rival characteristics off, to keep them at bay from each other. In so doing he was splitting his own nature.

He could be generous and kind and loyal to his friends. He could be charming, cultured and utterly charismatic. He could be loving, funny and tender. On the other hand he could be faithless, fickle, possessive and controlling. He could be prey to searing bouts of depression.

Those who know him best – really know him – have seen all sides of his nature, often staying longer with him than was perhaps healthy for them, because, so often, Julio's good qualities outweighed his flaws. What is astounding is that, regardless of the dark side of Julio's nature, friends and ex friends continue to talk about him with affection. It is a rare associate indeed who has nothing good to say of him. They rarely speak negatively about Julio and when they do, it is done with compassion and with the understanding that he has never been the happiest of souls, that his life presented him from the outset with extraordinary difficulties. It is also usually balanced out by something positive.

The world loves Julio – that is not the issue. The issue is whether or not Julio loves or even likes himself.

The myth makers are happy if the world perceives Julio as sad. It is part of the legend. It pleases them that women – who make up the bulk of his fans – perceive him as the lonely guy soulfully singing to himself in an echoey chamber. It is part of the myth, but it is also part of the reality. For there is certainly a side of Julio – the left-hand side, shall we say – that can never be happy, that constantly seeks and fails to find contentment, that is made all the more unhappy, the more successful the singer becomes.

'Julio,' says Alfredo Fraile, his former manager and close ally, 'is a man who feels somehow that the more he gains, the more he is losing. He has spent his life becoming a success and his sadness comes not just from his life experiences, which have been hard and terrible at times, but from a feeling that he has achieved the wrong things.

'I give you an example. In Miami, when they had finished building my house, which was close to Julio's, I invited some intimate friends and all my family to a housewarming. It was a beautiful evening, with love and friendship all around. I looked up and suddenly I see that Julio, who was one of the guests, had left the room and I went in search of him. Finally I found him. He was sitting on the jetty that was part of our house, looking out to sea. I went and sat beside him – two grown men dangling our legs into the water – and I look at Julio and he is crying. So I say to him, "What is it Julio? What's wrong?" And he looks at me and says, "Alfredo, I envy you so much. I envy your family and your happiness and your life. I am a man with everything – and nothing."'

Right side, left side all over again. It is certainly not beyond the bounds of belief that Julio saw himself in the following way: On the right side: my life is complete, I have more money than I ever dreamed of; I have international success; I have women flocking to my bed. I am one of the most successful recording stars of all time. But on the left: I have made a mess of my marriage; I have not been a good father; I have deserted all those who genuinely loved me for myself in favour of those who applauded the myth and knew nothing about me. I am a failure.

The schizophrenia of it was, at times, unbearable, which was why Julio continued to place the different aspects of his nature in compartments and to hide them in the shadows under the left-hand side of the bed. Yet, try as he might to keep the dark side of his nature in obscurity, he knew, too, that it was a vital part, not just of who he was, but of his success. Without the dark side he would not have been Julio Iglesias International Singing Star. He would have been just anybody.

'Julio used this sadness because he knew that it made him a creative person and he was one of the most creative men I ever knew in my life,' says Alfredo Fraile. 'He was always at his most creative when he was at his saddest. It was part of what made his creativity tick.'

It was also, at times, an affectation, a plea for sympathy, a way of getting a woman into bed or millions of them to buy a record. And he would use it shamelessly.

Photographer Gerry Davis recalls how he frequently took pictures of Julio in the early eighties: 'He was funny and charming. He was a wonderful guy. But he definitely wanted things done his way. We'd done a shot where he turns quickly to the camera, right profile first, and points at the lens, and he really liked that shot – so much so that every time I went to take pictures of him he wanted to repeat it.

'I think he liked it because it had caught a certain mellow-ness, a sadness perhaps. It made him look kind of soulful – which I guess was the image he wanted in all his pictures. But the funny thing was that I used to take these pictures back to my dark room and develop them and when I looked closely at them, I could see that his eyes were smiling at me, twinkling – laughing at me and everybody, really. It made me wonder what the joke could possibly be.'

The joke, in the end, was that nobody – not the cameras, not the fans, not the friends, not the people who loved him – could ever know him completely. The joke was that when he seemed saddest, he was often happiest and vice versa; when he appeared to be opening his heart to you, he was doing precisely the reverse and keeping it under lock and key. The contradictions went on and on.

If only he continued to keep the left side of his face from view no one would ever know him completely. But they could try. They could certainly try.

Chapter One

Julio José Iglesias de la Cueva was born at Madrid's old and now defunct maternity hospital at the Calle de Meson de Paredes on 23 September 1943. It was the last day of Virgo, the sign which is said to bless all those born under it with artistic, sensitive natures but to damn them also with moodiness, intransigence and the neuroses of the perfectionist. By definition, Julio's birthday was also on the very cusp of Libra – symbolized by a set of scales which constantly seek, but never quite find, equilibrium. Those born under its influence are lovers of beauty and peddlers of charm. They need to be adored and praised more than any of the other eleven signs of the Zodiac. They are fickle in love, ambitious in their careers, charismatic but never entirely trustworthy. They make tremendous world leaders – or schizophrenics. It all depends on how life rolls the dice for them.

Ultimately, Julio's nature was to fuse all the good qualities and failings of both houses – to be a divided spirit that exists half in the bright light of success and half in the gloom of the shadows. But on that day – 23 September 1943 – the late summer sun beamed for him, frying away every whisper of cloud in the blue Madrid sky. At the Avenida Cinema a queue, hoping to escape the relentless post Spanish Civil War doldrums, was forming to watch the matinée performance of *Buffalo Bill* starring Gary Cooper and Jean Arthur, and on billboards throughout the city, adverts trumpeted the arrival of Hollywood's latest offering, *Only Angels Have Wings*, introducing its newest star, Rita Hayworth.

Elsewhere in Europe, which remained in the grip of the Second World War, dramas of an infinitely more epic and tragic kind were unfolding. In Italy that week Allied troops had conquered San Cipriano, Monlecovia and Potenza and in Germany Goebbels pronounced that 'everything is possible in this war, except for the capitulation of the German people.' In Auschwitz, the final solution was attempting to dissolve an entire race. In the Far East, Allied troops were dying deaths of unthinkable brutality in Japanese concentration camps.

But in Spain, the people still struggled to come to terms with a recent war in which brother had killed brother and in which half a million people had died. Julio's own grandmother, a descendent of the noble de Perinan family, had, they said, died from starvation during the conflict. But for Julio's mother, Rosario de la Cueva, the issue on that day was of life and how to bring it successfully into the world.

It wasn't easy. And this despite the fact that Rosario – or Charo as she is universally known – was in the best possible hands. Her husband, Julio Iglesias Puga, though still in his twenties, was already a brilliant and highly acclaimed gynaecologist. In the fullness of time he would deliver the babies of Spain's most influential families – a veritable *Who's Who* of the good and the great. 'If you gathered together every baby that my father has delivered it would fill Madrid's Plaza de Toros,' Julio is fond of telling visiting interviewers. 'He was the stork's pastor. He was the best.'

Unlike others fathers then, who in those days were happy

to pace the corridors of alien maternity hospitals, Julio senior was on home territory, in the very hospital where he went daily to work. It seemed natural to him – though perhaps a little odd to others – to minister to his own wife along with his boss, the chief consultant of the maternity hospital. He had no way of knowing that the delivery of his own son would prove to be one of the most difficult, medically and emotionally, of his career.

'Charo,' he recalls, 'was just not built to deliver babies. The pregnancy was normal and happy, but when it came to the delivery, things were so bad that we called a priest to give the last rites because it was touch and go whether she would make it.

'The problem was that though her contractions were strong, even hours and hours of labour failed to dilate her cervix and so Julio remained wedged inside her.

'We had to make the difficult decision to perform a Caesarean – which in those days was by no means the standard procedure that it is today. In those days we didn't even have penicillin. But it was either that or lose both Charo and Julio.'

The decision made, Charo was given a hasty anaesthetic. Her belly was swabbed with vinegar and sliced open. In a gush of water and blood, Julio was tugged abruptly into the world, face first and eyes open.

According to his autobiography, which was ghost written for him by the journalist Tico Medina in 1981, at 2 p.m, the moment of birth, he exercised his lungs, as all babies do. But not for the first time. Charo, he says, had heard her baby cry when he was still in her womb. 'They say that these children who cry in the womb and are heard from outside before birth, are, later, privileged beings. Although ultimately they also become the most solitary – albeit that they are surrounded by a multitude – and unsatisfied beings on the earth.'

The description of *in utero* wailers serves Julio's own

poetic image of himself – the image of the solitary sad guy whose fame and privilege serve only to alienate him from the world. The image which has sold him to the fans – and sold his records too. Further, it helps to know that the same unlikely phenomenon is documented in the life of Napoleon Bonaparte who like Julio set out to conquer the world only, some would say, with a lot less success.

The fact is that no babies – not even Napoleon and Julio – ever cry in the womb. It is physically impossible for them to do so. But who cares? The story is simply one of the anecdotes which add to the Julio mythology. And Julio is nearly as good at creating his own mythology as he is at selling records.

Myth and counter myth, indeed, form the backbone of his life. 'In later years,' according to Alfredo Fraile, who helped, indeed, to create that very mythology, 'people would come to me and tell me something or other about his life and I would josh with them, "who are you trying to kid? I invented that story for the press pack on our last tour. Don't come to me telling me these things about Julio as though they really happened. Get out of here."'

But the myths and inaccuracies continued: that Julio is a qualified lawyer, whereas, in fact, he failed part of his final exam at Murcia University and never qualified; that Julio studied law at Cambridge University, when, in fact, he had a brief spell in England, first in Ramsgate (never mentioned for its blatant lack of glamour) and then at Bell's Language School in that hallowed university town – not to study law but to improve his English; that he had once been a professional goalkeeper for Spain's most famous soccer team, Real Madrid, whereas, in fact, he had been recruited on the junior reserve team, and never made it to the professional first eleven.

But the biggest myth of all was the image of Julio Iglesias as the product of a perfect, happy, loving family. Just as his

mother, Charo, carries the scar of his delivery, which is said
to still ache and grieve her during inclement weather, so Julio
bears the burden of his childhood – as the psychiatrists he
was to consult later in his life to unravel the mysteries of
his depressions, insecurities and infidelities, could doubtless
vouchsafe.

But does it, after all, take a psychiatrist to work out that
Julio Iglesias did not ultimately become a happy man,
because he was not a happy child? That coming from a
family where relationships were so dysfunctional meant that
life ever after was never likely to be easy.

Certainly, it was an interesting family to have been born into
– a family with roots deep in Spain's history. On his father's
side, Julio's ancestors came from Galicia (hence Julio's tribute,
'Un Canto a Galicia', which he recorded in 1971, and the fact
that in 1992 he was reputedly paid £1.5 million to appear on
a series of adverts promoting the area). Dr Iglesias, the fifth
of seven children, was born in Orense, the capital of the
province. 'But because my father was a colonel in the army
and was stationed at various places, all of us were born in
different cities – one in Santander, for example, another in
Toledo and the little ones in Tangiers. Though all of us felt
that we were Galicians.'

Julio's grandmother, Manuela, too, had come from an
influential and wealthy family of Galician landowners. 'She
was a very handsome woman,' Dr Iglesias recalls. 'And at
the time when she met my father he was a very handsome
and rather arrogant lieutenant.

'In those days to be an officer in the army was the most
prestigious job that a young man could have. So Julio's
grandmother, who was very beautiful and full of herself
and Julio's grandfather, who was handsome and successful
and full of himself too, married. And we seven children were
the result.'

Julio's grandfather, Ulpiano, was a vehement monarchist and staunch supporter of Alfonso XIII. When the King left and Spain became a republic in 1931, a law was passed decreeing that all those in the army who were not in favour of the republic could retire, not just with honour but with promotion. 'So my father accepted the offer and retired from the army with the rank and pension of a general,' Julio's father says.

'We moved to Madrid and he became a pharmacist with his own pharmacy. But all his life he never lost his military spirit or his passion for politics. He was born a monarchist and he died that way.'

During the Spanish Civil War he, and indeed his entire family, suffered for their political beliefs. Dr Iglesias was seventeen when the war broke out and already in his second year of medical studies. He describes his political beliefs, then as now, as those of a Conservative Catholic. 'But in those days there were reds and blues and if you weren't on one side then you were on the other.'

Julio senior became a card carrying member of Falange – the Spanish Fascist Party – though he claims that he never considered himself a fascist, per se. 'I signed up because I felt that we had to fight the communists who were killing us and bringing anarchy to our country, but I was never an active member of the party. I joined to show solidarity and to swell the ranks. But I gave as much thought to joining as you might to drinking a glass of water. I was a young guy who was only really interested in study and in sport. But I was punished for my political affiliations.'

In the political panic that gripped all Spain, Iglesias senior, along with other members of his family – his father and brothers – were identified as fascists and imprisoned. On several occasions they narrowly escaped execution by firing squads. 'My survival and that of my brothers was largely due to my ability to talk my way out of even the most perilous situations,' he recalls.

He could not, however, talk himself out of the prison at Aranjuez – some forty-five kilometres south of Madrid – where he was incarcerated for the duration of the war. After three years of imprisonment he emerged as a fortunate member of the Civil War's winning team and took up where he had left off – both professionally and personally.

He had already met Rosario de la Cueva y de Perinan before the outbreak of war, when they were both in their teens. 'She was not just a pretty girl, she was completely exceptional. The kind of girl who today could have won a Miss World contest,' Julio's father recalls. 'I was crazy about her.'

Charo's pedigree was that of a 'top drawer' girl. Her father was the well known Andalusian journalist and playwright, José de la Cueva, and her uncle Jorge was equally famous in the same profession. Politically, they were centre right. 'But they had the liberal views of intellectuals,' Julio's father says.

Charo's mother, Dolores de Perinan Orejuela de Camporedondo, on the other hand, was a direct descendant of Spanish nobility. Her uncle was the Marques de Perinan and her cousin, also a marques, was the Spanish Ambassador to London for twenty years.

Two centuries earlier, the last Spanish governor of Puerto Rico had been a Camporedondo and was related to Charo on her mother's side. He married a native of that country and it is now possible to trace Puerto Rican blood in both Charo and in Julio.

Julio's parents had met in 1935 at a dance run by a tennis club – of which they were both members – in one of the rich suburbs of Madrid. 'After that, Charo and I and a gang of friends would meet to play tennis and go to dances. But then the war came along and broke everything. When I was in prison I knew absolutely nothing about her – not even whether she was dead or alive. But I never stopped thinking about her and as soon as I got out of prison I went to find her, to pick up where we had left off.'

He found her still living at the same address but saddened by a war which had claimed her mother, Dolores, in 1938 and left her in charge of running a household and caring for her brother and sister. 'Strangely, she seemed plumper than I remembered her. But then in those years of hunger people ate anything they could get – rubbish food – and sometimes more of it than was good for them. It was a psychological response to the fact that you never knew where your next meal was coming from.'

The couple became official *novios* – girlfriend and boyfriend – which granted them the freedom to step out together unchaperoned, but no more. Julio senior immersed himself in his studies and by the age of twenty-two had qualified as a doctor. Knowing that he could now independently support a wife, and possibly a family, he and Charo married early in 1943, 'I was very much in love with her and in those days you married to liberate yourselves from the control that your parents still had over your lives.'

Dr Iglesias and his virgin bride lived first with his parents at the Calle de Luchano, moving six months later to the Calle Altamarino, in Madrid's Arguelles district, an upper-middle class part of town not far from the Parque del Oeste. Here, well-to-do families – including the Iglesias family – lived in luxurious city apartments. It was to this apartment that Charo brought home her new son and, being the devout Catholic that she was and is, prayed for a happy and harmonious family life.

The accident of our birth is something utterly beyond our control. Of all the events in life it is the most random. On the surface, at least, it seemed that Julio had been blessed.

He had been born into an affluent, professional middle-class family – the son of a man who was already beginning to wield influence in high places. 'The wives of anyone who was anyone were my patients,' the elderly and now retired gynaecologist confesses proudly. 'All of them at some time or another owed me one.'

The Iglesias family were among the privileged few and to prove it, Julio's father was the first in the neighbourhood to own a Mercedes. 'They always seemed to us to be a cut above,' recalls Ricardo Martinez, a schoolfriend of Julio's who lived in the same neighbourhood, or *barrio*. 'There was something glamorous about them. We were good friends with Julio because you couldn't help liking him and he wasn't stuck up in the least. But you never forgot that his family was special. We all felt that way.'

Certainly when the *años de hambre* (the hungry years) hit Spain in the late forties the Iglesias family were largely unaffected. After the Second World War had ended, the United Nations introduced a trade blockade against Spain's fascist dictatorship in 1946, and a widescale famine threatened. In Julio's home city of Madrid, trolley buses and trams stopped for an hour in the morning and an hour and a half in the afternoon to conserve energy. Cats and dogs disappeared from the streets, having either starved to death or been eaten. And in the countryside poorer peasants lived off boiled grass and weeds. But in the Calle Altamarino, where Julio spent the first three years of his life, there was always food on the table. 'It is not my fault that I never suffered hunger,' Julio says in his autobiography, before adding mysteriously: 'But then there are other hungers that toughen you up as well as not having bread to put in your mouth.'

What could these metaphorical hungers have been? Certainly not the hunger that arises from lack of parental love. By all accounts, both mother and father in their different ways, doted on their small son – a hypersensitive child who would cry and laugh at the least provocation; a child who was capable of feeling ecstatically happy and profoundly unfortunate by turns.

Nor did they love him any less when, eighteen months after his birth, a second son, Carlos, arrived on the scene. 'There was never a lack of love for either of the two sons,' recalls Gabi Fominaya, who became a kind of surrogate sister to the two boys. It was rather the lack of love – or the effects of a passionate love that had turned bitterly poisonous – between Charo and Dr Iglesias that underpinned and undermined their young lives. 'That,' the fiercely protective Gabi admits, 'could not have been easy to deal with.'

The rather tedious sidestreet architecture of Calle de Benito Gutierrez is relieved by the slightly surreal, almost Daliesque building at number 27. Unlike the flat façades of most of the other shops, bars, offices and apartments which line the street, the frontage of number 27, with its collection of black wrought-iron balconies arranged at muddled and jaunty angles, is a work of an eccentric creator.

It was to this building, right around the corner from their old apartment at Altamarino, that the up and coming Iglesias family moved in 1946 when Julio was three years old. It was the building that he was to regard as home right up until his marriage in 1971.

Inside, the rooms are spacious, high ceilinged and marble floored. Black shutters protect the inhabitants from the fierce Madrid sun, which in the summer roasts city dwellers with temperatures of up to 40 degrees centigrade. The same shutters also serve as protection from the prying eyes and ears of passers by. Fortuitous, perhaps, in the case of the Iglesias family.

Not that Dr Iglesias and his wife were given to high pitched rows and saucepan throwing. The marriage which had started with the passionate innocence of youth became instead a kind of cold war, falling apart by degrees in silent desperation.

'Charo did her very best to make the boys' home life as normal and happy as she possibly could,' comments Gabi, whose family occupied one of the apartments in the same building. 'She was always there. She lived for her children.'

Still, given the circumstances, the front she presented to the world required Oscar-winning efforts. And though Gabi, for example, never remembers a conversation with either Julio or Carlos about the reality of their parents' marriage – 'It was something we all knew about but didn't talk about' – the truth is that Charo's attempts to present the perfect, middle-class idyll convinced no one, especially not her sons.

'In the neighbourhood we would see Julio's mother, who always looked to us like a magazine model, glamorous and high class and with her head held high,' recalls Ricardo Martinez. 'But the truth was we felt sorry for her.' According to Martinez, she was widely considered to be *una buena madre*, which in Spain has a double meaning. It means, literally, that she was a good mother, but it also implies that she had to be good to put up with the behaviour of her errant husband. In other words, it was common knowledge that Julio's father slept around.

As a woman, of course, Charo had been born at an appalling time in Spain's machoistic history – a time of institutionalized discrimination. Right up until 1975 – after Franco's death, when Spain abolished the concept of *permiso marital* – when a woman married she was obliged to accept Article 57 of the Spanish Civil Code which stated that 'the husband must protect the wife and she must *obey* her husband'.

John Hooper, in his portrait of Spain, *The Spaniards*, paints the picture thus: 'Without her husband's say so, a wife could not embark on any sort of activity outside the home. She could not take a job, start a business or open a bank account. She couldn't initiate legal proceedings, enter into contracts or buy and sell goods. She couldn't even undertake a journey of any length without her husband's approval . . . Leaving the family home for even a few days constituted the offence of desertion, which meant – among other things – that battered wives could not take refuge in the homes of their friends or relatives without putting themselves on the wrong side of the law. And although adultery by either sex was a crime punishable by between six months and six years in prison, there were different criteria for men and women. Adultery by a woman was a crime whatever the circumstances, but adultery by a man only constituted an offence if he committed it in the family home, if he were living with his mistress or if his adulterous behaviour was public knowledge.'

But while the law said one thing, it was common for middle-class men to have any number of mistresses. 'Anyone who could get away with it, did it,' says Dr Iglesias. 'With a lot of couples that I knew, the husband was a womanizer and the wives turned a blind eye. It was quite usual. The way I see it, I was a womanizer, but even when I was sleeping with other women I loved Charo. Nothing really bad was happening, after all. She could have put up with it a bit.'

Charo, however, was not the 'putting up with it' kind. She had made her vows to Julio's father believing firmly in the sacrament of marriage. She had hoped to enjoin her life with a man just like her father, José, who had been a devout Catholic and a faithful husband. Instead, she married Julio Iglesias Puga – who, by his own admission, was incapable of fidelity.

'I admit, now, that the marriage failed mostly because I liked to play away from home. I liked girls a lot – just like Julio – I liked to work hard and to play hard and Charo couldn't forgive the womanizing, she just couldn't forget it.

'Slowly, slowly the hurt was incubating inside her until, eventually, she reached a moment when she stopped loving me. I used to try to have a relationship with her but she didn't want to know. I would come back from work early to be with her and she would be somewhere else. Maybe, at that time, I was still in love with her but when I saw that she was deserting me inch by inch I fell out of love with her too. By the time the boys were ten years old I had fallen in love with someone else – a woman who was my mistress for years. The situation between Charo and me had become impossible, but we stayed together for the sake of the boys.'

Julio and Carlos, in the meantime, tiptoed through the ruins of their parents' marriage. According to Dr Iglesias, they were never subjected to rows at home. 'But then,' he adds, without the faintest trace of irony, 'I have always been a very proper man. If I wanted to sleep with a woman I made sure it was between seven and ten o'clock at night or else I would tell Charo that I was going away to a study seminar for the weekend and I would take a woman with me.

'I didn't tolerate fights at home in front of the children and I made sure that they never saw me out in public with any of my girlfriends. Though I realize now that people, so-called friends of theirs, probably teased them about having seen me out and about with women who were obviously not my wife. And, probably, in some way it affected them . . .'

It was doubtless for the best that Julio senior and Charo only ever inflicted their marital woes on two children – though if Charo had been given her way there would have been others. When pregnant with both her sons she fervently wished that each would be a daughter. That she never gave birth to a girl was a consuming regret. 'I think perhaps that's why I became so close to Charo,' says Gabi Fominaya.

After the birth of Carlos in 1945, however, Dr Iglesias saw

to it himself that this would be her last pregnancy. 'When Carlos was born, Charo had exactly the same problems as she had with Julio,' he says. 'Again, she nearly died during the delivery. Again we called the priest.'

This time, however, while she was still under anaesthetic, her husband and Dr Iglesias's immediate boss at the obstetric unit took the extraordinary decision to sterilize her.

'My boss said to me, "So what do we do, Julio, do we sterilize her or not?" And I thought about it. At the time Charo and I liked to make a love a lot, but she was like a rabbit, she was one of those women who would become pregnant every time we did it. I didn't want people to think that I was deliberately making her pregnant to kill her or something – so I thought it better for the sake of her health to say "yes". So we tied her tubes there and then and, of course, from that day onwards she was never able to have children. It was a purely gynaecological decision and Charo never complained about it afterwards.'

That Charo herself was not even consulted was symptomatic not just of those times but of the very nature of the relationship that had existed between her and her husband from the outset. 'I think it's fair to say that Charo was completely annulled in that marriage,' comments Isabel Preysler who later, when she married Julio Junior, gained a first-hand understanding of the psychological effect that such an annulment had on the entire family. 'Charo,' she adds, 'just simply didn't exist, you know. It was always the father who decided everything – did everything.' Charo, in the meantime, had to do the cleaning of the house and the cooking and she used to look after the boys. Then he would come home and he used to complain that he didn't like the way she did anything. She was made to feel that she did everything wrong.'

The drip, drip effect wore away at her slowly. By the time Isabel knew her in the seventies she was 'a person who seemed very unfortunate in her life. She was one of those sad women who has come to love tragedy. They're always crying and they're always depressed. She was bitter, but then with the life she'd had you couldn't blame her really. Perhaps, in her position. I would have been the same.'

Chapter Two

Outside the Colegio de Los Sagrados Corazones, mothers are loitering by the gate waiting for the school bell to announce the end of lessons. In a few minutes the doors will open and spill forth a torrent of overenergetic boys of various sizes onto the pavement of the Calle de St Martin de Los Heroes – just across the way from the Iglesias apartment. Charo, dressed immaculately as always, her face carefully made up, stands slightly aloof from the others.

The daily ritual of collecting her small sons must be observed at all costs. 'They had a maid, Maria Luce,' recalls Gabi Fominaya. 'But it was always Charo who would go to the school gates to meet the boys. She never missed.'

She would spot first one son and then the other. Julio, who was pale and scrawny, with matchstick legs and untameable wiry hair, and Carlos with his honey-brown skin, softly angled body and large brown puppy eyes. 'There was never any question which one of them had the looks,' says Gabi, 'and I think Julio used to suffer a lot on that account.'

Charo, however, was careful not to show a preference for either son. She would squat down, arms outstretched to greet them, and plant anxious kisses repeatedly on their cheeks.

'I don't think there's any question that the more our marriage fell apart the more she invested in her sons,' Dr Iglesias says. 'Her love for them was extraordinary. It was, in some ways, a smothering love.'

Outside the school gates, Julio would accept the outpouring of affection as his friends looked on, nodding and winking. Then, like Carlos, he would take his mother's hand as she walked slowly and regally back to Benito Gutierrez, which was no more than 200 yards away.

'She was so striking to look at and so carefully turned out that on the walk back from school, men in the street would turn and look at her and there would be wolf whistles on all sides,' says Isabel Preysler. 'As a child, Julio hated this, for men to admire his mother. He hated for her to wear make-up or for her to come to school, as she often did, wearing a dress that was low cut and revealing. Later, when we were married, it was a sort of obsession with him – he couldn't bear for me to wear anything that showed a cleavage because, I suppose, it stirred up the feelings he'd had about his mother.'

These feelings, of course, were bound up with the usual male fixation with Madonnas and whores – which dominated the macho Spanish culture in which Julio was raised and underpinned his family life.

His father, after all, worked on the unspoken assumption that infidelity is wholly acceptable if you continue to 'love' your wife and to exalt and deify her as the mother of your children. You must set her aside from the 'whores' that you betray her with and no damage will be done. But to fulfil this ludicrous male fantasy, she must be stainless, blameless and virginal. Certainly not a sexual being in her own right.

This was confusing to Julio, who gazed upon his mother's curvaceous form, her archly painted ruby lips, her pencilled eyebrows and saw the theory falling apart. He wanted his mother to be the Madonna, just as he later required it from his wife. But Charo was human. Made of flesh and blood. Furthermore she had a passionate nature that had once allowed her to love her husband and which now consumed her sons.

Early on, Julio responded to his mother's overbearing love as most children would. 'When he was a little boy he adored her the way that all little boys adore their mothers,' Isabel Preysler says. 'But over time, because of the situation in that family, the relationship became complicated. Things began to fall apart.'

In the early years, of course, Julio's mother did what she could to protect her sons from the fallout of her despairing marriage. Julio and Carlos lived lives not unlike the other children at number 27.

'There were about eleven of us in all, with ages ranging from three to seven,' remembers Gabi Fominaya. 'We would play in the street or on the stairs. We lived in each other's places the whole time, though I was especially close to Julio's mother and would break away from the other children to be with her. I would follow her around like a little shadow.

'Perhaps for her I was the daughter that she's always wanted and never had. We were so close that she would even take me on holiday with the boys – we would go away for six weeks at a time to Plencia one year and to Galicia the next.

'Julio's father would arrive for a spell then leave again to go back to work in Madrid – but to me he was a shadowy figure. My main recollection was always of Charo with the boys when they were little. Charo on her own. Whenever you went to their home it was always Charo either cooking or cleaning, just being a mum, you know. Obviously I don't know what was going on beneath the surface, but certainly in those early years, the home seemed happy to me – and the reason for it was Charo.'

In those days the mother and her two sons appeared to present a united front against the world. Life revolved around the home, the strict Catholic school, run by priests, that both Julio and Carlos attended from the age of five, and the world of religion in general.

'Even now Charo is still a devout Catholic and the boys were brought up in the same way,' says Gabi. 'Often Charo's father, José, who was one of the kindest men you could meet, would come over. He would hoik one of the boys onto his shoulders and we would all go off to Mass together at the chapel in Julio's school. Again, I don't have any recollection of Julio's father ever going with us.'

In the early days, there is no question that Julio and Carlos were close – not just in age, but emotionally – though the usual rivalries existed between them. 'I do think, for example, that Julio had quite an inferiority complex about his looks compared to Carlos. Carlos was an exceptionally beautiful child with thick dark hair and beautiful long eyelashes. I think Julio got sick of people saying how lovely his brother was,' Gabi contends.

'I remember on one occasion in particular, when we were on holiday, his mother saw Julio turning away in pain when more people had come over to make a fuss of Carlos, and because she loved him so much she suffered for him. His aunt was with us at the time and Charo said to her, "Look, can you say something nice to Julio? Because it's really a bit much the way everyone pays Carlos attention all the time."

'So the next morning, at breakfast, his aunt came down and she looked at Julio and said: "My, you're looking handsome today, Julio, and so smart." And he didn't smile or look pleased or anything like that. He said, quite crossly really, "Come off it. My mother told you to say that."'

What Julio lacked in looks, however, he made up for in personality and there is no question that, skinny and spotty as he was when a teenager, girls loved him. 'You could never have called Julio good looking,' recalls schoolfriend Ricardo Martinez. 'But when we played football at school and he was in goal, all the girls from the Convent of Santa Ana, which was just around the corner from the Sagrados Corezones, would come and cheer for him. We all used to say to him, "So, what the hell have you got, Julio?" It was a mystery to us.'

What he had – apart from the obvious, fervent desire to gain more attention than Carlos – was an odd kind of charm. 'And girls always responded to it,' recalls Gabi. 'He could charm the pants off anyone.'

In the early days, when his career was in its infancy and he was still living at home, Gabi recalls how she could never get into the building without running a gauntlet of girls all keen for a look at him, a peck on the cheek or an autograph.

'To us, who knew him well, it was sort of weird and funny. Quite ridiculous really. But I can tell you now that it frightened his mother to death,' says Gabi.

In terms of women, the relationship between Julio and his mother was the first and most formative of his life. But long before he began to experience the delights of fame, fans and groupies, it had already taken on severely negative undertones. These would affect all his relationships with the opposite sex.

Precisely when the mutual adoration society between mother and son was replaced by an unspoken disharmony no one can say. There was no precise moment.

It was, rather, a gradual process – just like the drip, drip dissolution of the Iglesias marriage. By the time Julio wrote his autobiography in 1981 he was able to declare that though he had the usual feelings a son should have for his mother, it was his father who had been, without question, the person who had shaped his life with an enduring influence.

Somewhere along the line, it seems, he made a decision to

be on his father's team. 'And in the war that existed between the parents you had to be on one side or the other,' says Isabel Preysler. 'The parents were split, you see. It got to the point where they couldn't stand each other and so the children were split too. Carlos decided he would be with his mother and Julio decided he would be with his father and they were on completely separate sides. The two Julios on one and Charo and Carlos on the other.'

Unfortunately, however, it was an unequal war. 'Julio's father was the one with the career and the contacts and the power and later, when Julio became famous and successful, he had power too. So then everything had to be done the way they wanted it done,' Isabel continues. Charo and Carlos found themselves on the losing side.

But surely it was more than just the will to win that motivated the dynamics of the relationship between Julio and his mother? More even than the natural affinity that Julio and his father had for one another, an affinity which arose from the knowledge that they were hewn from the same block, that they *were* each other. There had to be more still to explain why Julio and his mother found themselves on opposing sides of the war. In his autobiography, again, there are the usual red herrings offered up as to what may have gone wrong between Julio and his mother. There are anecdotes, for example, told with infinite drama, about how Charo would, when Julio was naughty or failed to make the grade at school, lock him in the maid's tiny bedroom or in the bathroom for hours at a time. According to Julio, he would scream, 'Mama! Mama. Let me out. I'm suffocating. I'm dying!' His mother would be impervious to his cries.

Eventually, according to Julio he would be released, sweating and shedding hysterical tears. He would run onto the balcony filling his lungs with the air of freedom.

It's an interesting vignette, but one which Julio's father, for example, contradicts. 'The truth is,' he says, 'that Charo never disciplined the children. She could never say no to them, she was completely soft with them and if it hadn't been for me reining them in they would have been wild.'

Perhaps it was not Charo's strength that ultimately alienated her son, but her weakness in continuing to live under the same roof, sharing the same bed as the man who broke his marriage vows to her whenever the opportunity presented itself. Could it be that he lost respect for a mother who did not respect herself enough to fight and, in so doing, he lost respect for all women and never quite managed to regain it? It certainly seems possible.

The foundations of Julio's personality were laid, brick by brick, in those early years at number 27 Benito Gutierrez. Unconsciously and imperceptibly – the way that all personalities are built. But whatever was occurring deep in the young Julio's psyche, externally at least he struck all that knew him as a normal, happy kid. 'If Julio had problems he never talked to us about them,' says Ricardo Martinez. 'He seemed pretty happy to us.'

That he didn't talk to others did not, however, stop people talking about him and his family. According to Martinez: 'People knew about the situation at home with Julio's dad, yet Julio didn't seem to know anything about what was going on – or if he did, he never said so. We used to joke that he was so innocent and gullible that if we'd played football with him, we could have used him as the ball – kicked seven shades out of him – and he wouldn't have known the difference.'

More likely, Julio was all too painfully aware of his parents' predicament. Later, as an adult, he was to admit in an interview: 'Ever since I was three or four years old I would see that the relationship between my father and mother was not a good one. I think that's why I spent all my time away from the house.' But that he chose to present a brave face in public was entirely typical. Even then he was intent on being perceived from the metaphorical right side rather than the left. If he had problems, he was not prepared to share them with the other kids. Like any child, he wanted to be just the same as everyone else.

During his toddler years he would ride his tricycle up and down the street, the veins in his temples throbbing with the effort of going faster than the rest, heedless of his mother's cries to slow down.

As each summer school holiday arrived, Julio and Carlos would prepare for the long vacation away from Madrid. Charo complained that Galicia was too cold and from 1951 the family would holiday regularly in Peniscola – a mediaeval walled town on the Costa del Azahar. Here, Julio says, the family became an institution. Certainly, the two boys building castles on the beach and turning cartwheels in the sand as their mother looked on was a familiar sight. It was in Peniscola that Julio learned to ride his two-wheeler, performing feats of derring-do for applauding onlookers. He could ride with no hands, and perform death defying wheelies. He was, he says, a magician, a veritable circus act. People joked with him that they took their vacations in Peniscola just to see the son of Dr Iglesias riding a bike. Julio, of course, loved the attention – loved to be centre stage, even then.

Back at school, after the long summer, Julio would immerse himself in that other talent that singled him out from the crowd – football. He would stand between the goalposts, dancing restlessly from foot to foot, puffing air into his gloves, waiting for his moment to shine.

Later, in his autobiography, Julio pondered his motives for becoming a goal keeper. He was drawn, he said, to the fact that it was the goalie who had the most responsible position in any football team. He loved the idea that a game could be won or lost depending on his performance. Loved the idea, too, that in the most dramatic moments of any match all eyes would be on him.

In a school which nestled in the shadow of the Real Madrid training ground – and in which sporting powers mattered as much as academic talent – Julio's talents did not go unnoticed. By the age of five he was in the school junior team, already outclassing every other player. 'He certainly knew how to save goals,' says Ricardo Martinez.

As each school year drew to a close, the priests would loosen their garrote-like grip on the school, becoming almost friendly towards their pupils. Julio would be invited to play in goal in matches organized between teachers and other visiting teams of priests. An honour never before or since conferred on a pupil. The priests would run around the field, still wearing their long dark robes, sweating profusely and trying to boot the ball past Julio. Trying and generally failing.

Everyone, including the priests, liked Julio. He was a jock, a lad, someone whose personality radiated restless energy. He was always at the centre of whatever was going on – slapping his mates on the back, flicking his towel at them in the changing rooms.

Academically, however, he took his place behind most of his classmates, displaying none of the brains of either his father or his brother Carlos. His best results were invariably in literature and in art, while in Maths he was the dunce of the class. He was, he said in his autobiography, moved by all that was poetical, aesthetic or lyrical, while the world of science and logic left him cold.

If it were, he would have been given more opportunities at school to exercise his artistic as well as sporting capabilities. He was, after all, a child who loved books, and going to the cinema with his mother, who was herself a movie fanatic. With the showman qualities he displayed in the goal mouth, and later on stage, he would have been ideal for school plays. But, unfortunately, leading roles were handed out as rewards for those who did well in class. Julio's academic performance normally earned him roles as semi-animate objects – trees and so forth.

Attempts to join the school choir, too, were apparently thwarted and the story about how the choirmaster, Father Anselmo, threw Julio out after hearing him sing his first note has now descended into the Julio legend and is frequently trotted out in press packs. The story may or may not be true. At any rate, the legend goes that, on hearing Julio sing, Father Anselmo counselled him to stick to football – adding, in a staggeringly unprophetic way: 'Singing is not for you.'

In truth, however, in those days it was not. Julio followed the good Father's advice and concentrated his efforts – and dreams – on the football field. On his bedroom wall were the cherished posters and autographs of his footballing heroes – Alfredo Di Stefano and Ricardo Zamora, the latter being still cited by Julio as the greatest goalkeeper in Spain's history. All the snot-nosed kids of the area dreamed of one day being Zamora or one of his colleagues on the Real Madrid team. 'But Julio was the only one of us who ever stood a chance,' says Ricardo Martinez.

To prove the point, early in 1959 when still fifteen, Julio attended trials at the hallowed Real Madrid ground, the legendary Bernabeu Stadium, where he had stood on countless occasions in the crowd, cheering and dreaming with his father and Carlos. Julio was one of hundreds of hopefuls whose ultimate schoolboy fantasy was to pull on the white jersey of their Real Madrid heroes. The selectors obviously liked his style and he won a place as junior reserve goalkeeper in May of that year – no mean achievement considering the numbers desperate to try and break into a club who dominated European soccer. 'From the outset Julio always made it look kind of easy,' recalls Fernando Valls, who was one of Julio's Real Madrid contempories. 'He was a showman, you know. He would spin the ball around on the tip of his finger before booting it back into play. He was agile and daring. He always went for the ball, even in the most impossible situations. He definitely had what it might have taken to go all the way to the top.'

Back at Benito Gutierrez and at school, the news that he had been signed on schoolboy terms for the majestic Real Madrid won him fresh admiration from his friends. 'He'd always been popular,' recalls Alfredo Fraile, who not only later became his manager, but was also one of his schoolmates. 'But after joining Real Madrid he became a kind of local hero – someone that people looked up to. Maybe that was his first real taste of success and adulation and he never stopped needing it.'

Julio's life began to revolve around the football stadium and the thrice weekly training sessions run by the well-loved Enrique Martin Landa, the junior squad coach who died in 1992. 'The guy was like a father to all of us,' recalls Valls. 'He loved us all and we loved him right back.' Enrique would keep a tight rein on the boys. 'Cigarette smoking and drinking was forbidden and before each game we all used to say Mass. 'But we were an ordinary bunch of guys and probably none of us stuck to the rules. Julio, I'm sure, was just like the rest of us. Just what you'd expect from a teenager.'

Along with his school chums and the usual gang from number 27, Julio also began to hang out with some of his team-mates. 'Though his friends were mainly boys that came from well-to-do families like his own,' recalls another player, Fernandez Cecilia. 'He didn't have that much to do with the others who came from more working-class backgrounds.'

There was, however, sport between all the players both on and off the field. 'There was a lot of leg pulling and stick meted out between the players. And sometimes you had to be quite tough to deal with it,' says Valls. 'On one occasion I remember walking up to the stadium with Julio and another friend from the team. This friend and I were both singers in a choir and we started practising a Zarzuela – which is a traditional Spanish song – while we were walking towards the stadium.

'Anyway, Julio started singing too and we both stopped in our tracks, looked at him and advised him to shut up. Because as far as we were concerned he couldn't sing to save his life. Though, when you look at it, the career he ended up in made fools of us both.'

Still, the teasing and sometimes brutal banter which existed between team players could at times be merciless. For example, though Julio has confessed to being a skinny, pale guy with hair that stood up like a porcupine, he has never mentioned the acne which plagued him and which, according to Valls, was a constant source of cruel amusement to his team-mates. 'It was so bad that when he took off his shirt the other guys would take one look at him and say his back looked like a paella. It wasn't kind and he definitely had a complex about it.'

Not that it put Julio off his stride with the girls, who in those teenage years of rocketing testosterone became and remained a fixation for him. 'Even when he was already in his twenties a group of us would go out for a drink and we would joke with Julio that if we put a curly wig on top of a broom he would probably fall in love with it, he was so crazy about girls,' recalls Antonio Barahona, Julio's first official photographer and sometime friend.

There may have been some truth in this, though in terms of relationships he was never interested in just anyone but only in girls he imagined he could never get. Indeed, the more impossible the conquest the more deeply in love Julio would fall, not just as a teenager but throughout his life. Even as late as 1990, he was propounding the hard-to-get theory to journalist Chrissey Iley. 'It's so much better to love than to be loved. If someone loves you very much, you couldn't give a damn about them. Oh no, not them on the phone again. You want to be the one who is going, "Please, please, come on. Come on. Ring." I need that challenge.' But even in his teens, there were, as Ricardo Martinez testifies, plenty of willing girlfriends waiting on the touchline for Julio. But these were only ever regarded as ego boosters of the most dismissible kind. Their very eagerness meant they could never be serious contenders for Julio's affections.

Infinitely more interesting were the likes of his first love, who is remembered in his autobiography, and indeed by all those still living in the neighbourhood, simply as Maria. Her blonde hair and piercing blue eyes singled her out from the other girls with their sultry dark looks. Julio later recalled that all the boys were in love with Maria in that stupendously painful adolescent way. Each of them hoped to make her his.

Ricardo Martinez recalls that Maria became part of their gang. 'In those days in Spain, unless you were engaged officially to a girl it wasn't the done thing to go out with her on your own. So we went out in gangs, though everyone accepted that Julio and Maria were girlfriend and boyfriend.'

According to Ricardo Martinez, the relationship ended in tears. Maria, he says, finally left the *barrio* when she became pregnant. 'And none of us ever knew what became of her.' Nor, he says, did anyone know for a fact who the father was.

At the Colegio de Los Sagrados Corazones, however, Martinez states that there was a kangaroo court held to determine whether or not Julio had been the guilty party. But the fact that he remained at the school and was never expelled seems to imply that he wasn't – or at any event that no one could prove it.

Despite this, Martinez claims that at a fiesta, after sharing several jugs of sangria with friends, Julio bragged to his consorts that he had indeed been the father of Maria's child. 'Though no one believed him because none of us had even been to first base with a girl let alone got her pregnant. It was just the kind of thing that Julio would say to make himself look big to us.'

Julio's father has no recollection of the scandal and further adds that if Julio had said such a thing to his friends it would have been a complete lie. 'I happen to know for a fact that Julio was still very much a virgin at the time and that he remained that way until he was over twenty.' Julio could lie to his friends but never to his father. There was no aspect of Julio's life that his father was not privy to. Even the most private.

Chapter Three

The road from the small holiday town of Majadahonda winds like a serpent through mountain and forest towards Madrid. Cars journeying along its ten kilometre stretch swing from bend to bend in frantic loop-the-loop patterns, their back tyres spraying gravel as they go. At Plantio, half way home, the road doubles back on itself in the mocking shape of a horseshoe or an ear-to-ear smile. Not for nothing is it known by locals as the bend of death. On 22 September 1963, it nearly claimed the life of Julio Iglesias.

At the time, of course, Julio was a young man who appeared to have everything to live for. Just one day shy of his twentieth birthday, he was a rising star at Real Madrid and by now a law student at the Colegio Mayor de San Pablo. He was, everyone agreed, a guy with a future.

He had driven to Majadahonda in the sporty red Renault Dauphine car that had been a present from his father – the kind of gift that went with the rich kid lifestyle that he enjoyed. He and his friends, Enrique Clemente Criado, Tito Arroyo and Pedro Luis Iglesias (no relation), had been to the town for the annual fiesta in which youths proved their manhood and sexual prowess by chasing normally docile cows and taunting small bulls in the plaza. They had eaten outdoors, run with the young bulls and danced with every willing, pretty girl in the town square. None of them, however, liked to drink and if they did it was always the barest minimum.

Sportsman that he was, Julio was clean-living to the point of boredom. Moreover, at that moment he was within sight of realising his ambitions at Real Madrid. It was well known that the selection chief, Puskas, had his eye on the promising young goalie and Julio had recently astounded the powers that be by stopping one of the great di Stefano's legendary penalty kicks during a practice session. Things were looking promising for Julio and he had no intention of jeopardising his future or his fitness with drink.

At around 2 a.m. the four friends made their way back to the car, breathing in the misty air of the already approaching autumn. Julio, insisting he was fit to drive, turned the key in the ignition and felt the engine come to life. As he released the clutch and squeezed the throttle, the car growled and headed for home. The boys relaxed, wound down their windows and relived the highlights of the night. Who had been the bravest? Who had kissed the prettiest girl? Fired up, perhaps, by the macho rite of passage that Majadahonda and all Spanish fiestas represent to boys on the brink of manhood, Julio squeezed the throttle a little more and the others fell silent as the speedometer climbed from 40 to 70 miles per hour.

Enrique Clemente, who was not just a friend of Julio's from school but also a Real Madrid goalie, playing for the first eleven rather than the reserves, sat in the passenger seat, his foot pressed to an imaginary brake pedal. As the lethal hairpin approached, Tito Arroya spoke tersely from the back seat, fear registering in the staccatoed syllables with which he advised caution. 'Careful, Julio, brake a little. Don't accelerate, this is a very dangerous bend.'

'Don't worry, just sit back and watch an artist at work,' Julio yelled joyfully. His foot danced on the accelerator before hammering it towards the floor. He approached the bend of death at full throttle.

The car's speedometer registered 100 – just as Julio realized that the bend was beyond his and the car's capabilities. He remembers attempting to tug on the steering wheel and feeling it slip from his hand. He remembers the machine-gun sound – tac-tac-tac – as the car hit the series of cement pillars that bordered the bend, felt the back wheels seize and skid out of control before the car lurched and double somersaulted down a steep incline. The impact of its landing split the Dauphine in two and wedged it deep into the soil. In the eerie stillness that followed, the headlights continued to shine into the misty darkness while the ghostly sound of a dance band on the car radio mingled with the creck-creck of cicadas.

In the slow motion in which each of us is said to perceive the few seconds before our potential death, Julio's mind had flashed inconsequentially to the holiday he had spent that summer with his parents and Carlos in Peniscola. As he surveyed the slight morning dampness of the mottled tarmac, from the eccentric upside down position of the topsy-turvey car, he thought of the rain-drenched roads of Galicia where he would drive with his father when, as they often did, they would leave Charo and Carlos in Madrid to go away together. Just the two of them. The ever-winning team.

Having fully expected to lose his life, he was shocked to find himself still wedged in the driver's seat, white-knuckled fingers gripping the steering wheel, eyes gazing unblinkingly into the mist. He noted with shock the lack of visible injury. He wasn't bleeding or bruised. He looked around and saw that his three friends had been thrown out of the car – or had jumped. He listened intently for signs of life.

Slowly his three friends began emerging from the shadows with their clothes torn and covered in dust. One limped a little from a cut leg, another was bleeding from a wound on his face, another complained of backache. Julio, too, registered that his chest ached a little . . . and his spine. But nothing major. The three of them congratulated themselves on being alive.

Still shocked from the accident, however, they abandoned the bisected car and headed off in silence on foot to the first public telephone box they could find – at a nearby bar, which opened its doors to the visibly shaken and dishevelled band. Julio noted again with wonder how, of all the three friends, he appeared to be the least physically affected by the accident. Even his clothes seemed unmarked.

He telephoned his father's clinic, knowing that Dr Iglesias would not be there in the small hours, but asking for help from the night staff. They sent a car to pick the boys up and tended to their various wounds at the clinic before taking each of them home. It was 4 a.m. before Julio arrived back at Benito Gutierrez and explained the sorry saga to his parents. As usual, Charo wept and Dr Iglesias wagged his finger. 'I told Julio he was totally inconsiderate and that in future he would have to be more careful,' he says. 'But, the truth is that mostly we were just glad that he was alive.'

The trouble started shortly after the Majadahonda car crash. Julio had begun his university course early in October and was establishing a routine for the week whereby he would attend lectures each morning and train for Real Madrid in the afternoon. Tuesday, Wednesday and Friday the amateur reserves would meet at the Ciudad Deportiva (Sports City) and on Thursday it would be at the Bernabeu Stadium – where Julio, by all accounts, would do his best to ingratiate himself with the first team stars, slapping them on the back, feigning a camaraderie with them to impress the rubber-neckers who would constantly turn up at the ground.

Julio thanked God he was alive and threw himself into football with renewed vigour. He ran, jumped, produced miracle saves in the goal net. Counted his blessings. Then, at the end of October, the pain started.

It was, initially, an intermittent but agonizing pain – the sensation of a needle stabbing deep into Julio's flesh and penetrating to the very bone of his spine. Within weeks the pain became more and more constant – a raging monster that threatened to consume him. He couldn't sleep, he could barely breathe with the pain.

'Julio came to me and complained of this weird pain, which was obviously becoming worse by the day. He was grey with the pain. He was dying with it. For a father to see his son this way is a terrible thing,' Dr Iglesias recalls. 'He had always been a healthy boy – an athlete. But I could see the gravity of his condition written on his face. I rang every specialist that I knew and called in every favour I was owed to try to find out what was wrong with him. Sometimes if someone gives you an explanation for what is causing your pain then you can deal with it. But it wasn't to be that easy for us.'

By the end of October, Julio and his father had already consulted every major specialist in Spain. They carried out tests, took X-rays, passed him around from one to the other like Julio and his team-mates might pass a ball. None, however, was able to find a physiological cause for the pain and even suggested that Julio was suffering from psychosomatic illness. In the meantime, Julio continued to swallow painkillers by the handful. The pain was now so intense that, Dr Iglesias recalls, one afternoon Julio sneezed violently and was so pole-axed by the agony in his spine that he collapsed unconscious on the floor.

'It was totally obvious that my son was not suffering from a psychological disorder. He was in real physical trouble,' he says. 'But when no one can tell you what the hell is wrong, what do you do?'

The tests continued but to no avail. By November, Julio, who was persisting with his football career, began to notice that apart from the pain, which had become his constant companion, he was also losing power in his legs. Trainer Enrique Martin Landa would joke with him that he was a lazy, rich layabout who was shirking his training – all the while expressing concern to the powers that be at Real Madrid that something was seriously wrong with the promising young goalie. As indeed it was.

By December, Julio began to notice that he felt unsure on his feet. His father recalls with clarity how on one occasion just before Christmas, his son attempted to leave the apartment, but as he stepped onto the pavement his feet and legs gave way and he fell down. 'By this stage we were getting desperate and we had already seen maybe fifty doctors. But it was becoming clear to us both that there was a real physical reason for Julio's pain. I would watch him attempting to train at the ground and it was heartbreaking because he was not the same kid. He would be running and wincing with the pain and he had no reflexes left.'

The round of X-rays and tests continued. Christmas came and went, clouded by a fog of pain. Like so many sufferers of chronic pain, he recalls that he now felt as though it were a part of him. His best friend. It had taken him over body and soul. Then New Year 1964 dawned and on that very morning the pain became so vivid and excruciating that Julio simply could not bear it any longer. He was being destroyed by the pain and surrendered to it, screaming and crying for death.

Julio continued suffering until 6 January – the festival of the Reyes Magos, a day on which Spanish children traditionally receive their Christmas gifts and a day of great celebration throughout the country. Julio was unable to get up from his bed and also, according to his father, was unable to urinate.

A committee of specialist neurosurgeons was called to Benito Gutierrez, leaving their family celebrations to attend Dr Iglesias' son. Among them was Dr Franco Manero, resident neurosurgeon at Madrid's famous Caudillo Hospital. Manero concluded that Julio must be admitted as an emergency case since the patient was clearly suffering from a serious spinal compression that X-rays had failed to locate.

'In those days diagnostic methods were a good deal less advanced than they are today,' says Dr Iglesias. 'And I heard with horror Manero's recommendation that we should perform the Tiodoro on Julio.'

The Tiodoro was a relatively new technique, whereby a red liquid was injected into the nape of the neck and allowed to flow down the length of the spine while its progress was monitored by X-rays. Its purpose was to detect a blockage in the spine being caused by a growth or tumour. It was rarely used because of its potential dangers and was nicknamed 'the rabbit's death' since it required a patient to remain perfectly still like a rabbit frozen in the headlights of an approaching car. One movement, the medical team warned, and Julio would die. Julio had always longed for drama in his life but now he was about to star in his own potential tragedy.

Julio was transferred to Zero Block in Madrid's Eloy Gonzalo Hospital and was in a critical condition on arrival. He was taken immediately to the room where the investigation would take place. His father, as always refusing to be excluded from proceedings, was to be with him.

In his autobiography, Julio describes his fear at seeing the long needle that would pierce his spine, without an anaesthetic to dull the pain since the investigation required the patient to be fully conscious. He remembers the cold white walls and the metal table on which he would be strapped by the feet and hands to avoid even the slightest movement. He compares himself variously to a man awaiting death on the electric chair and Spartacus who was crucified. He stops a little short of comparison with Christ and yet there is a mystical, almost religious quality to his perception of himself seated on the table, arms and legs spread and tied. He recalls the moment at which the needle penetrated slowly through layer after layer of skin into the soft tissue and then the bone at the top of his spine thus:

'I think it was for me the greatest moment of anguish I have ever experienced. The moment of my greatest fear, my greatest sense of being a complete nobody, of feeling all the fear of a child or of a small animal. I had been a hyper strong kid, super strong . . . I had been one of the best sportsmen my school had ever had. I was a complete sportsman. I was an athlete from head to toes, but there I was with that liquid moving slowly down my spine with my head bowed. Like a rabbit, like a bull, like a ewe about to be put to death in the slaughterhouse.'

The cold red liquid trickled through the very marrow of his spine until it reached the spinal tumour which had been causing Julio's problems. This time, thanks to the Tiodoro and the X-ray machine, the team of specialists were able to see the growth that had until then evaded their scrutiny. 'You could see the problem clearly,' Dr Iglesias says. 'A soft cyst had been growing on Julio's spine and causing gradual paralysis by compressing the vertebrae and nerves. I didn't like what I saw because my immediate thought was that Julio had a spinal cancer of some kind. But, at least we could now see where the problem was coming from.

'Coincidentally, there had been recent reports in the medical press about similar spinal tumours affecting GIs in America after returning from the Second World War. The medical evidence seemed to suggest that these growths or osteocrestomas were caused by physical trauma of some kind. We assumed in Julio's case that it had been caused by the accident – though, to be honest with you, I was never entirely sure whether this was the case or whether his spine had been injured or traumatized while playing football. There was many a time when I went to watch him play and I'd see him get a kick in the back. The tumour could easily have been caused in this way too.'

In any event, it was clear that the tumour had to be removed at speed and Julio was quickly prepared, wheeled into the operating theatre and anaesthetized. Though it seemed to Julio, awaking in the recovery room, that he had been unconscious for just a few minutes, the operation had taken eight long hours and had been a life and death affair.

With consciousness came the appalling realization that he remained totally paralysed below the waist. As the nurses lifted him onto the stretcher he was aware that he had lost all feeling in his legs. They hung lifeless.

As the hospital drama unfolded, with Julio as its lead player, each of the satellite characters in his early life story began assuming the roles that by now were second nature to them.

Julio's mother had remained at the hospital praying and crying, willing her son to survive against the odds. During the night that followed the operation she sat in a chair beside his bed, refusing to leave Julio's room. Despite the rifts which had come to exist within the Iglesias family, she was, on this occasion, utterly on her son's side. She was devastated by his condition.

Dr Iglesias, too, suffered the acute misery of seeing his previously healthy son now paralysed and facing possible death from what could have been a cancerous growth. 'But Charo's love for her children and mine are two different things,' the doctor asserts. 'My love is more positive, more forward-looking, more functional. She was suffering for Julio – there is no doubt about that. But you can't just suffer, you have to do something.'

In other words, Dr Iglesias dealt with the situation by doing what he always did – by taking control of it and of Julio. 'I could not just sit and watch my son suffer. I had to go into battle on his behalf. And I can say that because of this, Julio owes his life to me.'

After the operation, at which Dr Iglesias was also present, he insisted on having the tumour analysed by not one but two of Spain's leading pathologists.

'One came back with the verdict that the growth was cancerous and the other said that it wasn't though, in his view, it was from the same family as cancer. In fact, more is now known about osteocrestomas, which are made up of giant benign cells. But in those days very little was known about the condition and Franco Manero, the surgeon who had performed the operation, insisted that Julio be treated with radiotherapy and with cobalt treatments, which in those days was a very invasive procedure. I was asked to make the decision on Julio's behalf.

'I told him that it should be done and they started the cobalt treatment the next day. But I wasn't convinced about it because it really was such an extreme form of treatment. By the third day I could see it was killing Julio. His blood count was getting lower and lower and the cobalt was burning his spine down to the marrow.

'I started asking every expert that I knew about Julio's condition and the treatment he was receiving. I went to Fernandez Castro, who was a professor of pathology and had been a pupil of the Nobel Prize winner Ramon Y Cajal, to ask for his advice. He said to me that he had heard of similar cases to Julio's and that in his view the condition was benign. He advised me to stop the treatment before Julio's spine was damaged beyond repair. He said that even if the treatment didn't kill Julio, he would never walk again afterwards and his kidneys would be so damaged that he would be unable to urinate. He would also be impotent and lose his bowel function.

'I was in a dilemma. Should I trust Castro and then later see my son die from cancer, or did I watch him being destroyed by the treatment?

'I remember going into the hospital grounds and looking up at the sky and it was like a mystical experience. It was as though God himself spoke to me and he said, "Stop this treatment before it kills your son." It was the seventh day of the course and I demanded that they stop immediately, which they did. So you see why it is that I say that Julio owes his life to his father.'

According to those who knew the family at the time, it was now that the relationship between father and son – which was already close and exclusive of others – began to deepen and mould itself into an almost unnatural intimacy. Both Julio's ex-wife and Fernan Martinez link the extraordinary depth of feeling which exists between the two men to this difficult and in many ways formative period. 'Julio often used to speak to me about what his father did for him during the illness,' Martinez recalls. 'It wasn't the normal kind of stuff that a father would do for his son. It was totally out of the realms of the norm.'

It was as though the doctor believed that he alone could save his son – that he alone could minister to him, thus making him whole again. 'I admit that making Julio well again became the only thing in my life, the most important thing,' Dr Iglesias himself concurs. 'I did not want anyone else to be responsible for his care except for me. I took on the whole responsibility for Julio. I could see it was going to be a long battle and so for two years I gave up my job to be with him. I thought of nothing else for that time.'

Julio remained at Eloy Gonzalo for fifteen days, consumed by pain and paralysis. There was no movement whatever in his legs and that of his arms was clumsy and restricted. He was unable to eat and was being fed intravenously. His weight had dropped to under eight stone and his psychological condition was very poor. 'He was frustrated. His brain would tell his legs to move and nothing would happen. I would go to him and he would be crying terrible tears and asking me, "Why has God done this to me?"' Dr Iglesias recounts. 'But this for Julio was a temporary phase because he is like me, he has a great deal of willpower, he refuses to let life beat him.'

Dr Iglesias took the decision to take his son back to Benito Gutierrez where he could take full control of his treatment. Julio's bedroom was converted into a quasi hospital room, complete with adjustable hospital bed, medicine trolley, hospital lights and so on.

'For the first five months after the operation,' the doctor recalls, 'Julio was unable to urinate or to defecate by himself. He wore a catheter in his bladder and three times a day I would clean my own son's urethra to prevent infection. I would use my own fingers to take the excreta out of Julio's bowels. Yes, it was obviously a very intimate thing for a father and a son. But I was a doctor and it did not shock me or disgust me. Julio was my son and there was nothing, really nothing, that I would not do for him.'

The closer that father and son became, however, the more distanced were Charo and Carlos. 'Obviously, I did not know Julio at the time,' says Isabel Preysler. 'But I do know what Julio has told me and it seems that it was really after the accident that he and his father became like one person.

'He always told me that the person who had cared most for him when he was sick was his father. That if his father had to stay up all night with him or look after his most intimate needs then he did it generously and without complaint. His mother was not so involved.' In other words, she could not compete with the intimacy that existed between the two men and, like Carlos, she felt herself excluded from it.

'Even today, Carlos has a kind of complex about it,' Dr Iglesias confirms. 'Since that time he has always believed that I loved Julio more than him. But that is not the truth. It was simply that Julio needed me and that there was not much room left for anything else.'

Once home, the uphill struggle towards recovery began in earnest – with the oft-quoted, by Julio, incident in which his father arrived at Benito Gutierrez with a wheelchair.

He has recalled both in his autobiography and in interviews the day when his father pushed open the door of his bedroom and sheepishly presented the dreaded object to his son. He viewed it in his father's hand in a folded position, wheels close together, a canvas seat hanging mockingly, the glint of steel spokes . . .

He does not recall speaking – or, indeed, needing to say a word. His father had simply to look at Julio's face to see the profound hurt that his action had caused his son. Dr Iglesias lowered his head and took the wheelchair out of Julio's sight. It was never again seen at the Benito Gutierrez apartment, though Julio has said that for years after he continued to be traumatised by the sight of any wheelchair.

It had been after all, a horrific symbol of his predicament and yet it also served as a spur to the crippled young man. After viewing it he vowed to himself that he would walk again, though, of course, there were to be no instant miracles on the path to recovery.

Both Julio and his father remember, instead, the weeks and months of effort necessary for even the most miniscule improvements. 'Julio,' his father recalls, 'would simply lie on his bed hour after hour, day after day, willing his legs to move. Sending urgent messages from his brain to his feet. Until finally, about four months after the accident, I came into his room and he said, "Look, Dad, I can move the big toe on my left foot."

'It was perhaps to other people a small achievement but it turned Julio around. It gave him hope that if he tried hard enough and willed himself to walk for long enough, then he would succeed.

'After that he would pester me all the time. Every time I came into the room he would ask me to touch his legs to see if there was more feeling in them and I would say, "But, Julio, I only touched them five minutes ago."'

As his strength improved and the feeling in his legs increased, he began at night time to heave himself onto the floor with his arms, dragging himself along the corridors of the apartment while his parents and brother slept. Though he was unable yet to walk, he needed the sensation of movement and when his parents came to see him in the morning they would find their son exhausted but triumphant after his night time labours.

But even if hope had returned, the promise of a career as a professional soccer player – a dream that Julio had cherished since he first played in the school team as a five year old – was shattered. For Julio, the sense of loss was devastating. He knew that he would never again pull on the famous all-white strip of Real Madrid.

'To taste performing in front of a crowd and then realize you never will again was terrible,' he told English journalist Simon Kinnersly years later. 'Knowing I wasn't going to play football again wasn't tough – it was death.' At this point, of course, Julio could not have known that in the future, there were to be crowds that even he had never dreamed of, performance on a different stage. A whole new dawn was about to break.

Chapter Four

In matters of sex, Julio has tended to always tell the world what they have wanted to hear – rather than the truth. Insanely, at one point he claimed to have slept with 3,000 women – a number his ex-press relations chief, Fernan Martinez, admits smilingly 'was probably invented by Julio with the help of his accountant.'

Equally, of course, in the post-AIDS era, when it was no longer fashionable and even considered repulsive to admit to more than three lovers, he retracted his hefty boast claiming at various points in later life to be celibate, uneasy in the bedroom, sexually frail. Somewhere in the middle, between the monstrously inflated tales of bed hopping and abstinence, lies the truth.

Back in 1964, however, the paralysed Julio faced the very real possibility that the spinal tumour and treatment which followed it could have rendered him permanently incontinent and impotent, the latter being for the young Spanish male an unthinkable fate. At the time of the accident he had a girlfriend – curiously not mentioned in his autobiography – Maria del Carmen Jimenez.

'We used to call her Pisca, which means a little scrap of nothing,' recalls Gabi Fominaya. 'They seemed very much in love and she was very much accepted as Julio's girlfriend by the family and especially by Charo, who had always wanted Julio to marry her. 'I think Charo saw in Pisca a good-hearted person who loved her son and would make him happy. But Julio had different ideas about what he wanted from a relationship.'

Though very much in love they had never made love, according to Julio's father, 'because those were innocent times and Pisca was a very innocent girl.'

In any case, after the accident the relationship began to fall apart and it was to his father that Julio turned again to express his tremendous sexual anxiety, although in his autobiography he says that he 'couldn't have cared less at the time about sex.'

'I distinctly remember a conversation with Julio when he said to me: "Papa, you know I must have done something very bad for God to be punishing me in this way. I am twenty and I have never made love with a woman. How can I accept the possibility that now I never will?"'

As the feeling began to return to his legs, however, he also began to recover his sexual potency. 'It was a very big step, for example, when Julio was able to urinate for the first time without the help of a catheter,' his father recalls. 'It was maybe six months after the operation and the whole family was getting away for a long weekend in Valencia, everyone was waiting in the car, but Julio insisted he wanted to try to pee naturally before we left and I can remember it like today. He was standing there with his penis in his hand for maybe forty minutes trying and trying to pee until eventually a couple of drops came out and he was so unbelievably happy. It might seem a stupid little thing to other people, but to him it was a major triumph.'

In other words, what Julio knew was that if you could pee

from your penis then chances are that in time you would also be able to do the other thing that God intended it for. While in later years, the over-abundance of sexual encounters was partly a result of his upbringing – his father was his hero and what else had he spent his entire adult life doing? – but it was also the panic-stricken response of a man who has confronted and experienced impotence and dreads its possible return. It was, ultimately, the sex life of a man with everything to prove – especially to himself.

In the aftermath of the operation, however, Julio tried to put his fears on the back burner as he concentrated on overall health and fitness and the one goal that was to be paramount in his life – to walk again. After two months at home on his sick bed he was able to stand for the first time, supported on each side 'like a newborn baby.' He remained in this position for ninety minutes, attempting to take his first step and finally succeeding. It was also the first major step on the road to recovery.

Two mirrors were put up in the apartment – one in his room and one at the end of the passageway so that his father could watch Julio and Julio in turn could watch his father. Julio continued with his nocturnal sorties into the corridor, endlessly crawling its length, backwards and forwards, sleeping for only four hours a night.

In the morning he would eat a hearty breakfast and be taken to a local swimming pool built especially for use by Madrid's disabled. He would swim lengths frantically, like a man possessed, for four or five hours a day, every day. Meanwhile, other paraplegics would sit sadly in their wheelchairs, feet dangling in the water, surveying the former sportsman rebuilding his broken body.

At mid-day, José Luis, the family chauffeur, would arrive with Julio's pet Alsatian, Rock, and ferry his master to Madrid's Casa de Campo, a 4,500-acre park with its own woodland, lake and zoo. Julio would have lunch in the park

– an enormous, rare steak, red meat being a commodity he ate with a cannibal's appetite. Not because he liked it, but simply in order to build up his strength and his muscles. Then, post lunch, Julio, his dog and José Luis would begin to walk.

At first Julio would go to the Campo on crutches, managing barely 20 metres in the initial stages of recuperation. Two years later the three of them would often walk 20 kilometres. There was no part of the Casa de Campo that Julio did not cover on foot. Even today, when performing in Madrid, he is apt to make his chauffeur pull up outside the park while he spends a few minutes revisiting what for him was the most important battlefield of his life. The memories of those times come back thick and fast. He recalls the times when his father would join him on his walk and other times when his mother or Carlos would be there too.

Julio and his brother would have pretend races that Carlos would always allow his brother to win. Generous, indeed, for it was perhaps the only race that he might conceivably have ever won against his brother.

There had, of course, always been competition between the two brothers. Close as they were in age, Julio had felt himself dispossessed, as many small children do, when Carlos had usurped his position as the baby of the family, and the competition that was born with Carlos has persisted throughout the two brothers' lives.

Julio, who was certainly not the looker of the family, began early on to draw attention to himself in other ways: by being the charmer, the wit, the sporting hero. Carlos, in the meantime, being the second son, seemed content to play a secondary role in the family, which as Julio and his father's relationship gathered steam, placed him also in the role of the underdog, from which he never quite emerged.

While Julio had been the class joker, the footballing star,

Carlos went quietly about his own life. 'He always seemed the more serious and the more subdued of the two brothers,' says Ricardo Martinez. 'But maybe it isn't so easy to compete against Julio.'

Academically, however, he was certainly the brighter of the two – a model student, who went on to show his father's brilliance for medicine. When he left the Colegio de Los Sagrados Corazones, he first went to Florida for two years to learn English, much to his mother's chagrin, and then entered medical school in Madrid, where he became a star pupil. By the time he was in his late twenties he was an internationally renowned breast cancer specialist.

Later, however, he was to give up his career to join his brother in Miami as his financial adviser – a move which increased his bank balance immeasurably, but which saw his self esteem plummet to bankruptcy level.

'I think Carlos looked at Julio's world and thought it was much more interesting and glamorous than his. He saw the girls and the hotels and the private planes and he wanted to be part of it. So he gave up his world to live in Julio's – though I don't think it made him happy,' says Gabriel Gonzalez, who knows both brothers.

According to Dr Iglesias, there are certainly undercurrents of jealousy and competition between the two brothers and there always have been. 'But though Julio always tells people that the person he loves most in the world is me, I honestly believe that it is really his brother Carlos that he loves the most – although, of course, the relationship is a complicated one.'

This last is certainly true. Isabel Preysler recalls that in the early years of their marriage the jealousy burned white-hot between the two brothers. 'Carlos had recently married and I remember that he came to Julio for financial help because they needed furniture and he couldn't afford it and Julio certainly wasn't poor at the time. He was doing quite well.

'I was certainly in favour of helping Carlos because he was

Julio's brother and that is what family is for. But Julio said "No, I've had to work for what I have and Carlos will have to work for himself."

'There was this funny kind of competition between them. It even extended to the point that when Julio was away on tour he never wanted Carlos and his wife to take me to the cinema or to have me to their house for dinner. It was really a jealousy thing on Julio's part.'

During the years when he was laid low by his paralysis, a short-lived parity seemed to exist between the brothers, despite the attention that was lavished on Julio by his father, driving Carlos more and more to the periphery of family life. But Julio had to be crippled to see himself equal to his brother.

He had, after all, lost so many of the props that sustained his ego. He had been the boy that the girls from the convent at Santa Ana came to cheer for at school football matches, the rich kid with the sports car, the local hero. Now he had become, understandably, morose and depressed, unable to walk, or even to go to the toilet without assistance. He suddenly had to view himself as another person entirely.

In the early days of his recovery it had not been easy to let go of the old self and the old dreams. Since he had first been chosen for the school football team his vehement ambition had been to be a professional goalie. But from the moment the spinal tumour was diagnosed, it was clear that Julio would never play football again.

'He took it badly, of course he did,' says Dr Iglesias. 'We had to get rid of his football boots completely, get them out of his sight. Seeing them only served to remind him of the career that he always dreamed of. It was very depressing for him.'

Believing as he does in fate, however, Julio has often remarked to interviewers that there is a purpose and grand plan that governs the major events in our lives. If his football career had not ended then his singing career would never have begun. If he had not found himself incapacitated and lying for months in a bed then the young male nurse that attended him, Eladio Magdaleno, would not have brought him a cheap guitar with which to entertain himself.

At the time, Julio had never played before, though throughout his teenage years he had been a music fan. Since buying his first record – 'Grande' by Spanish star Mina – he had gone on to collect those of Pedro Vargas and other popular singers of the day. Now, in his bed, he began to strum along to music as it was played over the radio. He became a Paul Anka fan, an Elvis devotee. He learned how to accompany the tunes of Jaime Morey, Luis Gardey and Manolo and Ramon (the Ramon half of the partnership being Ramon Arcusa who went on to produce so many Julio's records and to be one of his closest friends).

He was not, as he admits, ever to be a Segovia – a master of the guitar – but he learned to play competently and well enough to accompany himself as he sang. At the same time, he began to develop a sense that his future lay in his new-found abilities. He would peer at his black and white TV set as the song festivals so popular in Spain were televised to millions, with a growing intuition that one day he would be part of that world.

After watching the Festival of San Remo in 1965, for example, he remembers announcing to his father that he too would sing there one day and he made a similar announcement to his mother after watching the festival of Viña del Mar and then the Benidorm Festival.

'None of us took it particularly seriously – though knowing Julio, we should have done because when he decides to do anything he always means to achieve it,' says his father.

Julio continued to strum along, to send out for the records cut by his favourite artists. The strains of Elvis wafted down the stairwell at number 27 Benito Gutierrez.

'As time went on we would also hear Julio singing along

with his guitar,' recalls Gabi Fominaya. 'Though we all thought it was a tremendous joke when he said that he wanted to take it up professionally because none of us felt he could sing to save his life.

'I remember my sister had just had a baby and Julio would wake the child up with his singing, which would make the mother furious and produce loud screams of "Shut up, Julio – for heaven's sake."

'But Julio knew better than the rest of us precisely what he was doing, he knew that he would be successful.'

It is perhaps stating the obvious to say that Julio could never have been as successful – or as rich – as a footballer as he subsequently became as a singer. In that sense he came, in some ways, to view the disability that robbed him of his football career as a divine gift.

Yet, for all that, the gift came with a price of its own and Julio's illness left him strangely unconfident – not just shaky on his legs, but emotionally unstable too. 'What happened to Julio after the accident was a very big thing in his life,' says Alfredo Fraile. 'And perhaps after such an experience no one can ever be quite the same again.'

Within two years of the operation Julio's condition had improved immeasurably and, thanks to his determination, way beyond the expectations of his doctors who had considered it quite possible that he would never walk again. By 1966, he was a familiar sight at the Casa de Campo where he would amble along, albeit still with the aid of a walking stick. By 1968, he had abandoned the stick, but not the fear that one day his paralysis might fell him anew – a fear which has never truly left him.

'I can remember, for example, on one occasion when Julio called me in the middle of the night,' says Alfredo Fraile. 'He was sitting in a chair by the phone and was unable to get out of the chair. He said he was paralysed and I would have to come over to him immediately – which I did.

'When I got there he was already okay again. We talked and he thanked me for coming over. He had just been going through one of those psychological things which sometimes happened to him when he was tired or overstressed. The paralysis thing would come back every now and then and take him over.'

The fear remained, because despite Julio's superficial appearance as a kind of sun-tanned warrior, he has never fully recovered either emotionally – or indeed physically – from the trauma. Even today his rigorous exercise programme is a necessity rather than a vanity. His two-hour swim each morning and work out in the gym are what ensures that his back remains strong and his legs continue to work. 'Though even now you notice with Julio that when he's on stage he can often look shaky and not too stable,' says Alvaro Rodriguez, who has photographed Julio on numerous tours.

'People have even sometimes commented that he looks a little drunk – which is never the case, he is simply still not that secure on his feet. It's for this reason that he likes to wear special shoes on stage that have very thin, cloth-like soles that allow him to grip the ground. If you look at his feet, he uses them like claws to hold onto the ground. I have taken pictures where you can see them bunched and hanging on for dear life. Though his disability is not something he really cares to talk about too much. He is sensitive about it for obvious reasons.'

His father, of course, knows more about his son's physical condition than most and corroborates Rodriguez's observations. 'To be honest with you, I would say that Julio is maybe only 80 per cent recovered and no more and that's as good as it will ever get. Sexually, however, he is 100 per cent.' And who could possibly doubt it?

Chapter Five

The ancient ramparts of Peniscola rise hundreds of feet from the beach on the Costa del Azahar like an elaborate sand-castle built earlier in the day by an over-enthusiastic child. Despite its teetering and precarious appearance, the walled town has stood since mediaeval times, defending itself from the belligerence of various invading armies. Once it was the Moors who tried to break through its defences and possess its fairy-tale beauty. Now it is the tourists who overrun its quaint, labyrinthian cobbled streets, the visiting foreign film crews who clamber over its battlements.

In 1961, for example, Peniscola formed the back drop for *El Cid* – an epic tale of eleventh century love, war and passion. It was in Peniscola, too, in 1966, that Julio used the dramatic surrounding as the backcloth for his first epic love scene. For it was here, according to his father, that Julio made love for the very first time.

The girl who finally relieved Julio of his virginity that summer before his twenty-third birthday has never been mentioned by Julio either in interviews or in his autobi-ography – precisely, one imagines, because he was not keen for it to be known that by the standards of most other men his first sexual experience had occurred rather belatedly. His father, however, recalls her as being a young French girl on holiday with her family.

Julio himself had gone to Peniscola that year with reluctance. On previous holidays he had arrived a picture of health and hope – a young man on the brink of a brilliant football career, someone who could run faster, swim better than everyone else, a kid who entertained the crowds that gathered to watch him performing wheelies on his bicycle.

Now, however, though recovering well from the operation, he still couldn't walk without a stick and dreaded the pitying gaze of those who, like the Iglesias family, came every year to the town and had watched him growing up. He had convinced himself that he would not have a good time that summer. He could not have known that a young brown-haired girl with broken Spanish would see to it that he did.

Dr Iglesias's recollections of her are a little hazy. She was young and pretty, of course. She would sit on the beach watching Julio swimming back and forth in the same obsessive way that he trained at the paraplegic's pool in Madrid. She would help him out of the sea and they would sit and talk for hours on the sand. Julio would make her laugh, he would use his inestimable charm on her. He wanted to make love to her very badly – that much was clear. But then again, in that summer of 1966 and with his virginity still tauntingly intact, he wanted to make love to anyone.

The romancing and hand-holding went on for several weeks until Julio and his French girlfriend made love beneath the stars in the shadow of the walled town.

'After it had happened, Julio came to me immediately and said, "Dad, I've finally done it. I've finally made love for the first time",' his father recalls.

Whether or not it was the usual inept fumblings of inexperienced youth or the symphony of erotic sensation that Julio normally likes to claim for his lovemaking, no one apart from Julio and his unnamed, unremarked upon lover will ever know. 'But I can tell you that Julio was very happy that he had made love. I know that he didn't have any regrets about it.'

The romance continued until the end of the summer. 'Maybe Julio wrote to her afterwards, maybe not,' says his father. 'I don't particularly recall him mentioning her again. She was not, I think, a big love in his life.'

When the summer of 1966 had ended, Julio prepared to resume his law studies. His course at Madrid University had been interrupted for two years by his illness and in the effort to get well again he had lost touch with the academic world, which, by his own admission, had never been a particularly natural habitat for him.

By 1965 most of his friends and peers from the university had already graduated and by 1966 were in the middle of their military service – which even now remains a requirement for all young Spanish males. Julio, however, was exempted due to his invalidism and was free to continue with his studies, financed by a father who was happy to pay indefinitely for his son's education. 'I always wanted both my sons to be something in life,' the doctor says. 'Carlos was already an exceptional student and it came easily to him. But for Julio, studying was always more hard. He wasn't a natural like Carlos. But I insisted that at least he tried.'

His father had seen to it that even during his son's illness he was registered for each new year at Madrid, thus keeping his place open. But as the new term at Madrid approached Julio viewed it with increasing dread – partly because he did not want to be reminded of the happy years when he had studied at the university and trained at Real Madrid, years that had been filled with so much hope. Neither did he relish having to make up lost ground on a course that he had found difficult even before his operation.

He considered his options and decided that instead of returning to Madrid University he would take up a new place at Murcia. Not only were the course and qualifying exams reputed to be easier, but also Julio could live and work away from the shadow of the Bernabeu Stadium which continued to cast gloom over his life. So, against his mother's will, he left for the university in October. His fervent hope must have been that, having had his first full-fledged sexual experience, there would be many more such encounters in the months to come.

It is doubtful, however, that Murcia proved to be as sexually bountiful as Julio might have liked. Though other parts of Europe were experiencing a sexual revolution in the sixties, Spain lagged helplessly behind in this regard. While London swung, Murcia and the rest of Spain remained a tightly corseted society gripped by a church and a state that were deeply suspicious of physical enjoyment of any kind – particularly sexual enjoyment. It is not surprising that Julio's first sexual experience had been with a French girl. In sixties Spain, nice Spanish girls simply didn't do it.

Whatever the reason, it seems unlikely that Julio's two years at Murcia – a time which generally goes unremarked upon by him either in his memoirs or elsewhere – were a high point in his life, either sexually or academically.

He sat his final exams in 1968, but despite later informing journalists that he was a lawyer, he failed to qualify. According to his father, he flunked just one part of his finals. 'And I could have fixed for him to go back to Madrid University where a friend of mine in the law faculty was willing to pass Julio without him even having to sit the exam again. All he had to do was sign on at the university and it would be done.'

It is small wonder that even now Julio continues to refer to his father as the person to whom he owes most. For, so often in Julio's early life story, he emerges as chief puppeteer. Mr Fixit. On this occasion, however, his son decided not to take up his offer, for reasons which, in the summer of 1968, became quite obvious.

Having sat his finals in April of that year, Julio returned to Madrid in a disconsolate mood. Though it was now four years since his operation, its aftermath continued to affect his life. Despite his persistent exercise programme and towering will to triumph over his disability, he remained unsteady on his feet and paranoid about what he perceived to be other people's pitying reactions to him. Once again, it was his father who came up with the idea of sending Julio to England for a while – partly to learn the language and partly to conquer his paranoia. 'I had so many complexes about people seeing me that my father sent me to England on my own,' he told *Hola* magazine in the 1980s.

The arrangement was not popular with Julio's mother. 'She hated the idea of Julio being so far away in England, just as she had hated it when Carlos had wanted to go to America for two years to learn English. She put up a real fight, but Carlos went and so did Julio, although Charo argued that it was cruel to send Julio off to England on his own when he couldn't even walk properly. But I told her in no uncertain terms that Julio must go,' says Dr Iglesias.

Later much confusion was to arise over where, precisely, Julio went that summer. The Julio mythology has it that he went to Cambridge University to study law – and this is a notion that Julio himself does little to discourage.

In fact, his studies in England began at a language school in Ramsgate, but, finding the place unutterably boring and provincial, he swiftly transferred to the Bell Language School in Cambridge, an establishment which is still to be found in the town – though no one quite remembers its now most famous pupil.

No one except Enrique Bassat, who was to become a lifelong friend of Julio's. They met in May 1968 – a date which has historical importance as well as being personally significant for the two young men. It was, after all, the month in which student riots were shaking Paris with the effect of an earthquake – and the after tremors extended to those young Spaniards whose families had sent them abroad to study.

'Unfortunately, money being sent to us by our families had to clear through the bank in Paris first, don't ask me why,' says Enrique. 'It was just the way it was. Because of the riots everything in the city was upside down and our money simply wasn't getting to us.'

Julio had used what money he had brought with him from Spain in Ramsgate and had expected to find more waiting for him from his father at a bank in Cambridge. But nothing had arrived. Enrique was in the slightly more fortunate position of being able to borrow funds from family friends in Scotland. 'But to be honest, I had almost nothing to live on and the situation was desperate.'

It was on the day of Julio's arrival in the town that Enrique – who was from a wealthy Catalan family and had already been studying English in the town for a year at one of the rival language schools – first encountered the man who was to be a key figure in his young life.

'I was driving through the centre of Cambridge in the little Seat car that I had brought with me from Barcelona, and as I pulled up at some lights I noticed this guy sitting on a suitcase on the pavement with a guitar beside him, and he looked kind of dejected, almost down and out, you know.

'He must have noticed the Barcelona plates on my car, because as soon as he saw me he waved me down and came walking towards me and I noticed instantly from his walk that he was handicapped.'

Enrique wound down the window and the two men exchanged pleasantries. 'He told me he was from Madrid and he explained that he had absolutely no money and I suppose, seeing him there so vulnerable, I felt sorry for him and I said, "Okay, you can come with me. You can share my room and you can share my money and we'll both live on what I have until the situation improves."'

Julio returned to Enrique's flat, which was nothing more than a glamorized bedsit – 'one chair, one table, a couch, a kitchenette and a bed that came out of the wall.'

'And because we were young and we had no money,' says Enrique, 'there was very little to do. So we talked and we talked and Julio told me the history of his life.'

It was to Enrique that Julio spoke, not just about his family life, but about the devastating effects of the spinal tumour. 'You know, Julio was scarred, not just physically. He was scarred emotionally by what had happened and he struck me as someone who had no sense of self worth at all.

'You have to understand that before he became ill, he had been such a popular guy. He had played for Real Madrid and, really, he was sort of famous. But then he had the accident and the way he told it to me every one of his friends abandoned him. So he got to thinking that no one had ever liked him for himself, that they had only liked what he represented. So, he didn't trust friendship, you know.'

He came, however, to trust Enrique: 'Maybe because I liked him at that time when he didn't like himself and I liked him because he was Julio, pure and simple, not because of any advantage I could gain from knowing him.

'We were living together and talking together and spending almost every day together because, to be honest with you, he wasn't even remotely interested in learning English. He thought he could pick it up just by being in the place, which was ludicrous. But he influenced me, too, and then I stopped going to classes. We were just two young guys in England, at a time when it was good to be there and we were brought close together by extraordinary circumstances. If they hadn't been so extraordinary maybe we wouldn't have been so close.'

Extraordinarily, for example, the two men who had both come from the cushioned world of the Spanish ruling classes, experienced hunger for the first time in their lives. 'It was quite ridiculous really,' Enrique recalls. 'We would go to a café and order a chicken quarter and share it between us. Okay, we weren't exactly starving, but we were absolutely broke. Really, I am not exaggerating.'

On one such occasion, it struck Enrique that they must find some way to bolster funds. 'I said, "Julio, we can't continue like this, so what can we do? Do you have a talent of any kind?" And, of course, he could sing a bit and play the guitar and I could play the piano. So I said, "Okay I've got a plan that can earn us some money."'

Enrique, whose English was more accomplished than Julio's, began touting for live music work in Cambridge pubs. On the outskirts of the town, at the Airport Pub (which has long since been converted into offices) the landlord agreed to hire the double act at weekends for £6 a night – 'which wasn't a fortune, but considering that even when our money came through from Spain, neither of us had more than £100 for the term, it was quite good money.'

Enrique sold the act to the landlord not on the basis that either of them was particularly accomplished – 'because, to be honest, I didn't think either of us was – but on the basis that between them they would pull in every loyal foreign language student in the town. 'I promised him that 100 people would come and see us every time we played – so it was a good business proposition.'

In the event, Julio, whose skill had improved immeasurably since first being given his guitar by Eladio Magdaleno, proved better than Enrique or the landlord had anticipated. 'The first night at the pub I accompanied Julio on the piano but he outclassed me by a million miles. So I said, "Hey, you're good enough to do it on your own, so I'll become your manager instead."

'I would go with him most weekends and I also started drumming up business in other pubs, too. We used to play at one in Ely just outside Cambridge. Julio would sing songs that were popular at that time – Tom Jones, Engelbert Humperdinck, The Beatles – and people responded to him because he had something then that he still has now, something that you can't really quantify. He had a kind of light that shone from him. A kind of charisma. I think people responded to that more than they did his singing.'

The two shared the proceeds as they had shared their food and Enrique's flat. But they also shared something else which took on a profound importance for both of them – the love of the same woman.

It was perhaps a mark of their intense friendship that Enrique Bassat introduced Julio to Gwendoline Bollore at all. Having been in the same class at their Cambridge language school, he had been attempting to woo Gwendoline for six months before Julio arrived on the scene and he was, by his own admission, helplessly in love with her.

She was, as Enrique recalls, everyone's idea of a 'fairy-tale princess' – petite, with blonde hair tumbling down her back, blue-grey eyes and high Slavic cheekbones that she had inherited from her mother, who was the Russian Princess Borochencho. 'It was, on reflection, absolutely normal that both of us should fall in love with her,' says Enrique. 'Julio was a very romantic boy. I was a very romantic boy. And she was the girl that every romantic boy dreams of falling in love with. We were looking for the same thing – physically and mentally. We were looking for Gwendoline.'

Before Julio's arrival, Enrique had done his best to make her his own. Eternally broke as he was, he would take her out for a meal, hoping to charm her. 'The first time, she said she would come to a Chinese restaurant with me – and so, to impress her, I went earlier to the place and asked the waiter to teach me how to pronounce everything on the menu in Chinese.

'Later we ordered and I felt pretty good about it. But, then, Gwendoline suddenly started speaking to the waiter in fluent Chinese. It turned out that, though her mother was Russian and her father was from a top French family, they had lived in Beijing until Gwendoline was ten. She was a girl who was absolutely full of surprises.

'She was utterly remarkable – not just physically, but mentally, intellectually and spiritually. Is it any wonder that when Julio arrived he fell in love with her too?'

Despite the intimate conversations that went on between Julio and Enrique, the latter had kept his innermost feelings and aspirations about Gwendoline private: 'Because, I suppose, I wanted to keep this precious thing for myself. But I think that Julio must have known what my feelings were towards Gwendoline. I think everyone must have known because my feelings would have been written on my face.'

Julio, however, once he had been introduced to Gwendoline by Enrique, was equally besotted – and, as it happened, Gwendoline responded to the charisma that Enrique was all too aware of. She was powerfully attracted to Julio too.

According to Julio's version of events – which fails to mention the Enrique connection – it was Gwendoline who made the first move. She waited for an occasion when, presumably, she knew that Enrique would not be there, and went to find Julio at the Airport Pub. When he emerged after closing time, she was waiting outside in the shadows for him. She took his hand and they began walking back to Cambridge together. When they kissed, each must have understood that they had betrayed Enrique.

Julio walked Gwendoline back to her digs before returning to York House, a hall of residence to which he had moved from Enrique's flat after money finally arrived for him from

Paris. Though it was to all intents and purposes the swinging sixties, there was a strict single sex code in the building and girls were not allowed back.

'So the next thing I know, Julio has come to me and he says, "Enrique, I need to ask you a big favour. I need to borrow your flat so that I can be alone with a girl. And so I gave Julio the keys without question.

'But, of course, he didn't tell me which girl it was. So when I came back I was shocked to find it was Gwendoline. I was upset – he wasn't. But then, I guess, he was the winner and I was the loser. Conscience did not come into it.'

Gwendoline, witnessing the pain on Enrique's face, asked to be taken home immediately by Julio, and it was several days before the two men could face speaking to one another.

'Then I remember that Julio came round and, unworldly idiots that we were, we went out and bought a bottle of Cherry Brandy to drink together.' Anaesthetized and soothed by the sickly-sweet and strongly alcoholic brew, they sorted out their differences and reaffirmed their friendship.

'We put our cards on the table,' Enrique continued. 'I said to Julio, "I was in love with that girl and you knew it, so how could you do that to me?" And he said, "Well, I was in love with her too, Enrique, so how could I help myself?" And because I knew Julio, and knew the way that he was, I could see that this was how he justified it to himself. What could I do?'

Enrique attempted to forgive and forget. 'I understood that he had a very deep need to reaffirm his own personality and a deep need to be loved,' he reasoned. 'More than this, Julio is a man who needs to be loved by the very best – the best of the best – and that was Gwendoline. Unfortunately for me, he had to have her because second best just wouldn't do for him. He could never make do with second best.'

Defeated, Enrique resigned himself to being a loser. 'I knew I was the loser, but I kept the feeling inside myself. Julio understood it and Gwendoline understood it. But we carried on, the three of us, the best of friends, because I couldn't bear to lose the friendship of either of them. But Julio understands that I had to sacrifice a very important thing in my life at the time for the sake of friendship – Gwendoline – and I know that he has never forgotten that.'

In many ways, Gwendoline was to be the prototype for all the women that Julio was ever to fall seriously in love with. Like his mother, she was strikingly beautiful, a top drawer girl who moved with the grace of a swan, but without a trace of haughtiness. She was warm, open and full of life, and she had none of the sexual hang-ups of the girls that Julio had grown up with.

Importantly for Julio, however, at just eighteen she was also a virgin which made her easy to venerate and to love, and easier, conversely, to lust after which Julio did – falling for her with the force of an avalanche.

Thus it was that Gwendoline, who later became the subject of one of Julio's most famous songs – a song named after her that he took to the 1970 Eurovision Song Contest – became without question the first great love of his life. Before the accident he had been fond of Pisca, but it had been a relationship operating under the constraints of Spanish society and sex had not occurred between them. He had experienced sex with an anonymous French girl in Peniscola – but sex was all it had been. With Gwendoline, however, sex and love merged together powerfully. It was a big passion, a revolutionising relationship.

Unlike the legion of women who later gave themselves to Julio, Gwendoline was made special because her motives were beyond question. 'She didn't see him as a star and she didn't see him as a handicapped person. She saw him simply as a man that she loved and she gave herself completely to him,' says Enrique.

It was an intensely sexual relationship which was made all

the more ferocious by the doubts that Julio had entertained about his potency in the aftermath of his operation. It was also a relationship that he needed on other levels. 'Because,' as he says, 'it was an uncertain time for me. I was not the same person that I had been. I wasn't a footballer any more and I wasn't a professional singer either. I was just a Spanish boy who got some applause in the Airport Pub. I had few illusions and a lot of sadness and loneliness.' Gwendoline, it seems, arrived in the nick of time.

How deeply and how permanently she changed Julio's perception of himself is another question. According to Enrique, the change was, in fact, superficial and transient. 'He seemed a little happier, but then, as now, you only have to scratch the surface of the man just a little, and you see that underneath, in his soul, he is unsure.

'Underneath, he still sees himself as the small Spanish man who is without confidence in himself. A man who is trying to reach the sky and touch the moon because that is the only way that he feels he is worth anything. He is a man with more money than anyone can imagine – but someone who is never on the ground long enough to enjoy any of it. It is significant that he owns his own plane because that way he can spend most of his time in the sky, which is where he feels happiest.

'I think Gwendoline must have asked herself many times why things did not work out between her and Julio and maybe it was simply this – that she would have made a life for Julio here on the earth. But Julio can't stand to have his feet on the ground. Julio needs to fly.'

In the event, fate and circumstance were to separate the two young lovers, at first temporarily and later indefinitely and irrevocably. But during those months in Cambridge they appeared inseparable. 'They seemed very much in love,' says Enrique. But then something happened to Julio that was infinitely bigger than his love for Gwendoline. And that something was his career.

Chapter Six

June in Cambridge gave way to July. Julio and Gwendoline, the lovers, and Enrique, who had taken on the role of dear friend and selfless lender of single-bedded flat, appeared to be living a charmed life. Julio and Gwendoline would make love while Enrique made himself scarce, then he would return and the three of them would step out arm in arm and head for the famous river Cam, where they would laugh and drink wine and sun themselves for hours. 'We were friends,' says Enrique Bassat. 'Everything was okay with the world – it was sunny and bright and we were young.'

It was a perfect time to be young, in a perfect place, during a perfect English summer. But the idyll was about to be shattered forever. 'I remember the three of us were together when Julio received a telephone call from Spain to say he'd been selected to sing at the Benidorm Festival. I think all of us knew in our hearts that things would be never be the same again.'

Ironically, it was Julio's song, 'La Vida Sigue Igual', which translates into 'Life Goes On The Same', which had – with Julio's father's help – met with the approval of the selection panel of one of Spain's most prestigious popular song festivals. Two days after the call, Julio waved goodbye to Gwendoline and Enrique at Heathrow Airport. 'And when he was gone we instantly missed him and clung together because our love for him was now the main thing that we had in common. We were friends, just good friends, because our relationship had moved on. Love is one thing, friendship is another, and though I had loved her I saw that you didn't have to sacrifice one thing for the other.'

They talked, but mostly about Julio. Both were a little shell-shocked by the events that had taken him away from them. 'We'd heard him sing "La Vida Sigue Igual" a million times and we thought it was a pretty song,' says Enrique. 'But we didn't stop to consider how it might change his, and our lives.'

The song had been conceived by Julio during his recuperation period in Madrid. The lyrics carried a message that seemed pertinent to his state of mind while lying in his sick bed. They spoke of each individual's struggle to make something of his life – even though that life was by definition transient and temporary. The song remained unfinished until Julio went to Cambridge. But there, encouraged by Enrique and another mutual friend, a Czech student called Milan Marick, he put the finishing touches to it.

Emboldened by his affair with Gwendoline, he made a crude recording of the song and, in June, sent it to every recording company that could be found at that time in the Madrid telephone directory.

Most replied with a polite rejection letter. They were not interested in taking on new artists and more than this, Julio's style did not impress them. In Spain, after all, at this time the most celebrated performers were artists like Karinna, Miguel Rios and Los Bravos – all of whom sung rather inflated Hispanic numbers, often with a semi-political protest content. The songs were rooted deep in the Latin culture and pulsed with an unmistakable Latin rhythm. 'La Vida Sigue Igual', on the other hand, was a simple song written from the heart and without any of the affectations of Spanish contemporary music. What Julio had created, perhaps unconsciously, was a song that had international appeal. It was a song whose lyrics, melody and delivery relied on a unique simplicity. In short, it was a song which, like all the others that followed it, ordinary people could relate to.

Later, when asked for the magic formula which lay behind his success, Julio would repeat with constancy this idea of simplicity. 'The lyrics are about simple ordinary things, the stories between couples everywhere in the world. It is a musical chat. Not intellectual. Not sophisticated. It's how people talk to each other when they are close,' he told journalist Donald McLachlan in 1982. Adding in an interview with *Titbits* magazine in the same year, 'My lyrics are stories that are very simple, even naive. They come out like a conversation you might have in a street. I sing little stories about love and lovers. That's the secret.'

It was a secret, however, that only two record companies had the foresight to want to share. The first was Hispavox who offered Julio a contract whereby they would purchase rights to the song, 'La Vida Sigue Igual', though Julio himself would not be required to sing it. Columbia, on the other hand, wanted both the song and the singer and saw Julio and 'La Vida Sigue Igual' as potential entrants for Benidorm, which was a showcase for both new and established recording artists.

At first Julio demurred, saying he would be happy to go to Benidorm simply as the author of the song. Enrique Garea, who was head of the Spanish wing of Columbia at the time, was insistent, however, and Julio interrupted his Cambridge idyll briefly to return to Madrid where Columbia had arranged for him to be whisked into their studios to record the song.

Much later, as an established and internationally acclaimed artist, he developed a reputation for obsessiveness in the studio. He would record and re-record in his quest for perfection – unlike one of his heroes, and later good friend, Frank Sinatra. Legend has it that when they recorded 'Summer Wind' for the latter's *Duets* album in 1993, there was a hilarious difference in the studio technique of the two men. Having done one simple take, the sound engineer was said to have turned to Frank and asked, 'So, Frank, you want to do any more?' Sinatra then replied, 'Nah. Only faggots do overdubs.' Julio who by this stage was rarely intimidated by anyone, was said to have shrunk in his seat.

It was perhaps reminiscent of that occasion back in 1968 when Julio was very much the ingenue – wide eyed and waiting for instruction from his elders and, to his mind at that time, betters. He recalls needing a stool to sit on while his first ever single was being recorded – not because of his still traumatized spine, but because his legs were shaking so much with nerves. The sound engineers, however, made short work of the job and 'La Vida Sigue Igual' was cut with the minimum of fuss.

The original record is now owned by Costa Rican TV magnate Pierre Baldi. The crackly and unsophisticated recording is, without question, a collectors' item for which Baldi has been offered vast sums of money, always turning it down. It demonstrates the raw Julio, with his untrained and immature voice, singing a song he had written from the heart. It was a song which, for all its lack of sophistication, Julio has never wanted to change by so much as a note. It became a kind of anthem, or hymn whose message seemed timeless and permanently relevant.

With just ten days to go before the festival, Julio returned to Cambridge, while Garea submitted the disc to the Benidorm

Committee. Despite the mythology – and the memoirs – the song was not at first accepted by the panel, who were unsympathetic to the number for the same reason that so many of the record companies had been.

'It was eliminated,' says Dr Iglesias. 'So I went to the chief of the committee, Pepe Solis, who was one of Franco's ministers, because, you see, I was his wife's doctor. In fact the wives of all the people who were in charge, the bosses, the people who fixed things, the bankers and politicians – the *Mandama*s – all of their wives came to me and I didn't charge them a thing. So I said to this Pepe Solis, "Why, after everything I've done for you, have you done this to my son? You're a pack of bastards." So Solis agreed to chuck one of the other entrants out and to put Julio's song in its place. I don't know which song they chucked out and I don't care.'

The main thing was, of course, that Julio's father had fixed it for Julio again.

After touching down at Madrid's Barajas Airport in the second week of July 1968, Julio went directly to Columbia for a meeting with Enrique Garea, who offered his congratulations and the news that another entrant signed to the label, Manolo Otero, who was being plugged as the new Frank Sinatra, was hoping to travel with him to the festival. Julio and Otero left the capital together on 14 July in Julio's tiny Seat 850, perhaps the most modest car that the singer was ever to own.

With temperatures topping 40 degrees centigrade, the two men, whose careers have constantly intersected in the intervening quarter of a century and who have remained good friends, travelled with the heater on and the windows open, hoping to reduce the temperature of the engine. They lost count of the number of times the overheated car spluttered to a halt during that 450 kilometre drive.

It was at around 6 p.m. when the car and its passengers

finally limped into Benidorm and the two men headed for the Hotel de Madrid, the official festival HQ, to register. On signing in, Julio was advised that he would be the first singer to perform at the event, at which point he seriously considered turning tail and heading to Peniscola where his mother, by all accounts, would have welcomed him with open arms.

'I think it's fair to say that Charo was not in the least bit keen for her son to take part at Benidorm,' says Gabi Fominaya, who had remained close to Charo, still living at number 27 Benito Gutierrez. 'She would have been happier if Julio had never embarked on a singing career. The way she saw it, the life would never make her son happy.' But, as usual, her doubts went unheeded.

Poles apart, as ever, from Julio's father, she remained in Peniscola while her husband booked in at a Benidorm hotel to be near his son. Yet, in the singer's memoirs, he states that his parents were unaware of his participation at Benidorm – perhaps to deny his father's behind-the-scenes involvement. According to the singer, when his parents read about Julio Iglesias in the paper on the morning following the event they assumed it must be another Julio Iglesias that was being referred to and not their son.

'No, obviously I was at Benidorm,' says Dr Iglesias. 'How could I not have been there for such an important event?'

The evening of his arrival at the coastal town, Julio met with his father before returning to Manuel Otero with whom he was sharing a room. The two went to the beach for a late swim, admired the girls and after a supper which both were too nervous to eat, they turned in for a fitful night's sleep.

In the morning Julio was up early for his allotted rehearsal time at the Plaza de Toros, which doubled then, as now, as a venue for various visiting acts and musical festivals and as a bull ring. He surveyed the seemingly endless tiers of empty seats, which some 36 hours later would be filled with critical spectators and considered, once again, throwing in the towel.

His confidence was boosted, however, by the arrival of the all-girl trio who had just returned victorious from that year's Eurovision Song Contest. They had been the backing group for Massiel and her winning entry 'La, La, La'. That Columbia had arranged for them to now back Julio at the festival seemed to him to be almost a lucky portent of success, though being totally unused to performing with backing singers or an orchestra, he was to need every available hour before the competition to master these new skills.

The first round of the competition itself was scheduled to take place on 16 July, and Julio viewed the approaching ordeal with gathering alarm. Despite the charm and charisma that was already a part of his nature, he was infinitely more diffident then, at the launch of his career, then he ever was later. He had grown up liking and needing the limelight, basking in the applause and attention of others, but on the opening night of the tenth Benidorm Song Festival, the unconfident Julio that lurks behind the confident smile threatened to take over entirely.

As Julio recalls it, he ventured onto the Plaza de Toros, his already shaky legs almost unable to support him. He stood in the wings of the stage, dressed in a lightweight navy blue suit – the other suit he had brought with him, a plain white affair, he had decided to keep in the unlikely event that he made it to the finals in two days' time, though he had little faith that he would be needing it.

As he surveyed the general rumpus around him – the bands of visiting press men, and the teams of cameramen sent from all over the Spanish-speaking world to televise the event – it occurred to him that he would shortly be watched not just by the crowds that now filled the Plaza de Toros to capacity, but by an international audience of millions. Engulfed as he was not just by the suffocatingly warm and wet temperatures of that sticky night but by a stage fright that gripped his throat and nailed his feet to the floor, sweat began to pour profusely from his body.

Even now, according to his father, the singer sweats so much during each performance that every one of the expensive, hand-tailored suits that he wears on stage is utterly beyond redemption and has to be thrown away at the end of every show. 'But then Julio can afford that, you know.'

On that particular night, however, thoughts of such extravagances were as distant as the stars which shone from the black sky like spotlights above the Plaza de Toros. Julio looked at his suit and noticed for the first time that the legs on it were too short. He surveyed his shoes and considered them cheap and tasteless. Though it was just seconds before the start of the competition, he wondered insanely if he had time to go back to the hotel to change, and was only stopped from doing so by Enrique Garea who had turned up at the competition to give his support to his two protégés – Manolo Otero and Julio. He placed a firm and calming hand on Julio's shoulder.

The clock ticked in thudding rhythm with Julio's heart and on the beat of 8 p.m. the emcee climbed onto the stage and read from the piece of paper he held in his hand. 'The first song,' he said 'is entitled "La Vide Sigue Igual". The music and words are by Julio Iglesias and the composer himself will sing the song.'

Legend has it that at this moment, Julio was so paralysed by fear that he remained rooted to the spot. A minute passed and then two – by which time the audience who had been applauding began shuffling around in embarrassment. Enrique Garea, who stood by Julio's side, beseeched him through clenched teeth to get up and sing. Mule like, Julio shook his head from side to side, refusing to move.

Another minute elapsed before Garea took the law, and

the singer, into his own hands, shoving him forcefully from behind into the glare of the spotlights. Julio stumbled onto the stage. Without a guitar to caress for comfort he thrust his hands awkwardly into his pockets – a defence mechanism which characterized all his early stage appearances and which so infuriated Columbia chiefs that they ordered the pockets of his stage suits to be sewn up. Julio's eyes blinked uncomfortably like a badger caught in the headlights of the car. He was blinded by the dazzle – but clearly visible before him was his destiny.

'A simple guy with spots singing an honest song,' is how Gabriel Gonzalez, the Columbia executive who was later put in charge of Julio's career, describes Julio on that night. 'Physically, he was a disaster – skinny, acne ridden and with a huge inferiority complex about his looks. But people liked him for some reason. They liked his innocence and they liked the song because it was something they could relate to.'

For all his gaucheness, Julio heard the orchestra playing the opening bars of his song 'and it sounded good'. He found the voice and the courage that moments before he imagined had deserted him forever. And he sang.

He sang the song which he had written during those bleak months back in Madrid – the song he had sung a thousand times to friends during the happy days in Cambridge. But he sung it that night like he'd never sung it before and when it was over he heard for the first time the intoxicating applause of a stadium full of admirers. It was to remain for him as alluring a sound as the siren's song has been to sailors and, in some ways, every bit as deadly.

'If you take that sound away from Julio then you might as well kill him,' comments Feliciano Fidalgo, the journalist and renowned Julio-watcher who is also a long-time friend of the singer. 'That sound is, basically, what the man lives for.'

That night, with the first taste of success in his mouth, he bowed gratefully, and with childish delight, to the audience, unable to believe the sound he was hearing. Leaving the stage he hugged Garea and Otero and waited in the wings to see the latter perform. He applauded his friend heartily, while secretly hoping that Otero's song would not oust his from the competition. The audience reaction to 'La Vida Sigue Igual' had, however, left him feeling strangely confident.

After all the evening's entries had been heard, each song received a different interpretation from a popular group of the day. In Julio's case 'La Vida Sigue Igual' was performed by Los Gritos, whose version was also very much appreciated by the Plaza de Toros crowd.

Julio waited for the announcement that he and Los Gritos had been selected to take part in the final, two days later. He went back to his hotel room with Otero, who had also been chosen, and slept that sleep of the just. He had victory in his sight and he knew it.

Thus it was that on 18 July, a more confident Julio, dressed in a white suit with stripy shirt and dark kipper tie, took the stage once more at Benidorm. This time he was ninth in line to sing and he waited calmly for his turn. When it arrived he walked calmly into the light aware, as he puts it, that my train was passing . . . that this was my opportunity. That I must not miss it. This was my moment.'

He determined to give the performance his all, to climb on board the train that was his destiny. He drew his voice, he says, from his liver, from his soul and from the depth of his very testicles. (Testicles mattering infinitely more to the Spanish male than tonsils ever could.) And once again, as the audience exploded into applause, he felt his soul soar above the Plaza de Toros.

There was one more act to go, followed again by the group interpretation of each song. Then the sixteen-man jury retired to consider its verdict. Two hours later they returned and announced Julio Iglesias and Los Gritos to be the winners of the tenth Benidorm Festival. A jubilant Julio climbed onto the stage to be presented with a cheque for 150,000 pesetas (around £750) and a festival trophy which he held aloft triumphantly, as though it had been the World Cup.

In the moments after the presentation ceremony he was descended upon by the usual press posse. First to interview him for TV was Raoul Matas for the Chilean TV Station, Canal Trece, followed by Miguel de Los Santos and Emilio Loygorri for the Spanish press.

In his report from Benidorm, the latter gave the opinion that Julio had won by a fluke and that 'La Vida Sigue Igual' would probably not have been the people's choice. He described the as yet unknown singer as 'a young guy, with a toasted suntan and with a special appeal for the girls.' Incorrectly, he also said that Julio was a qualified lawyer.

'But when the press asked him, he had told them himself that he was a lawyer,' says Dr Iglesias, 'even though he had failed one part of his exams. Then, of course, having told them this, he felt he couldn't go back to sit the exams or sign on at Madrid University where my friend was willing to pass him without him having to even re-sit the exam, because he didn't want the press to find out that he wasn't actually qualified. So he decided to chuck the whole thing in. He abandoned his legal career there and then.'

Whatevers his reasons for turning his back on the legal profession, Julio saw clearly that he had another career with which to concern himself – not the respectable, safe and lucrative one that his parents had wanted for him and not the one that he had dreamed of as a boy. It was one of those strange, almost surreal coincidences that on the very evening of his victory he bumped into Ricardo Zamora, the goalkeeper Julio had hero-worshipped as a boy. In the conversation that took place between them, Julio apparently announced his intention to be as successful a singer as Zamora had been a goalkeeper. With those few words Julio abandoned his past dreams and embraced his future.

The next day, the press accompanied Julio on board the victory float that wove its way between the jubilant crowds of Benidorm. At twenty-six years old he had not yet begun to insist that he was always photographed from the right side. He posed this way and that – he gave them his all.

Since the accident, he realized, something had been missing from his life and that something was adulation. He felt once again that he was the local hero and the feeling was good. He welcomed its return like a long-lost friend and vowed never to be parted from it again.

When the camera crews packed up and left so too did Julio and his father. The two headed back to Peniscola to share the moment of triumph with Charo. Julio's mother, in the meantime, had witnessed her son's victory on TV and had read about it in the morning papers. When the two men arrived at the family holiday home they found her in the depths of despondency.

'To be honest with you, when Julio walked in she took one look at him and burst into tears,' says Gabi Fominaya. 'The father was delighted by Julio's success and by all the attention, but Charo was really devastated. Look at it from a mother's point of view. She knew that her son's life could never be the same again and she knew that success is not always a recipe for happiness.'

To Charo, then, the title of her son's winning song seemed staggeringly inappropriate. With a mother's instinct she understood that his life was not about to go on the same but to metamorphose dramatically.

Chapter Seven

On 20 July 1968, Julio left his parents in Peniscola and headed back to Madrid. His journey to Benidorm had been fraught and it's likely that, in a practical sense at least, the journey back to the capital was no better. But such was Julio's state of mind that it seemed to him that he was being carried back to the city of his birth on wings. He had left it in May as a semi-cripple, despondent and disillusioned, and now he was returning to it once again the hero.

As his car spluttered to a halt outside number 27 Benito Gutierrez, he immediately noticed a gaggle of girls who had been keeping a vigil, waiting since morning for the conqueror to return. 'From that day onwards, the truth is that whenever Julio was known to be in town there would always be a crowd of girls outside the apartments,' says Gabi Fominaya. 'There were days when you could hardly get through your own front door.'

Julio knew then, as he does now, that the support of the fans is lifeblood to any performer and he has never underestimated their worth. He has described them as 'guardians' without whom a singer would be nothing. It was, he said, the fans who know all the minutiae about you, who follow your career with the attentiveness of a detective and the love of a mother. It was they who remained faithful to you during the bad times.

In time, he became used to the screaming girls and the groupies, to the obsessive housewives and the downright eccentrics – like the Japanese woman who would buy a first-class ticket on any flight that she knew Julio was on simply to be near him. But he never took it for granted.

He was – and is – always utterly charming. 'Because,' says Fernan Martinez, 'he understands that these people buy his records and also he is genuinely grateful to them for their support. It is an unspoken rule with Julio that the more someone appears to be humble the more important he likes to make them feel. He will take on important people and fight with them if need be, but I have never heard him be rude to a fan or scream at a chambermaid. He is always completely warm and completely civil to them. Why else do they continue to follow him the way that they do?'

That sweltering afternoon of 20 July, Julio began as he meant to continue. He stepped into the crowd, signed autographs, pecked cheeks and posed for pictures. He was flattered by the attention and amazed that, despite the 42 degrees of heat which held Madrid in its relentless grip, the girls had camped out on the hot pavement refusing to leave without a sighting of the new celebrity. He flashed his straight white teeth at the girls before entering the building.

If he had wanted to, he could doubtless have tried to seduce any one of the girls who had stood waiting so patiently for him on the baking pavement. But at that precise moment there was only one woman on his mind and that woman was Gwendoline. Before heading off to the Benidorm Festival, he had, according to Enrique Bassat, left her with the thought that when the competition was over he could take her on holiday to the beach resort of La Manga del Mar Menor, near Murcia. 'And all the while that he was away we talked about the possibility. Gwendoline asked my advice about it.'

In the event, after winning Benidorm he called her immediately and they arranged to meet in Paris. 'So I took my little car and I drove her to Heathrow, knowing she was going off to be with Julio again. You can imagine what my feelings were at that moment, though obviously I didn't tell Gwendoline because she was in love with Julio and she wanted to be with him. I knew I was losing her forever, but what could I do?'

By the time Julio arrived in Paris, four days after Benidorm, Gwendoline was at the airport to meet him. The young man arriving in the capital of France with money in his pocket and a beautiful girl waiting for him on the other side of customs remains, for Julio, one of the greatest images of triumph that he has ever known.

He was, after all, besotted with Gwendoline and he has always claimed her to be one of the most important people in his life. She was his first 'liberal' love, and theirs was the first coupling that he had been able to enjoy without restraint – though, sexually, that month of August was to prove problematic. On arrival in Paris, and without the permission of Gwendoline's parents – who were currently in the throes of a traumatic divorce – the lovers booked into the Hilton, with its romantic outlook on to the Eiffel Tower. After a night of passionate lovemaking they were disturbed by a knock on the door which proved to be Gwendoline's by now furious mother. She had, she told them, rung fifteen hotels before finally tracking her daughter down at the Hilton. She demanded to know what was going on, though the double bed with its rumpled sheets made the answer obvious. She wanted to know what Julio's intentions were towards her daughter – did he plan to marry her? To which he replied that though the two of them were very much in love, neither at that moment entertained thoughts of marriage.

It was not a good start, particularly since Julio had arrived in Paris hoping to persuade Gwendoline's parents to allow him to take her on holiday with him. Clearly La Manga del Mar Menor was now out of the question, so cannily, when Gwendoline's mother had calmed down, he suggested a holiday in Orense, Galicia, where his uncles still lived. Over the next two days various telephone calls occurred between Orense and Paris in which Julio's uncles assured Gwendoline's mother that her daughter's virtue – already, let's face it, violated by Julio – would suffer no further abuse in their house. Julio smiled at Gwendoline's mother, charmed her the way he charmed everyone and finally received her blessing.

On 25 July the couple flew from Paris to Barajas airport where Julio had left his Seat 850 in the car park and they began the long drive to Galicia. Julio's uncles anticipated that they would need to drive all night – allowing no time for hanky panky. Julio, however, put his foot firmly on the throttle and the couple made it to Orense by 10 p.m. the same evening. They had arrived in time for one last night of unrestricted passion. They attempted to check in as man and wife at the San Martin Hotel. But the concierge, whose job it was to uphold a law which made it illegal for unmarried couples to sleep together in hotels, suspected at once that these were a courting couple and no more, a fact confirmed by their passports. He could only allow them to stay he said, if they took two single rooms. This they did, though only one of the rooms was ever occupied.

That night was to be the feast before the famine. Julio's uncles had decided that Gwendoline would stay with one of them and Julio would stay with another, in a separate house. Julio, who had become used to the luxury of sleeping with his girlfriend whenever he chose to in England, now experienced the unfamiliar sensation of being able to look but not to touch.

It was an August of making love hurriedly in uncomfortable cornfields and, when the frustration became unbearable, of announcing that he and Gwendoline were off for a few days on their travels. They drove to the nearby Galician coast, attempting to book in this time at the Gran Hotel in La Toja – and failing. They spent the next few nights in a roadside bed-and-breakfast where they shared a bathroom with lorry drivers and a bedroom with cockroaches. It was not exactly the romantic tryst they had imagined.

Julio vowed to Gwendoline that, despite appearances, their future was bright. He suggested that after the summer they might go together to the United States to learn English. There in the land of opportunity – particularly sexual opportunity – no one would ask if they were married and, hell, if need be he *would* marry Gwendoline. Of course he would – though deep in his heart he knew even then that he was simply creating pipe dreams.

That summer, after all, 'La Vida Sigue Igual' was being played all over Spain – even though, much to his frustration, the version mostly heard on the radio was the recording by Los Gritos. But, still, it was his song and if he could write one successful song then surely he could write others. Why, that summer in Galicia he had already begun work on another song – this time about the beautiful woman currently sharing his life, about Gwendoline.

The world of music was beginning to take its inexorable hold and a whole new set of ambitions and dreams were being born in the young singer.

Their birth, however, signalled the death of Julio's relationship with Gwendoline. In mid September he suggested that she should return to her mother, who would be worrying about her, in Paris. He himself would return to Madrid to speak with the Columbia chiefs. But shortly – very shortly – he would return for Gwendoline and they would pick up the idyll where it had left off. He swore it.

In the event, back in Madrid, Columbia were keen to put their newly signed recording star to work. 'We wondered whether he had any more songs up his sleeve,' says Gabriel Gonzalez. 'Because at that moment he was a one-record wonder.'

He told them frankly that he did not – but that he soon would have. He spent the remainder of the summer on the balcony of Benito Gutierrez composing new songs. By October 1968 he had written ten new numbers, including 'El Viejo Pablo' and 'No Lores Mi Amor', which translates into 'Don't Cry, My Love'. The fact that his girlfriend in Paris would probably be doing precisely this was an irony that was, sadly, lost on him.

She wrote to him every day and he, in the beginning, did the same. Then, as time went on and the world he was inhabiting began to take over, he would write less frequently. Their plans to go to America were put on hold again and again until, eventually, both stopped mentioning them.

Julio, after all, was intent on other travels – to the top, as Gabriel Gonzalez recalls. 'He was probably the most ambitious person I had ever met, even in those days. He had it in his head that he was going to be successful and nothing would divert him from that. To be honest, in those early days, none of us believed that he had what it took – we regarded him as a bit of an annoyance. He had this one song that had done well at Benidorm and that was it. But whenever you turned round he was there in the corridors of Columbia with his guitar, or he was on my back pleading with me to go with him to all the radio stations to get his record played.

'We would traipse off to all these places and Julio would wait downstairs while I went up to plead his case. I used to say to him, "Look here Julio, I've got bigger fish to fry." Because at that time I was also in charge of marketing The Rolling Stones and Tom Jones and Engelbert Humperdinck in Spain. But the guy was unbelievably persistent – and when it wasn't him it was his father, who was even more unrelenting, asking me what I was doing on behalf of his son's career.'

Gonzalez corroborates the story that Julio's father had used his influence with the Benidorm judges – and contradicts Julio's assertion that his father would have been more keen to see his son follow a career as a lawyer or, even, a diplomat (which, given his subsequent history, he would have been rather good at). 'No,' he says, 'his father was always there in his shadow egging him on, helping him and encouraging him. Even when he had a manager, his father was still in there giving his opinion. The mother remained outside the whole thing, not wanting to participate. But you could never have said that about Julio's father, he wanted to be completely involved at all times.'

Infuriating as Julio junior – and senior – proved to be to Gonzalez, it was, he says, impossible to dislike them. He and Julio became firm friends. 'We were both young and full of hope and we had a lot in common. Most of our conversations in those days were about football.' As for Dr Iglesias, he swiftly ingratiated himself with Gabriel by becoming his wife's gynaecologist. 'I was married in 1968, the same year that we signed Julio, and that same year Dr Iglesias delivered my first child.'

Julio, in the meantime, who often refers to his fresh compositions as 'newborn infants', returned to Columbia with ten tracks ready to be recorded. In October 1968 Columbia flew him to London to record the album, *Yo Canto* (I Sing) at Decca's studios, where in 1962 The Beatles had famously cut some of their first tracks. Absurdly, the company's publicity machine also arranged for pictures of Julio to be taken in the streets of London dressed in a bowler hat, a city gent's overcoat and carrying a black brolly. On his return from England's capital they had other similarly daft publicity stunts up their sleeve to promote their newest star.

One was a short documentary made for newsreels (NO-DO, the Spanish equivalent of Pathé). It was watched by cinema audiences all over Spain and featured a brief history of Julio's colourful and romantically tortured life. The camera crew had taken him to the Bernabeu Stadium, dressed him once again in a Real Madrid goalkeeper's strip and had him leaping unconvincingly around the goalposts that now symbolized for him another incarnation. It should perhaps have been fun, though, in fact, the making of the film was a rather depressing experience. Julio, who was and is to this day partially handicapped, could not help recalling the days when he would leap between the goal posts, with the grace and agility of a cat – the times when he was whole and strong and could leap towards an oncoming ball with death defying ease.

The pictures taken on the day of the filming show Julio beaming, but the occasion remained a sad reminder of what might have been. The consolation was that Julio's future as a singer was looking brighter than it ever had for him as a footballer. This was to be the last time he would look back.

No looking back – even for the sake of Gwendoline who continued to pine for her lover in Paris. Julio, however, was already cheating on the woman who had given her virginity and her heartfelt love to him. How was she to know that he was unable to be faithful?

The demise of the relationship, says Julio, was due to the distance between them – and certainly the miles that separated them could not have helped. But already a pattern that was to repeat itself again and again in Julio's life was emerging. He was, after all, conditioned by events in his family background, by his father's constant infidelities to his mother, and by a society that supported the idea of male profligacy. He was driven to infidelity, it appeared, by his very genes and he had moved into a domain where infidelity was a constant possibility – even a necessity. Poor Gwendoline – beautiful she may have been, but she did not stand a chance.

He continued to write to her, but with a growing sense of unease and, ultimately, with the guilty conscience of a man who has already betrayed his love. On one occasion, indeed, he went to pick up letters from Gwendoline with his new girlfriend – or one of them, since there were several on the horizon: girls from Columbia, journalists, backing singers.

The couple were, of course, now moving in different worlds, and after returning from London, he broke the news to Gwendoline that Columbia were about to send him to the Viña del Mar Festival in Chile. There was no mention of her accompanying him.

It was Julio's first long-haul flight – eighteen hours from Barajas to Pudahuel airport in tourist class on a plane that made constant stops. Julio, wishing to experience all the new sensations that South America would offer him, remained wide awake throughout. It was when the plane touched down in Brazil that the exotic quality of the continent struck him like a punch in the face. He recalls the smell of petrol, asphalt and ripe fruit. It was his first sensation of the smell, the heat and the colour of Latin America. It was the start of a lifelong love affair.

Viña del Mar, his ultimate destination, was reached eventually and filled the impressionable Julio with a similar sense of wonder. It was an up-market seaside town whose main claim to fame was its music festival, which each year attracted the good and the great from all the Latin territories. Staying at the O'Higgins Hotel, with its pale gold façade, he began to get his first taste of the luxury that success might afford him. He noted with the awe of the newcomer that fellow guests were artists like Leonardo Favio, and that he – Julio – was the least known and fêted of them all. Nonetheless, his performance of an Italian number, not his own, was well received in the Quinta Vergara where the festival took place. 'But then, in the early days, Julio had that ability to make the audience feel sympathetic towards him. Perhaps they even felt sorry for him,' Gonzalez suggests.

In the years to come, Julio would return to Viña del Mar often. It was in South America, indeed, that he began to lay the foundations for what was to become a fabulously successful international career. Later he would arrive at Pudahuel airport to receptions not unlike those given to The Beatles, with thousands of screaming girls carrying placards and wearing T-shirts bearing his name. (And popularity-wise, though it may seem odd to the English market which has persistently regarded him with scorn, he *was* and is the Latin equivalent of The Beatles.) But on that first trip, just one woman took pity on him and asked him for his autograph. She was the first snowflake in what was to become one of the most phenomenal snowballs of success.

On his return to his native land, Julio embarked on a tour of Spain. Back in Paris, Gwendoline no longer expected her love to fulfil any of his promises to her. After all, the Spanish tour was followed by a trip to Rumania with film-maker Valerio Lazarov, who was keen to test out new filming techniques using lasers and zoom lenses. He suggested to Julio that there could be mileage in making a film of him performing at the Debrasow Festival, in Bucharest and Julio, who already saw that every country represented a potential new market, agreed. He sang one song in Spanish and another in Romanian – the first time he sang in a foreign language – though he would later record albums in Italian, French, Portuguese, English, German and even Japanese. Though the reception was warm, his memories of Bucharest, where he was billeted in a grey, unfriendly-looking hotel with cold labyrinthine corridors and plugless baths, are of being chilled to the marrow. There are pictures of Julio in the streets of that city, with his collar turned up against the biting wind that blew from Siberia, looking pale and vampire-esque, attempting to imagine himself elsewhere where the sun was shining. Sun being to Julio what snow is to the polar bear. Essential.

Seeing Julio's rather depressed state at this time, it was Lazarov who suggested that the next leg of the trip, which was to take them to another festival in Vienna, could be interrupted with a brief visit to Paris – where Julio could once again see Gwendoline. Julio's desire to see his lover outweighed his doubts that she would want to see him. He called her and they arranged to meet.

It was March 1969 and even in Paris the chilly winds blew. The couple rendezvoused at a Paris night club. Gwendoline brought a friend with her and Julio brought Lazarov. The additional couple were, in a sense, there to protect Julio and Gwendoline from each other. Their presence insured that the couple did not have to confront the real issues that existed between them – that, in reality and despite Julio's promises to Gwendoline, there was to be no future for them.

Gwendoline, bitterly hurt and heartbroken, was cool towards him and distant. Julio in return convinced himself he didn't care and hid behind his macho pride. But when they said goodbye, mouthing the usual platitudes about remaining friends forever but knowing that this could never be possible, there was genuine sadness. Later, Julio was frequently to wonder what might have become of his life if he had indeed married Gwendoline, and to curse the universal truth that love and the right moment for love so rarely coincide. But it is doubtful that life would have been so different for him. She loved him and in his way he loved her, but perhaps love for Julio has taken second place to success. Most likely it would have been Gwendoline who ultimately served Julio with separation papers rather than the woman he did marry – Isabel Preysler. And that is probably the only difference. But if it consoles Julio to think otherwise, who could blame him?

As for Gwendoline herself, according to Enrique Bassat,

after the break up with Julio she met a Dr Ritzentaler in Paris and married him, more or less on the rebound, and they moved to Lyon, where Gwendoline lives to this day.

'But unfortunately,' reflects Enrique, 'she had a great deal of medical problems – gynaecological problems – and she was never able to have children, which was a great tragedy in her life. Probably because of that, her marriage didn't work out and she was divorced. But maybe what had happened between Julio and her was also partly responsible – I don't know. We never spoke about what really happened and when you see that someone has lost something so precious you don't like to dig the knife in the wound. Though, as someone who knew her, I would say she was pretty devastated by what had happened.'

Even now, a quarter of a century later, Gwendoline invariably calls Enrique, 'and we talk about old times and we talk about Julio.' Since Bassat lives in Barcelona and Lyon is fairly close by, he has often suggested meeting up with her. 'But she always says the same thing: "No, Enrique, I don't think that's a good idea. I prefer for you to remember me the way that I was when you first knew me." And it is always said with such a sad voice.'

Julio, too, prefers to remember Gwendoline as she was – as he puts it, 'in a glass case, alive and fresh like a rose in a glass of water' – which is pretty much how he liked to think of all the women he genuinely loved, even when they were still living with him.

'But Julio, too, always asks me for news of Gwendoline whenever I see him or speak to him. Even last year when I saw him in Miami we spoke about her,' says Bassat.

The ties forged between Enrique and Julio remain strong. 'Perhaps because I liked him when he was nobody and he never forgets that. He understands that I was really his friend, that I didn't want to know him for any advantage I might gain from knowing him. I was simply his friend. And I will always continue to be his friend because I know the real Julio – the good and the bad.'

Bassat completes his recollections of Julio with an anecdote about a particularly memorable meeting between the two men. 'It was maybe fifteen years ago, when Julio was already a very big international star and he was coming to give a concert at the stadium in Barcelona. I went to see him at the hotel where he was staying before the show and I took my little daughter, who was only four years old at the time, with me.

'When we got into the room the crowd around Julio was ten maybe twenty deep. But as soon as he saw me come in he raised his arm and shouted: "Enrique!" He waded through the crowd and embraced me and then he took my little girl and he hauled her up onto his shoulders.

'He was about to leave for the stadium, but instead of putting her down he took her with him to the lift, still on his shoulders. And then he put her in his limousine and I raced for my car and I was in frantic pursuit trying to keep up with his limousine because I didn't want to be separated from my daughter. And you know, I felt rather desperate.

'Later, it occurred to me that actually, at that time, my little girl was a fairy princess too – just like Gwendoline had been. And that once again Julio was making off with the girl I loved most in the world. And I felt that same panic and jealousy that I had felt over Gwendoline.

'When I finally caught up with him Julio embraced me again and handed me my daughter. He smiled at me and, of course, he knew.'

Chapter Eight

On the beach at La Manga del Mar Menor, the place where Julio had originally wanted to take Gwendoline in that summer of 1968, the still only slightly-known singer is in a passionate embrace with another beautiful, cool blonde with high cheek bones and blue-grey eyes. She could so easily be Gwendoline.

It is now, however, the summer of 1969 and Julio and Gwendoline have parted company some months before. Besides, when you look more closely the blonde is Anglo-Saxon not Slavic and her hair is a little shorter. She is, in fact, the English actress Jean Harrington and not Gwendoline at all and her embrace with Julio is at the behest of film-maker Eugenio Martin, who had the dubious honour of directing a movie which bears the same title as Julio's first single, *La Vida Sigue Igual*.

The film, which starred Julio as himself, was vintage B-movie stuff of almost wonderful awfulness. It was made to promote Julio's career and was loosely based on his life. In the film, Julio is portrayed as the crippled superhero, limping his way to the top, conquering the hearts – and, doubtless, the hymens – of various girls, but especially that of Louisa (played by Harrington), a hotel switchboard operator who helps nurse Julio back to health.

With the love of Louisa, Julio, who in reality at that stage had never sung in a Eurovision Song Contest, gets to sing in one and to win it with . . . 'La Vida Sigue Igual'. But he is never too busy or too successful to think of others and it is thanks to him that a crippled eight-year-old also gets to walk again.

When not tugging the heart strings of the audience, he is plucking the strings of his guitar and breaking into song at unpredictable moments. That an equally dreadful sequel to *La Vida Sigue Igual* should have been made ten years later seems almost unbelievable. And, indeed, with charming self-denigration, Julio himself was to say of his sorties into film acting: 'They're the worst films you can ever see. I was the most ridiculous actor.'

No matter, there was a certain poignancy to the film location, La Manga del Mar Menor, which was chosen by Julio. And to the similarities between Gwendoline and Jean Harrington. Perhaps it was because of these very similarities that Julio insisted on her taking the lead female rôle, despite the fact that she spoke no Spanish and was horrendously overdubbed in the final version of the ninety-minute film – her mouth moving out of synch with the words, as though she were appearing in another movie entirely.

Julio had met her while recording his second album, in London. Still wounded from losing Gwendoline, he embarked on a lukewarm affair with her. In his memoirs she merits only a small mention as *'una media novia'* – a half girlfriend – and though he remembers her beauty he doesn't remember her name correctly, referring to her as Jane instead of Jean. Yet, for all that, the liaison continued for nearly a year with Julio flying frequently from Madrid to London to be with her for the weekend – the affair being terminated, in the end, only when Julio met the woman who was to become his wife, Isabel Preysler.

The level of freedom afforded him by his long distance love, however, was very much what Julio needed at that time. He immersed himself in his work, travelling that same year to Guatemala to sing as a guest of the Red Cross and participating in the Festival of San Remo in Italy. By the time 1969 came to a close he had already travelled hundreds of thousands of miles in pursuit of his dream – which was, quite simply, to conquer the world with his music.

On 21 December of that year, the conqueror joined forces with the man who was to become a kind of commander-in-chief of the battle plan, Alfredo Fraile. Fraile had been at school with Julio back at the Colegio de Los Sagrados Corazones, though at that time they had not been best friends. 'We knew each other, sure, and my mother and his mother were long-standing friends. But we mixed in different circles,' Fraile records.

After school, Fraile went to university and earned his degree as a physicist. He had lost touch entirely with Julio until, in 1968, shortly after the Benidorm Festival, he received an unexpected call from his old classmate. 'He rang out of the blue and said he needed my advice. He said he wanted to sing professionally and that he needed a manager. He came to me, I presume, because my father was a movie producer and a camera operator and we had good contacts in the world of show business. At the time I didn't think to suggest myself for the job and I thought that Enrique Herreros Junior would be a good choice. Enrique Senior was also a manager of film artists and a painter and his son had gone into stage management as well. So I organized a dinner for Julio at my mother's house and we introduced Julio to Enrique and so it was that Herreros became his first manager.'

It was Herreros who booked the early gigs for Julio, while

Gabriel Gonzalez at Columbia continued to plug the records on Julio's behalf. Between them they had given what Gabriel Gonzalez, for example, never believed to be a particularly promising career, as big a kick start as they could muster and Julio was doing better than anyone expected. 'So at the end of 1969, in December, Herreros came to me and he said, "Okay, you introduced Julio to me, but now I need somebody to help manage him. Will you come and work with us?"' Alfredo Fraile recalls. 'And it must have been the right time in my life, or perhaps because I'm an intuitive person, I could see that Julio was going to be a big success and so I said, "Yes", really without thinking about the consequences for my life.'

These were to be deep and far-reaching. Over the next fifteen years, the two men worked together, travelled together, ate together and even slept together – though in a strictly heterosexual sense. 'Julio always used to joke that he had slept with me more times than he had slept with his wife. And, of course, it was absolutely true.'

Over time, Fraile was to become not just his manager, but his intimate friend. 'He used to call me his "hermanager" which is a cross between *hermano* (brother) and manager – because what we had was not just a business relationship, it was like blood. Julio became like family to me and I became like family to him. I am partly who I am because of him and he is partly who he is because of me. And I would not want to change that.'

The Fraile-Iglesias marriage was one of opposites. Physically, for example, Fraile was pale and plump and shorter than the slender and obsessively sun-bronzed Julio.

Early in his career the singer discovered that a suntan could improve both his spotty skin and his image immeasurably. Indeed, later it was said to be written into his contracts that he would only perform in places where the sun shone. His world tours were organized to arrive at each destination in the height of summer. Later, in the eighties, rumours and press stories abounded that Julio's constant exposure to the sun had caused skin cancer – though this was never substantiated.

The difference between the two men was not just physical, however. Mentally, too, they were poles apart. Fraile had the brain of a scientist and applied strict rules of logic to the Julio campaign – while its protagonist supplied the eccentric and often irrational creative flair and charm.

'He told me that sometimes when he was flying out of control, I pulled him back down to earth. And sometimes when I felt that my feet were too firmly on the ground he helped me to fly a little,' says Fraile, reiterating the flying metaphors applied to Julio's personality by Enrique Bassat.

Fraile had grown up in show business. His father was one of Spain's foremost authorities on world cinema. But he lacked first-hand knowledge of managing artists and was content to play second fiddle to the more experienced Herreros. He used that time to observe Julio, to get the measure of the man.

'I did a lot of watching and listening. But I believed in Julio from the very first moment because I could see that onstage he had this way of communicating with people. It's not a question of the way he sings, it's more a question of the way that he communicates the songs and the stories in the songs. These songs of Julio's, they always sound so simple – and he always talks about how simple they are, everyday stories of everyday people. But maybe they are not so simple after all. Maybe their simplicity is a brilliant illusion. I certainly began to see this.'

Early in 1970, Fraile had a classic example of this illusion of simplicity to back up his argument. While on holiday with Gwendoline in Galicia, and deep in the throes of his passionate love for her, Julio had begun writing a song dedicated to her and bearing her name.

It was a sad song, a testament to the love that the two had shared. It was a song whose melancholic undertones suggested that at that time Julio knew in his heart that the love affair would not last. 'It was a song that was written from the depths of my soul that I wrote for her. Only for her.' But ultimately, of course, like all artists he recognized that the experience with Gwendoline and the song that resulted from it could and should be used.

So it was that the song he had sung gently into her ear that summer of 1968 was, by the summer of 1970, being played in discothèques and on radio stations all over Europe. Why waste a good thing?

The song was an anthem of love in which Julio expressed his innermost feelings for Gwendoline. He sang of the warmth that she had made him feel – a warmth that he said he stored inside himself to ward off the pain caused by the distance that now existed between them.

As the song progressed it invoked Gwendoline by name, and recalled the time they had spent together. It was a bitter-sweet song whose first verse earned Julio the nickname in the press of '*El Termo*' – the thermos flask. But for all the jokes made at his expense, the song nevertheless spoke to audiences and seemed to reflect every sad love affair that had ever been experienced between a man and a woman – as so many of Julio's songs went on to do.

The potential of the song was enormous. A fact recognized by Arthur Kapps, the Viennese musician who had been living in Spain for some years and who Julio had met through Columbia while making his third album *Soy* (I am). This early album, which was re-released by Julio's current record company, Sony, in 1993, has now become a collector's classic and demonstrates the vulnerable and highly romantic quality of Julio's early work. It featured tracks like 'Mi Amor Es Mas Joven Que Yo' (My Love Is Younger Than Me) which, given Julio's romantic history, could serve as the anthem for his life and 'Vete Ya' (Go Now).

Kapps – who had heard Julio singing a crude version of

'Gwendoline' – suggested that he should polish the number up and submit it for the Festival de la Canción in Barcelona, which was to take place in February of 1970. The festival served as an arena for selecting Spain's entry for that year's Eurovision Song Contest and Kapps advised Julio that, from what he knew of the other entries, 'Gwendoline' was almost certain to win.

Julio heeded Kapps' advice and duly entered the festival. His mentor had been quite right – 'Gwendoline' was a triumph at Barcelona and in March 1970, Julio found himself on stage in the Eurovision Theatre in Amsterdam, representing his country.

It was the days before the Eurovision Song Contest had descended into kitsch. It was watched by millions all over Europe and its winners were held in universally high regard. Sadly, 'Gwendoline' was pipped at the post by Dana's famous entry for Ireland, 'All Kinds of Everything,' but, nonetheless, in the summer that followed Julio's song was number one all over Europe and Latin America. Only Britain, which has never been too keen on songs sung in foreign tongues, remained impervious to Julio and he was to wait until 1981 to have any measure of success in the UK.

Sentimentally, Julio came to view this song as Gwendoline's legacy to him – her parting gift, as it were. If it had not been for her then he would not have experienced that summer of success all over Europe. In his memoirs, he closes his chapter on their ultimately doomed love affair with the words: 'Many thanks again, dear Gwendoline.'

In the old black-and-white movies of the forties and fifties, when films like *The Glen Miller Story* celebrated the lives of the famous, it was a well-used cinematic technique to indicate a star's most successful and industrious period with a montage of quickly-changing newspaper front pages, showing the protagonist first in one town and then another, on and on. The sound of trains tooting and puffing in the background would give the idea of incessant travel.

In any film of Julio's life they might apply the same technique to illustrate the year 1970. For though his career has always been characterized by a non-stop quality, an endless orbiting of the globe, that year was a particularly relentless one.

Keen to consolidate his success in Europe, and particularly in Spain, Julio immersed himself in a daunting programme of work that was to take him, directly after Eurovision, to the MIDEM festival in Cannes and on to the Luxembourg Radio and TV Festival in Germany. Later that year he was also to take part in Japan's Osaka Festival. It was his first trip to a country that would become a huge market in which Julio would be worshipped by hundreds of thousands of devoted fans. That year, too, ended on a professional high when he was selected to sing at an exclusive concert to inaugurate Marbella's Puerto Banus in the presence of Princess Grace of Monaco and the Aga Khan. 'Life was very full in that year,' recalls Fraile.

Opening up massively lucrative markets like Japan and singing for your supper in front of royalty were the more glamorous highlights of a year which, in other ways, had been pure back-breaking hard work.

'The real hard work that year went on mostly in Spain,' recalls Alfredo Fraile. 'That year we worked like crazy to make Julio a household name all over his own country.'

There was to be another album in 1970, Julio's fifth, featuring ten songs, including 'Gwendoline', which became the title track. Then in June of that year, Julio and Fraile hit the road in the time-honoured tradition of pop stars the world over. There were ten of them in all on board the tour bus: Julio, Fraile, a band of musicians, a record company executive and a driver who would have the daunting task of ferrying them safely between an exhausting forty-one Spanish cities in just one month.

'We were working like crazy all over Spain because we understood that until Julio conquered his own country he could not properly expect to conquer the others,' says Fraile.

Already, Julio was showing the punitive work ethic that was to characterize and to create his success. 'In the end, you saw that a lot of his success was due to plain hard work and I never knew a man who worked harder than Julio,' says Gabriel Gonzalez. 'Even when he's sleeping he's working. He's one of the hardest workers that ever existed in the world of music.'

Over the years Julio would constantly reiterate to journalists that this work ethic was fundamental. In 1982, for example, while riding the crest of almost unbelievable international success, he informed journalist Joy Nelson:

'As for holidays, I haven't had one in the last ten years. Holidays are for people who don't enjoy work. I don't know what Sunday is. I don't want to have a Sunday. It's the worst day of the week. I really don't have any time for it at all.' It was a philosophy of work and of the achievement of excellence. 'Julio's philosophy is this,' says Fernan Martinez. 'If you're going to join the army then don't settle for being a sergeant – be a general. If you're going to do the high-jump, jump three metres not just one. If you're going into the priesthood, be the pope. Always be the very best at what you're doing.'

Yet, caught up in his need for triumph, he came eventually to understand that its hold on his life had cost him dearly on other fronts. In 1991 he reflected in an interview with the *Daily Mirror* in England: 'I've made seventy-nine records in twenty-two years. To some people that means fame, wealth and success. To me it represents about fifteen years locked inside a recording studio.'

These years, presumably, could have been spent in pursuit of the one thing that continued to elude him: simple happiness of the variety that all the success and money in the world (which he certainly appeared to have) can never buy.

In those heady days of youth and hope and tireless enthusiasm, however, Julio had not begun to consider the cost of the tariff to be paid on the long and relentless road to fame.

'We were earning just about enough to keep the tour bus on the road. But it wasn't anything like it is today, where everything is first class and luxurious and jet set,' recalls Fraile. 'We would travel miles and miles on the bus, stay in second and third-class hotels. Sometimes, because maybe it wasn't such a great lifestyle after all, Julio would say, "Okay, we'll do this for a while, maybe four years or so, make some money and then we can go back to our professions. I'll go back to the law and you can go back to being a physicist." Though I don't know whether he saw it as a genuine possibility.'

It was in those relentless days of touring, sharing rooms in run-down hotels, that the two men began revealing their life experiences, as Julio had done with Enrique Bassat back in his Cambridge bedsit.

'But Julio is not a man that you get to know so easily,' insists Fraile. 'He can be very defensive and sometimes he didn't want to open up because, even though he was still young, he had already suffered a great deal in his life and he was afraid of being hurt.'

Fraile is referring not simply to the accident and its aftermath, but to Julio's family background, which had, to his mind, left scars every bit a deep as the one that he bore on his back.

'Julio was the result of everything that had happened to him, as we all are. There was the accident and the paralysis and that was a very big thing in his life. But there was also the thing that had existed between his parents and it was my instinct that he suffered because of that.

'I was with him for fifteen years and so I know many

things about him. But sometimes we didn't speak about the things that really mattered. There were subjects that were understood between us, but they were subjects that we didn't discuss.'

What Julio sometimes failed to articulate, however, Fraile interpreted by his actions. 'In those early days, when I first started touring with him, we would go to a hotel and, naturally, when we got into the room I would unpack all my luggage, hang everything up and put things away in the drawers.

'But Julio never used to do that. He'd just take the jackets out to stop them creasing and then a shirt – as and when he needed it – and that was that. Everything else remained in his case. It was almost as though he thought: "Well, maybe people won't like me and I'll have to leave quickly in the dead of night." He never explained it to me in this way, but I knew that was how he felt.

'Probably it was the result of the insecurity that was in his background, from the relationship between his mother and father, and maybe that was why in the end he settled for me as his manager. I gave him the security he needed and he gave me the element of doubt that I needed. That's why we worked so well together.'

Despite Julio's father's rather jaundiced and embittered assertion today that Fraile was simply 'the man who carried the bags', his importance in Julio's life was manifest and obvious to all who knew them.

In her memoirs, Virginia Sipl, who became Julio's safe harbour after the breakdown of his marriage to Isabel Preysler, makes it clear that Fraile played a key role in Julio's life, not just professionally, but personally. He was one of the few people Julio was prepared to listen to, she says, and the very first that he would go to in times of trouble.

Fraile himself, who planned Julio's early campaign with the

precision of a latter-day Rommel, claims, rather modestly, to have been 'maybe ten per cent responsible' for the star's phenomenal success. But he does not underestimate his value to Julio as a friend.

'The problem is that Julio has very few friends. Even though he thinks he has many, in his heart he knows he has few. Sometimes he confuses people worshipping him for people liking him. This is a big tragedy in his life.'

As the years went by the professional relationship – which was always fiery – blazed a trail throughout the world and, as it did so, the personal relationship deepened.

There is, for example, symbolic significance in a ritual that came to be observed by the two men after each performance that Julio gave, a ritual that demonstrates the precise nature of their relationship.

As each show came to an end and the crowds continued to cheer and scream for more, Julio would take his final leave of them still smiling, blowing kisses at them, still charming them. Then, leaving the stage, he would be engulfed in the darkness in the wings. Waiting for him there would be Fraile, always holding the same warm shawl, that he would carefully wrap around Julio's shoulders.

The buoyant, irrepressible Julio was left on stage and the vulnerable Julio, shivering and unsteady on his feet, emerged in those few paces between the limelight and the shadows.

'Julio would always talk about the cold that he felt when the lights went out and it was spiritual as well as physical,' says Fraile. 'After a show, artists feel empty because they have given so much. And Julio would be drained to the point of falling over.'

With the shawl around him, he would put his arm through Fraile's and the two men would walk slowly, and in Julio's case unsteadily, like an old man, back to the dressing room. The ritual never changed until Fraile ultimately decided he could no longer support his friend, 'his brother in arms', for reasons which will become clear later in the story.

Cut to Madrid in 1990 and a chance meeting between Fraile and Isabel Preysler, where, according to the former, the following conversation took place. 'Isabel said to me: "You know, Alfredo, you and I are the only ones to have ever divorced Julio." And, of course, she was right. But that we had done so was, perhaps, also a measure of how much we had loved the man.'

Chapter Nine

What Julio liked most about her was her youth. Above all, her devastating youth. It glowed from the cashmere-caramel bloom of her skin, shone from her large brown enigmatic eyes, danced on the shimmering velveteen blackness of the hair that flowed around her shoulders and announced itself in every graceful movement of her gazelle-slim body.

Isabel Preysler Arrastia was not the kind of girl that you normally encountered in Madrid. She was unfamiliar, oriental and serene with none of the giggly gaucheness of the usual eighteen-year-old. She was as poised as a princess, as stylish as a *Vogue* model, as innocent and yet as overwhelmingly exotic as a camellia in full bloom. Julio gazed upon her loveliness, drank in her full fragrance, saw the amused detachment with which she regarded him – and was utterly lost. From the moment he saw her, he knew that he wanted her more than he had ever wanted any woman. And what Julio wanted – let's face it – Julio, generally got.

Even in her own country, the Philippines, Isabel Preysler was regarded as a cut above the rest. She was the daughter of a wealthy, well-connected conservative Catholic family who were aquainted with Ferdinand Marcos himself. Indeed, a cousin of the latter – an unsuitable older man – had paid her court back in Manila, and her parents, keen to protect their innocent young daughter from his attentions, and from the gaze of newspaper photographers' lenses, had packed her off to relatives in Madrid.

Ostensibly Isabel was going to the city, as her elder sister had done, to improve her Spanish – which was, after all, the language of her forbears. At the same time she was to embark on a secretarial course and duly registered at the Colegio de Las Irlandeses – a school run by nuns. 'I had been educated by nuns back in the Philippines, too, and I think my parents were comfortable with the idea of me carrying on with them. They thought I would be safe.'

She arrived in Madrid in March 1970, as the almond trees were coming into bud, and moved into her aunt's house. 'Perhaps to others I gave the impression of being more sophisticated than I really was because the truth is, I was a convent girl who had lived all her life in her parents' house and now I was living under the protection of my aunt. So you see, I was in fact a very innocent girl,' she says. Implying, indirectly, that at this time she was also a virgin.

'I was fortunate because my godfather was also living in Madrid and my parents had many important friends in the city, who took care of me. And so I was immediately intro- duced to Madrid society.' Her friends included members of the jet set, Chata Lopez Saintz and Carmen Martinez-Bordiu Franco (General Franco's granddaughter – who remains a close friend and ally today). 'And these people started inviting me to parties where the young people used to go – they made a real effort to help me enjoy myself.'

In May 1970, Isabel found herself at a party being thrown in honour of the Flamenco dancer Manuela Vargas in the luxurious home of nightclub owner Juan Olmedilla. It was to be on that very night that she came face to face with the man who was to be her destiny. With Julio. Though her recollection of that precise moment – the moment that would change her life irrevocably – remains hazy, only half-remembered.

Julio, on the other hand, was later to recall his first sighting of the Filipino beauty with tremendous force. He saw her among the crowd and was bewitched by her skin, her large mysterious eyes, and her enormous style. He pestered Juan Olmedilla until he introduced her to him.

'But we didn't stay together at that party and to be honest I can't recall what I thought about Julio at that time,' says Isabel.

Most of the gathering at Olmedilla's house knew precisely who Julio was – the majority of them were his friends and the rest knew him from his appearance at the Eurovision Song Contest only two months earlier. Isabel, however, was either unaware of or unimpressed by Julio's celebrity. 'I don't think I really knew or cared who he was at that time.'

Julio, however, was captivated by the mysterious beauty and let it be known among his group of friends. Two weeks later, Olmedilla called him again to invite him, this time to a Saturday-night party at a house in the country. Julio at first declined the offer because he had a previous arrangement to meet with Jean Harrington in London that weekend. But when another mutual friend of both Julio and Isabel's called him to say that Isabel was also invited to the party at the Casa de Campo, he instantly cancelled his tryst with Harrington – who by now was more than used to her semi-boyfriend's fickle nature. He and his friends then concocted an elaborate scheme to ensure that this time, Isabel could not fail to notice the singer.

'I was in a car with my friends on the way to the Casa de Campo and we pulled up at some traffic lights', recalls Isabel. 'My friends started talking excitedly and pointing to the next car and they were saying "Oh look, there's Julio. Julio Iglesias in the car next to us."'

Before the lights could change to green, Julio's male passenger leapt from the car and came and opened the passenger door next to Isabel. 'Julio needs one of you to ride with him to the party,' he insisted without explanation. 'And the next I knew I was being pushed out of the car by my friends and I was saying, "Why me?" But the lights were about to change and I had to get in the car with Julio.' So it was that they found themselves travelling the same road, metaphorically, for the next seven years of their lives.

'Why me?' The words that Isabel shouted at her laughing friends on that occasion when they first set her up with Julio. It was a reasonable enough question and one that over the years she would come to ask herself again and again.

Julio describes his initial powerful feelings towards Isabel as *'un coup de foudre'*, implying a kind of madness at work. But the politics of attraction are surely, on analysis, more rational than this and there was indeed a rationale behind his obsession with Isabel.

Apart from the obvious – her looks, her class, the fact that she, like him, had come from a conservative, Catholic background – there were other more veiled and ultimately more important aspects to the attraction. There was her virginity, for a start, that once claimed by him as his wife could never be claimed by another man.

He would possess her entirely and place her in the glass case – the fresh rose in a vase of water that only he was at liberty to enjoy. And this became a fundamental in their relationship.

There were other important issues, too – that of her very foreignness for example. Julio viewed her shyness and her inscrutability – the gifts of the culture in which she was raised – as an indication of inner compliance, but, as she later proved, they were only ever an indication of her inner strength.

Most important of all, though, was her youth and this was the key to the attraction. As journalist Feliciano Fidalgo puts it: 'Every man, if he's honest, probably would prefer a young woman to an old woman, and the older he gets the younger he likes them. But for Julio it is something more than this. He likes young women because he can mould them and if you can mould them, then you have created them and the thing is yours and yours alone.

'Yes, Julio certainly wants to control his women. But he also wants to control men and to control the very table at which he eats. You must remember that Julio needs to dominate and to be king of all he surveys.'

On that night at the Casa de Campo, he surveyed Isabel and he wanted to rule her, to possess her and to call her his own. The fact that she was still unimpressed by her suitor acted as a fan to the flame. Where is the joy of conquest when it presents itself on its back?

After the party, Julio insisted on driving her home. She insisted, in the meantime, that he also take her friend Chata and drop her, Isabel, off first. On leaving his car, she shook her head and refused to give him her telephone number. She might as well have asked him to slip a ring on her finger there and then. In the event, Julio was leaving for London within a few days, but saw to it that one of his friends furnished him with Isabel's telephone number before he left. While he wined and dined Jean he was plotting how he would make Isabel his. He called her from London and she, finally impressed by his efforts, agreed to meet him in Madrid the following week.

On that first date they went to the Carlos III cinema

and saw Juan Pardo sing. After the show they slipped into a café in the nearby Calle de Serrat and without more ado, Julio made his feelings plain to her. 'He said to me: "You know, you are the perfect woman that I have always dreamed of marrying." And then he told me, "I'm not asking you to marry me, but you are just what I have always imagined I would like my wife to be." '

That evening she was wearing a high-necked dress and a silk sari on top. She was the Madonna and the high priestess of love rolled into one. More importantly, sitting there with barely a lick of make-up on her innocent face, her body shrouded from view like a nun's, she was the very opposite of his mother. And these things mattered – they mattered deeply – to Julio.

Julio, for his part, insists that from the moment he met her he knew that this was to be no ordinary flirtation. It was, for him, The Big One. Isabel, on the other hand, expresses doubts that he was 'really that crazy about me. Though I think that in trying to convince me, he also convinced himself.'

That night they left the café and went dancing at the then famous night spot, Gitanillos. They met the next night and the next and the next and Julio began to erode her scepticism. She was intrigued and flattered by his attentions. 'Though I still wasn't sure how genuine it was. I could see that Julio was a man who liked all these romantic things and I suppose I didn't entirely trust that. But as time went on I was taken in by his charm – and no one in the world is more charming than Julio. And when you are young, you don't have the defences or the cynicism of an older person.

'I saw, too, that he was very hardworking and I admired the fact that he was very *recto* – upstanding and correct in the way that he was. And, of course, when someone seems to be so very much in love with you, so attentive to you, then it is very difficult to resist. It is very attractive.'

Isabel felt her resistance slipping away and she, too, began to fall in love with Julio, although in the summer of 1970 – that non-stop summer of touring – their time together was snatched and frantic (as it would be later in their marriage). Julio would call her daily on the telephone from wherever he was and would fly from airports all over Spain to be with her, no matter how briefly. She was holidaying at Guardamar, near Malaga, an exclusive resort where the couple were later to buy a property of their own. It was, as 1968 had been with Gwendoline, a decisive summer of love.

He had, of course, talked of marrying Gwendoline – though not, he later realized, in any genuine way but rather in the flush of youth and passion. With Isabel, however, it was different, and he claims that from the moment he met her he decided that she was to be the 'love of his life', and that he would, indeed, marry her.

In October he was back again in Latin America, consolidating his success with the single 'Gwendoline', which had been number one in that territory throughout the summer, and he called Isabel on a crackly long-distance line imploring her to be his wife. She turned him down. But in December, back once again in Madrid, he asked her again. And this time she said yes. They had known each other for precisely seven months.

The engagement, brief as it was, met with no one's approval, says Isabel: 'My family did not particularly like the idea of Julio because he was a famous singer, which was not what they had in mind for me. But in time, after they had met him, they came to see that he was just a normal boy.

'More than this, when he met my parents he was very

charming to them. And you know how it is with Julio, no one in the world is more charming and in the end they came to love him and he won them round.'

For all this, in that December Julio and Isabel stood alone in their desire to marry. Indeed, it seemed that the only people in favour of the marriage were the couple themselves. Isabel's parents maintained that the couple had known each other for insufficient time and that their daughter was still too young to marry, while Julio's mother, Charo, made it plain that Isabel was not the kind of woman she had envisioned for her son.

'She had wanted a woman like Pisca for Julio,' says Gabi Fominaya. 'Someone who would be solid and look after Julio. I think Isabel seemed very foreign to her and a difficult person to understand. But, of course, she could not go against her son's wishes.'

As for Julio's father, he could see the attraction – but there again, he could doubtless have seen the attraction in any woman that Julio chose, such was his nature. Furthermore, he was not about to alienate his main ally in the cold war that persisted at number 27 Benito Gutierrez. If he had misgivings he kept them to himself. 'If this is what Julio wants then Julio has my blessing.' It was all rather predictable.

It was already the middle of December and the wedding was planned in haste for 20 January, immediately after the 1970 Christmas celebrations. Julio and Isabel – along with Alfredo Fraile who at that time was, says Julio, 'like a brother to me' – began touring Madrid looking for an appropriate venue.

Some days they would see a hermitage and it seemed too small, the next a cathedral that would seem too big. Sometimes they would set their hearts on a venue only to change their minds the next day. Finally, they alighted on the chapel of José Luis in Illescas, in the province of Toledo.

And there in the shadow of that ancient city, famous for its stunning Visigothic architecture and for having spawned El Greco, whose paintings can be viewed at every turn, Julio promised to forsake all others except Isabel.

The wedding was set for 6 p.m. on 21 January 1971. The couple had hoped for a quiet affair. In the end it was immediate family and close friends . . . plus a few hundred fans and an army of photographers and camera crews. For already, Julio's endless love affair with the media and with his dogged followers had begun. By 5.45 p.m. the pavement around the small chapel was packed, the crowd swelling despite the rain which had fallen persistently throughout the day. Two Guardia Civil were called to direct traffic and to ensure that onlookers did not break through the barriers – particularly when Julio himself, dressed in morning suit, arrived at precisely 6 p.m.

He looked, according to the newspapers at the time, rather gaunt and obviously nervous – though he smiled for the crowd. 'How are you feeling?' the journalist from NO-DO newsreel inquired. 'I'm happy to be about to marry the woman of my dreams,' he replied, before adding, 'I don't think it's her beauty I fell in love with. It was her goodness that struck me. And as for Isabel, I don't think she fell in love with a famous singer, but with a simple, normal guy, Julio Iglesias.'

Before disappearing into the chapel, he stopped to shake hands with the crowd as though he were visiting Royalty. Five minutes later, Isabel's car arrived and as she stepped out, a small bridesmaid holding her train to protect it from the wet pavement, she drew a gasp from the onlookers. She was a stunning sight to behold. She had chosen a full-length, long-sleeved bridal gown made of shot white silk. The spectacular veil was of pure white tulle. In her hand she carried loose white spikenards – a flower as rare and exotic as Isabel herself. In her ears she wore simple pearls. Her slender waist was accentuated by a wide silk belt and her hair was swept back into a soft bun, revealing a swan-like neck. Her bosom was carefully shrouded beneath the neckline of a dress that could have been worn by a vestal virgin.

It was, for many of Julio's fans, the first sighting of the woman who was about to do what they had always dreamed of doing – marrying Julio Iglesias. Similarly, inside the church, there were many who had yet to be introduced to Julio's bride, including Gabi Fominaya. 'Julio had certainly kept Isabel very much to himself and that day – their wedding day – was the first time I ever saw her. Naturally, she was very beautiful, exceptionally beautiful and very young and very much in love with Julio,' she recalls. 'But none of us knew what to predict for the marriage because she was very much an unknown quantity.'

Though Julio had stated publicly that he hoped for a quiet and simple wedding, photographers crammed into the pews and Isabel was illuminated by flashguns as she walked down the aisle. The priest, Father José Aguilera, an old friend of Julio's who had also officiated at the wedding of Alfredo Fraile and his wife earlier that year, took exception. As adviser to the Catholic Youth Action Group he was already well known to the press. He barked at those familiar faces that surrounded the altar with cameras in their hands that 'this is not a show, it is a religious ceremony. Both Julio and Isabel deserve more respect.' The service began. Isabel, lit from behind by a full-length stained glass window depicting the suffering Christ, read from Ecclesiastes: 'A good woman is a good partner.' Julio in turn read from St Paul's letter to the Corinthians.

'Though I speak with the tongues of men and angels, and have not charity, I am become as sounding brass or tinkling cymbal. And though I have the gift of prophecy and understand all mysteries, and all knowledge, and though I have faith so that I could remove mountains, and have not love, I am nothing.'

It could serve as an anthem for Julio's life.

At 6.30 p.m. the exchanging of vows began. As she made her promises to Julio, Isabel was overcome with emotion and delivered her answers to the priest's question with tears. Julio smiled indulgently at her, handing her his hanky. He made his own vows to her with confidence. At 6.40 p.m. Father Aguilera declared them man and wife and Isabel walked joyfully from the church, her arm through Julio's, to the sound of the 'Hallelujah Chorus'. Outside, the crowd hailed them ecstatically and the cameras lit up the evening sky with their flashguns.

The newlyweds and their guests repaired to a nearby function room for a stupendous party. There was the traditional wining, dining and dancing. As the couple cut the seven-tier wedding cake and exchanged a passionate kiss, the guests cheered, stamped their feet and smashed glasses on the ground for good fortune. On the loudspeakers came the inevitable sound of Julio singing 'La Vida Sigue Igual' – that song which always seemed to crop up at moments when its title seemed most inappropriate. For after marrying Isabel, life clearly could not and should not be the same again. Julio informed his guests that from now on every time he sang it, it would be for Isabel alone. If only he had really meant it.

They left the very next day for their honeymoon in Las Palmas de Gran Canaria, staying at a luxurious beachside hotel at Maspalomas. The previous occupant of their suite had been Neil Armstrong – the first man on the moon.

Later, part of the media mythology that surrounded the marriage implied that in those early days of his career the couple were impoverished. 'People even said "Oh, poor things, they couldn't even afford a proper honeymoon,"' smiles Isabel recalling some of the press reports that emerged, plotting the history of the marriage and of Julio's success.

'But though we certainly didn't live then as well as either of us lives now, we weren't poor by any stretch of the imagination and our honeymoon suite was luxurious. We went to the Canaries simply because I was anxious to get back to see my family in Madrid, since they had flown over especially for the wedding. Also Julio was about to leave for a tour of Mexico and I would be going with him. The honeymoon was really a stop gap.'

Caught up, once again, in a romantic idyll, Julio wrote a song for Isabel, just as he had written one for Gwendoline during the summer of 1968. This time the song, written on the golden crescent-shaped beach, was 'Como el Alamo al Camino' (Like a Poplar Tree on the Road). It was, he said, a song that set out the principles of a good marriage. It begins with the idea of perfect love in which fidelity and constancy are paramount. It dwells on the idealised, eternal nature of the love that he feels for the song's heroine – presumably Isabel.

So far so good – even if, in time, the words were to prove rather staggeringly unprophetic. But later the song descends unpromisingly into the idea that the love is doomed. It ends with a lament of the 'what went wrong?' variety and becomes a sad hymn of regret in which Julio accepts that he had lost his love forever and, yet, will always keep a place in his heart for her.

It was not exactly what you'd call an optimistic song to receive as a bridal present from a new husband. But, then, neither had 'Gwendoline' been full of the joys of spring. It was almost as though Julio could only admit in his songs what he knew in his heart – that faithful love and commitment, till death us do part, was for him never a real possibility.

After the honeymoon, the couple returned fleetingly to Madrid. Julio left his new wife with her family while he went for a few days to perform at the Festival of Knokke in Belgium. On his return he and Isabel set off with Alfredo Fraile and the rest of the team for a first ever tour of Mexico, Panama and Puerto Rico.

'In those early days, Isabel would travel with us a lot,' recalls Fraile, 'and she was very, very good for Julio. She made him happy and she kept his spirits up. She would be on the bus with us and she never complained about it, or suggested it was beneath her. She was a young woman who was very much in love with her husband – that much was obvious.'

In between touring commitments the couple made two trips back to the Philippines to visit Isabel's family, with whom she maintained close ties. In this way Julio learned more about the woman to whom he had enjoined his life and the realisation of what, precisely, he had done began to sink in.

Not that he felt that marrying Isabel was something he should not have done, though, in interviews later he confessed that he and Isabel should perhaps have attempted to get to know each other before making a lifetime's commitment.

As it was, they had known each other just seven months – barely time to understand even the most superficial aspects of two personalities that were unusually deep and complex. Isabel, too, confesses that she married on the hop, without stopping to consider what her expectations of Julio ought to be. 'When you marry and you're nineteen years old, you don't really have many expectations. You simply know that you're happy and that you're in love and you think that this will see you through.'

So why the haste? It's tempting to jump to the conclusion – perhaps the wrong conclusion – that Isabel agreed to marry Julio that December for the most basic reason of all. She said yes because she had just discovered she was pregnant. Perhaps or perhaps not. Perhaps their first child, Chaveli, born on 3 September 1971, just thirty-two weeks after the wedding night instead of the standard thirty-eight, was indeed, as Isabel maintains, simply early.

Dr Iglesias claims that 'Isabel certainly wasn't a virgin when she married Julio.' And since, rather bizarrely and some might say inappropriately, he became Isabel's gynaecologist after she married his son, he presumably should know.

Whatever the truth – whether Chaveli was conceived before marriage vows were exchanged or not – Isabel remained at her husband's side during those early months of the marriage, her body swelling visibly and beautifully with his child.

As the time for delivery approached, Julio took his father aside and instructed him to go with Isabel to Portugal. 'So we stayed together at a hotel in Estoril for a couple of months,' says Dr Iglesias, 'and I arranged with a friend of mine at the Red Cross Hospital that we would deliver the baby together.'

Certainly there are differing accounts here. Isabel suggests that the baby arrived in Portugal early and unexpected, while Dr Iglesias asserts that the delivery was planned to take place in Portugal. Otherwise, what on earth was he doing there in the first place?

'For some reason, Isabel did not want to have the baby in Spain,' he says – though she was more than happy to give birth to her subsequent children, Julio José and Enrique in Madrid.

What could possibly have motivated this bizarre decision? '*Ni puta idea!*' says Dr Iglesias, becoming visibly tight lipped. 'No bloody idea!'

Perhaps it would be jumping again to the wrong conclusion

to deduce that Isabel wanted to have her baby in another country away from the glare of a Spanish press who were already obsessed with her marriage to Julio, and who would doubtless have arrived at the hospital carrying not just cameras, but calculators. Or perhaps not . . .

Chapter Ten

There is a poignant picture of Isabel, Julio and Chaveli, taken at the Red Cross Hospital in Estoril. Isabel remains in her hospital bed, smiling a wan smile, while Julio is by her side holding his tiny daughter. He looks neither at Chaveli nor at Isabel, but smiles beamingly for the camera. He is wearing a suit like someone on a visit to the bank manager and his expression, too, is of someone on his way to somewhere else. Someone who has just popped in, as it were. He holds Chaveli as a rugby player might hold a ball in the fleeting seconds before he hurls it to his team-mate. It is not the picture of a man besotted by his wife and the miracle of new life that she has performed for him.

Though the baby, christened Maria Isabel after her mother but known, universally, as Chaveli, was born on 3 September, it was, according to Isabel, several days later before her father dropped in at the hospital. 'Well, he was working, he was on tour, which was the way it always was, and because of that he could only stay for a couple of hours,' Isabel recalls. 'But yes, yes, that hurt a lot even though in a funny way it also gave me strength because I thought, "Well, I have given birth alone – so I can be mother, father . . . I can be everything." '

Not that either of them in those early days – just over seven months into the marriage – stopped to analyse their feelings. It was only later, surveying the wreckage of their relationship, that such events would take on their proper significance. Julio, for his part, later confessed that Chaveli's birth was not perhaps as earth-shattering for him as it ought to have been.

'It was something, at first, let's say, just natural. A child after marrying? Of course. Isn't that a simple biological story – the most basic albeit the most beautiful story in the world? Doesn't it happen all the time?'

Well, perhaps. But not to him and not to Isabel, who carried the hurt of her husband's rejection with her throughout her marriage – even though, at first, she bore the wound of this and other betrayals unconsciously. She was, after all, a young bride and a new mother. On the surface, at least, she remained full of hope and optimism. She did not peer into a metaphorical crystal ball and predict the ultimate devastation of her marriage. 'I believed in my my marriage to Julio,' she says. 'I believed I had married for life.'

She had believed, too, in the romantic idyll of marriage, as depicted to her by the thoroughly romantic man with whom she had exchanged vows. She had bought into the 'once upon a time' and 'happy ever after' fairy tale that he had been so charmed by but was unable to fulfill. 'It wasn't, I suppose, until I'd been married a while that I came to realize with Julio that what he said, what he did, and what he felt were three different things entirely.'

While Julio toured in those early days she suppressed her misgivings, returning with Chaveli to Madrid and to the apartment that the couple had rented after their nuptials in the Calle de Professor Waksman. Despite all the later tabloid tales of breadline poverty, Isabel insists that materially, at least, 'we lived well from the beginning.'

'Okay, maybe we didn't have even a tenth of what Julio has now and definitely there was no comparison between our apartment and the house that I now have in Madrid. Definitely not. But I lived better than most of my friends – really very well indeed.

'The apartment belonged to a Catalan interior designer and it was very nice and very well placed. There were two bedrooms, two bathrooms, a kitchen, a dining room and a maid's room. A normal place for a couple starting out. My mother sent me a maid who'd been in the Philippines with me since the age of fourteen. Materially I had no complaints at all.'

Emotionally, too, the honeymoon period persisted for a while. 'We had rows – of course we did, like all couples. But they were small rows. You know the kind of thing – he tells you he's going to come back at a certain time and so you plan something and he doesn't come back . . . And since you don't have any problems bigger than that, you concentrate on those.'

There were periods of prolonged separation, which Isabel accepted as being part of the territory. Somewhere along the line, Julio had fooled himself, just as he attempted to fool both Alfredo Fraile and Isabel, that his singing career was a transient thing. 'In the beginning, Julio never thought he would sing forever. He thought he would reach a certain level, make a certain amount of money and then that would be it. And I believed him, yes, why not? I mean, he had a year to go to finish his law degree. He could always finish it. Don't get me wrong, I didn't sit at home wishing it were true, hoping every day that he would give it up. I suppose that even then, though I was young, I was also very much my own person and maybe being with Julio I became even more so, because I had to rely on myself so much.'

During the absences, there was, of course, Isabel's network

of society friends. There was also, to a lesser extent, Julio's family, though this constituted, as Isabel explains, a rather uncomfortable set of relationships. By marrying Julio she had unwittingly stumbled into the emotional minefield that constantly threatened to blow apart the very walls of Benito Gutierrez. 'But, of course, in the beginning I wasn't aware of that.'

Looking back she now understands that many of Julio's later problems, insecurities and infidelities stemmed from the uneasy dynamic in that family. 'Julio is a very complicated person,' she says, simply. 'His childhood was difficult. His family life was uncomfortable.'

Not, she admits, as uncomfortable as it must have been for Charo and Carlos who found themselves, to use her metaphor, on 'the losing team'. 'I had become part of the winning team without even realizing that it was happening to me,' she says.

That she had, in a sense, become its cheerleader does perhaps begin to explain why Charo harboured such deep-seated feelings of resentment towards her daughter-in-law. It would be easy to assume that these feelings stemmed from the usual Latin mother obsession with her son. 'But you know, Julio was not her favourite son at all.' The resentment sprung more from the idea that, with Isabel having joined the conquerors, she had tipped the scales still further against Carlos and Charo – and you cannot, to Isabel's mind, overestimate the division that existed within that family.

'But I tell you one thing: while I was married to Julio, I never realized how his mother felt towards me. Because since Julio and his father were the ones who used to decide everything, the ones with all the power, she was always very diplomatic towards me. Her feelings were only ever expressed behind my back and a lot of it I didn't even hear about until after our separation.'

There were superficially petty, but deeply telling examples.

'If someone said to her: "Oh, Charo, your daughter-in-law, how pretty she is, how well she dresses" she would say, "Oh, well, what do you expect with all that money?" She was bitter and I don't blame her because her life was very unhappy and my existence didn't help. Julio's father, for example, would constantly draw comparisons between us. He would say: "Look at Isabel, she's a fantastic homemaker, she does everything so well." We would go dancing – because Julio's father loved to dance – and he would say to Charo: "Oh, Isabel dances so beautifully, she's like a feather. Not like you – you're a lead weight." So I was constantly used as a slap in the face for Charo, but because I was on the privileged side I just didn't see it.'

Isabel did her best to be a dutiful daughter-in-law and to become one of Julio's family. She did her best to forge links between herself, Carlos and his wife, Mamen: 'I liked them a lot, though I suppose they could possibly have gotten to hate me, too. I always tried to be nice to them in the bad moments, because in the early days they didn't have a lot of money. For example, whenever Mamen gave birth I used to send her my maid and she would go three times a week to help out and I would send her all the children's clothes. Well, you know, sometimes you think you're doing people a favour but you don't realize that it can be upsetting. Maybe Charo, who was very close to Mamen, thought I was looking down my nose or being patronizing.

'I don't know, it's not something I've ever discussed, but I always wonder why she had that attitude to me when I never did anything consciously to hurt her? But how can you get inside someone's head?'

How indeed? How also to get inside Julio's head? What, for example, motivated his order that Isabel should not visit the cinema with Carlos and his wife while he was away on tour? 'I can't explain it to you. But it was funny. It was very funny. Also, though I got along very well with both my brother-in-law and his wife, we never, ever had dinner, the four of us, together. It was strange. But then it was again about this competition that the parents had placed between them. They loved each other but there was this enormous obstacle between them. This terrible competition.'

It was rather gratefully, under the circumstances, that Isabel would retreat from Madrid back to the Philippines whenever the opportunity presented itself. In the early years, during the long separations imposed on the marriage by Julio's touring, she would, she says, spend practically six months of the year back in her native land.

'When I had Chaveli, my mother used to come to Spain a lot and then every September, until she was about six or seven, when her brothers were also on the scene, we would go back to the Philippines. I would stay there September, October and November then, in December, Julio would join us for Christmas. He would leave again in January and come back for us just before March when we would all go back to Madrid together.'

There were many motives for the arrangement – not all of them sinister or negative. 'I was very close to all my family, to my sisters especially, and so it was Julio who used to call my mother to fix it up for me to go to the Philippines, because that way I wouldn't be alone.'

The arrangement was then, on one level, motivated by care and concern for his young wife but also, she now believes, it was a way of ensuring that she was kept away from her society friends in Madrid, away from the public eye, away, too, from the attentions of other predatory males. In short, kept out of trouble.

Not, Isabel says, that her husband had the slightest cause for concern. The birth of Chaveli, she says, had for her, at least, sealed her destiny with that of her husband – there was no competition. 'Maybe without Chaveli it would have been different. He was travelling a lot and I was in the Philippines.

If I hadn't had a baby what would have stopped me from thinking: "Well, I don't feel very married." But I did feel married, you see. I was happy with my daughter. Happy with my life. I was completely faithful to him, and it never once entered my head that he could possibly be unfaithful to me.'

Why, indeed, should it have entered her head? After all, Julio, the man who 'said one thing, felt another, and did another again', told her he was faithful. In his memoirs he reiterates the version of himself that he doubtless gave to Isabel at the time – that after marrying her he became more disciplined and more responsible.

He had moved his position, he said, from that of a man who thought of his life in terms of himself alone to one who now considered the needs of two people – himself and Isabel. Julio recalls that 'a terrible anxiety about success was being born in me'.

Career-wise at that time, after all, success ebbed and flowed and it was certainly not possible to rest on his laurels. Yes, he had been enormously successful after the Eurovision Song Contest. He had sold his first million records and his tour of Spain had brought him to the forefront of the music world. 'But to be honest, by the beginning of 1971, things were beginning to go a bit flat,' says Alfredo Fraile. 'You know how it is in Spain, the people like to build you up so they can knock you down. So we decided to leave Spain for a while and try our hand in other territories – which is why we planned that first trip to South America, to Mexico, Panama and Venezuela, after Julio's wedding. We thought we should give Spain a rest.'

Julio's waning popularity in Spain at that time undermined Enrique Herreros' confidence in his protégé. In name, at least, he remained in charge of Julio's career but it was Fraile who had emerged as the main mover.

'I remained convinced that Julio could be a big success, because I had seen with my own eyes the way that he communicates with people and I knew that what he had was something special and unique,' Fraile says. 'So I suggested to Herreros that we could make a big international career for Julio. But Herreros disagreed.'

Unconvinced, Herreros commented with a historic lack of insight that 'we will never make any money out of Julio.'

'So he said to me, "Alfredo, here, you take Julio. I give him to you as a gift with a ribbon on." And I said, "Yes, Enrique, I relieve you of him very happily."'

That was in the late spring of 1971, but Fraile's stewardship did not begin until the final months of the year since Julio still had commitments that summer that he needed to fulfil for Herreros – various shows that his manager had already pencilled in for him. Since Herreros and Fraile had effectively split, Fraile was left kicking his heels that summer, unemployed, with the responsibility of a wife and child himself. 'But I knew absolutely that Julio was worth waiting for.'

When Julio's commitment to Herreros ended, Fraile – again in complete contradiction to the notion that he was 'the man who carried the bags' – approached his father and asked to borrow 250,000 pestetas (roughly £1300). With this he rented a small office in the Avenida de Brasil, and set up a kind of campaign HQ – the campaign being Julio's bid for world fame.

'It was like a war in which you have to conquer each country in turn and in each country you need a different battle plan, because in each the language is different and the approach is different. I said to Julio that success is a ladder, and while you're climbing it you can never afford to relax for one reason – because you always have people climbing up behind you wanting to throw you off. But believe me, in me in those early days the battle wasn't easy. It was a real struggle. And that kind of struggle . . . well, it costs.'

Despite the ease, then, with which the public imagines its stars achieve their fame, clichés of the meteoric rise variety generally shroud the truth that all fame and success is achieved with back-breaking hard work and always at a price. In those early years, Julio's intense programme of work, his non-stop touring, was a question of necessity rather than choice and for this he is not to blame – although the price to be paid for it was normal family life. A price paid not just by Julio but by Fraile, too.

'At that time it was what we had to do if we were to have any chance of success. We played to very small audiences for very little money. The only proviso we made was that if we were invited back we would only do it for more money the next time – call it psychological warfare, if you like. We worked on the theory that the more people pay for you, the more they tend to appreciate you. It was not a question of the money, it was a question of the success it represented. So, for example, we had a lot of success in Mexico and the impresario who arranged the tour wanted us to come back within six months. But we said, "No. Sorry, you'll have to wait a year." It was about playing hard to get. We made the people pay for Julio and we made the people wait for Julio.'

Julio, whose enthusiasm for the task and whose need for approbation sometimes outweighed his good sense, was often uncomfortable with this approach. 'At that stage he probably would have said yes to everything – because he was, as they say, hot to trot. I was hot, too, but I made believe that I was cold. I played poker with people. I didn't think it was good to let people know that we were delighted by every offer that they made. I played it cool and it drove Julio crazy. But soon he could see that it was working for us. It was the only way.'

The conquering campaign trail in 1971 encompassed not just Latin America. There were trips to Japan, where Julio recorded a Japanese version of Como el Alamo al Camino,' the song he had written for Isabel. It translated into 'Anatomo Uramo' and established what was to become a trend for Julio – singing in languages other than his own.

By the end of 1972, Herreros was doubtless already both eating his words and licking his wounds. It was in that year, Gabriel Gonzalez recalls, Columbia awarded Julio a prize for being the company's top-selling international artist. His song 'Un Canto a Galicia' (A Song for Galicia) occupied the number one slot in Latin America, as well as Europe, North Africa and certain Middle Eastern countries. An album, this time recorded in German, was also about to be released. Herreros' doubts that Julio had a career in Spain, let alone an international career, had metamorphosed into an ugly monster that took joy in poking its tongue out at him.

And as for Julio, he recalls that 'a terrible anxiety about success was being born in me.' He knew, beyond a reasonable doubt, that he would never return, as he had promised Isabel, to his career as a lawyer. He knew, too, that he was hooked on success. His anxiety revolved simply around how to achieve more and more of it. He became, as it were, a success junkie – always, but always, looking for his next score. No matter what the cost, either to himself, or to those around him.

In 1985, in an interview with English journalist David Thomas, he referred directly to this problem, calling it by its name. 'It is an addiction,' he said. 'It's more than an addiction because an addiction you can take to the hospital and cure. Here the only cure is when you die.'

Back in 1972, thoughts of death were light years away. Success itself would make him immortal.

Right from the start it became clear that Julio and Isabel were, by necessity, travelling on different roads. More specifically, Julio travelled endlessly and Isabel stayed at home, a situation which she accepted as part and parcel of having married someone who – for all his protestations about the temporary nature of his career – was, in fact, a man with a burning ambition. A man with a mission, almost. She, like 'the people' that Alfredo Fraile spoke of, would be made 'to wait' for her husband's attentions. She did so without complaint.

She was his wife after all. 'And when Julio came home after a tour what he most wanted to do was to shut out the rest of the world and go to bed with her,' says Dr Iglesias, who, as usual, was privy to even the most intimate details of the relationship between his son and his son's wife.

Isabel, like his own wife Charo, conceived easily and joyfully. In August 1972, she fell pregnant for a second time – Chaveli was less than a year old at the time. She would give birth to their second child and their first son, Julio José, on 23 April 1973 at roughly the same time as Julio himself was giving birth to his sixth album, *Asi Nacemos* (which translates appropriately into 'This Is How We Are Born). Julio, who had unfortunately missed Chaveli's birth entirely, this time arrived at the hospital 'at literally the last minute' as Dr Iglesias was guiding his grandson's head into the world. His wife had been about to set off to the airport to pick her husband up from a tour when she had gone into labour. Her friends, Carmen Franco and Chata Lopez, were dispatched to the airport instead to meet Julio and bring him to the hospital. That Julio should be brought to her side in the midst of panic and high drama, all but missing the delivery, was, for Isabel, all too predictable. It was simply the way life was.

Again, not long after welcoming his son into the world, he took off for some far-flung corner of it to continue his tour. There were the usual Latin American territories to be seen to as well as Europe. It was also in 1973 that he began to make his first assault on the American market which, for him, would come to represent the Great Promised Land. In 1973, however, given the limitations of his music, which was 100 per cent Mediterranean in origin and style, he confined himself to playing cities with large European and Latin populations.

Although he had not even begun to crack what he was later to call the 'Anglo-Saxon' market – that is to say, the English-speaking nations and especially the United States – there is no question that his following elsewhere was already becoming a tidal wave. By the end of 1973 he had sold ten million records for Columbia to prove it.

Early in 1974 he released the album *A Flor de Piel* (Skin Deep). It featured ten tracks – many of them love songs – including 'Por el Amor de una Mujer' (For The Love of A Woman), 'Desde Que Tu Te Has Ido' (Since You've Been Gone) and 'Un Adios a Media Voz' (A Whispered Goodbye). 'Manuela', the third track on the album, was released as a single and swiftly went to number one in the usual territories – Europe (bar Britain), Latin America, North Africa and Japan. No Spanish popular music artist had ever stretched the frontiers of appeal as Julio had. Yet, as far as Julio was concerned, there were still far bigger conquests ahead and even in the early seventies he became aware that true international success could only ever be achieved by penetrating the American market. On 25 May 1975, he tested the water with a concert at New York's Carnegie Hall. But though tickets sold well and he played to a capacity crowd, the 2,800 seats were occupied by New York Italians, Spaniards and Latin Americans and the reception from the critics was mixed. Latin music critic Agustin Gurza, for example, marvelled that 'a prolonged standing ovation that Julio received was well out of proportion with the actual substance of his performance.' Fortunately, Julio's audiences have rarely – indeed never – agreed with his critics and they have always received their hero with faith and enthusiasm. Even back in 1975 – nearly ten years before his American breakthrough – the delirium that was to overtake his audiences there was already beginning.

Even then, of course, the majority of his audience were women – women who listened to Julio's songs and imagined that he was singing his words of love for them. There were frequently hysterical scenes in which hormone-charged women would camp by the stage door, follow him back to his hotel, attempt to gain access to his bedroom – and by all accounts, the best-looking ones generally succeeded. The public perception of Julio at this time was of a happily married family man. The private reality was another matter entirely.

Nineteen seventy-five was to be another milestone year – both for the private and the public man. In August of 1974, Isabel had conceived her third child, just over a year after the birth of her second. Small wonder, perhaps, that she was to complain to her father-in-law that 'if Julio had his way I would be permanently pregnant.' Enrique, however, born on 8 May 1975, was to be the last child that she would bear him.

This time, Isabel says, her husband was present throughout the delivery. It was to be – for both of them – a novel experience. Again, coinciding with the arrival of his son, Julio presented his followers with a sixth album, *A Mexico* (For Mexico) – a country which had indeed produced some of his most faithful fans.

The flavour of the album, rather like the title, was Latin American, and it featured tracks like 'Cu, Cu, Ru, Cu, Cu'. The release coincided with a tour of that country and other Latin American territories. That year also saw him again in North Africa, Canada, the Middle East and friendly US cities. His debut appearance at Carnegie Hall was to be one of the chief coups of the tour.

In the summer of that year, however, Julio was to turn his attention once more to the home front with a series of appearances in Spain. And it was here that he was to make the fateful acquaintance of Maria Edite Santos who would later – much later – appear as if from the woodwork to claim that Julio had fathered her child.

He met her, she said, at San Felíu de Guixols, a chic resort at the northern end of the Costa Brava, in those days popular with well-heeled Spaniards. That same summer Maria Edite Santos, then a young, rather timid Portuguese girl, was working in the resort as a dancer. She had left Lisbon with a dance troupe headed for Spain at the beginning of 1973, persuaded by arguments that there would be plenty of opportunities for pretty young dancers on the booming Spanish costas.

Maria had been born in the dirt-poor town of Cercal de Alentejo in Southern Portugal. She moved to Lisbon with her parents when she was three. Dark skinned with big brown eyes and masses of long, brown hair she was a good-looking teenager. At fifteen she had won her first beauty competition – Miss Costa de Caparica (Costa de Caparica being a stretch of coastline near Lisbon). She went on to win two other beauty competitions and appeared in TV commercials, occasionally working also in small theatrical roles. She was however, a trained dancer and dancing was her passion. So it was that in the summer of 1975 she found herself working in the Las Vegas Dance Hall at San Felíu.

Julio was singing at a nearby venue which shared its dressing room facility with the Las Vegas. Maria and other members of the dance troupe found themselves in the same tatty low-slung building as Julio and his backup singers and musicians, even though the singer already enjoyed celebrity status all over Spain.

Maria certainly knew who Julio was but, finding herself breathing the same air as the celebrity, treated him, she says, like any of the other artists that worked the costas. He was easy to get to, she says, in those days – just a normal guy doing his job. The paraphernalia of security heavies would come later.

According to Maria, Julio, who had not long since left his wife and children, including the now three-month-old Enrique, back in Madrid, began to romance the nubile, childless dancer. Though she spoke little Spanish she recalls that Julio, with his Galician roots, used his knowledge of Gallego, a Portuguese dialect, to woo her. 'He used to call me *La Portugesina* [the Portuguese girl]. He was all charm whenever I bumped into him.'

'I soon realized I liked him a lot. For me, his attraction was his personality. I wouldn't describe him as good looking either then or now. He attracts women with his charisma, class and style.' She says that Julio, who has never either admitted or denied his liaison with her, was clearly attracted to her and began to invite her to spend afternoons at the beach with him and his friends.

'He used to drive about in a big Mercedes at that time which everybody recognized. I had a battered black Austin Mini. So he used to ask me to pick him up in the town and we'd drive to the beach in my car, so no one would follow.'

She shared a flat in San Felíu with one of the other female members of the troupe. Julio, in the meantime, was staying in a villa out of town which had been lent to him by a friend from his footballing days at Real Madrid.

After one lazy afternoon on the beach, Julio apparently suggested that Maria might like to come over to the villa that evening, and when she agreed he duly sent the Mercedes to pick her up at the flat. Since, she says, she had no intention of staying, she followed the car back to the villa in her Mini. She had every intention of spending the night in her own bed.

But she said Julio was persuasive. He ribbed her about her smoking, shared his hopes of one day conquering the American market, wooed her with compliments and assurances. Made her feel, in short, that she was the only woman in existence. Despite her plans to return that evening, she claims she woke up the next morning in his bed, just as she did on another four mornings during what was to be a ten-day courtship.

She was not, of course, Julio's ideal woman. She was not, for a start, a virgin. She had slept with a few Portuguese men, she says, but never with a Spaniard – and certainly never with a man of Julio's sexual skills. Like other women who were to share his bed – including Virginia Sipl, who later wrote her own memoirs – she reports that Julio was as tremendous between the sheets as every one of his female fans might have imagined.

'He was,' she says 'a marvellous lover. He was as kind and considerate in bed as he had appeared to be out of it. There was nothing selfish about his lovemaking, he made sure that I was enjoying it. With Julio I honestly felt that it wasn't sex. We made love. It was quite unforgettable.'

What had been forgotten, however, according to Santos, was the use of any kind of contraception. 'I told him I didn't have a boyfriend and that I wasn't taking anything. He just shrugged and didn't seem to care. I didn't see a contraceptive in the house.' Also, she says that she did not see any visible signs that Julio was a family man – though like everyone else she was aware that he was married to Isabel and had three children. 'But there wasn't a photograph of them anywhere – not even by the bed,' she says. 'And he never talked about them, which I thought was strange.'

It was, nevertheless, Isabel's appearance in San Felíu which she says put an end to the ten-day fling. 'On one occasion we had arranged to meet after work. I turned up where he was singing and I saw his wife. I went back the next night and there she was again. That was the last time I ever saw him.'

Two weeks later, however, she missed a period. A doctor confirmed her worst fears: that she was pregnant. Her first reaction, she says, was to tell Julio, but his tour had moved on and she had no way of getting hold of him. Abortion at that time in Spain was illegal and women seeking terminations ended up either in expensive foreign clinics or in the hands of back-street butchers. She was, she says, too poor for the former and too frightened for the latter. She decided to have the child and a son that she named Javier was born on 19 April, 1976.

Over the years, she says, there were to be various attempts to contact Julio. In 1977, she attempted to track him down while he was performing in the Canary Islands. A friend had seen Julio and shown him a picture of Maria. He had apparently signed it on the back: 'With love from Julio.' Spurred on by what had doubtless been a message signed on a million programmes, autograph books and T-shirts, Santos took it as encouragement and flew out to the Canaries to confront Julio. By the time her plane landed, Julio had left, and it was to be another thirteen years before she attempted to speak with him again.

It was September 1990 when she took Javier to see Julio performing at the Mestella Football Stadium in Valencia, the city where she now lives. She went along with tattered photos of Julio and herself, taken in the dressing room in San Felíu. Julio's father, who was on tour – as he often is – with his son, granted her an audience. 'I showed him the pictures and said: "This is your grandson." I repeated that all I wanted to do was to tell Julio that he had a son growing up in Valencia.'

Maria Edite recorded that she was thrown out of the stadium a few minutes later by security guards. Once again she had failed to speak to Julio. But it was not to be the end of the story.

She returned home and brooded throughout the winter, finally contacting lawyers at the beginning of 1991. In February 1991, she became the only woman to bring a paternity suit against him.

She won the first round in October 1992 when judge José Luis Rubido de la Torre of Valencia's Number 13 court found in her favour. The ruling was based largely on Julio's refusal to provide a blood sample for testing.

His lawyers, however, appealed against this ruling, alleging that Julio had not been fully informed of his rights. In October 1994, Valencia's provincial court ruled in *his* favour – he had not been notified correctly by Judge Rubido about the blood sample required for paternity testing. But Maria Edite's lawyer, Roque Gambaro, has now appealed this ruling to the Supreme Court in Madrid, demanding that Julio is asked once again to submit to a paternity test.

Maria's lawyers remain firm in their conviction that 'the sample is such a simple thing to provide and, given that it stands forever, makes a nonsense of any excuse Señor Iglesias might give that he would be spending all his time in hospitals if he had to attend to every demand by women claiming he is the father of their child. It is absurd.'

In the meantime, Maria Edite – like all the women who have ever claimed to have slept with Julio – has become a rather tragic sideshow. A Spanish TV programme in 1993 notched up record ratings when they invited her to take a lie detector test in front of the nation, which she subsequently failed. On the other hand, in a similar test on a Portuguese show she was thoroughly exonerated. Notably, Julio himself has never agreed to such an intrusive investigation into his honesty.

Julio's alleged son, Javier, rather predictably, has launched his own recording career, releasing a record called 'Soy Como Tu' (I'm Like you). It is not, he says, a reference to 'his father', which is just as well since there is no one quite like Julio – except, perhaps, Julio's father, Dr Iglesias.

And, as usual, Dr Iglesias has some typically blunt words of wisdom on the potential likelihood of his son having fathered the Santos child. 'I'm not saying that Julio didn't go to bed with her,' he says. 'But if everybody who'd been to bed with him claimed to have a child by him then, maybe, there'd be 3,000 children running about the place.'

He does not doubt that there certainly *could* be unknown grandchildren in far-flung places. Didn't Julio admit in 1992 that he had made love to women in seventy-one different countries? 'In fact, there are maybe men who imagine a child is theirs whereas, in fact, it is really Julio's,' he adds, not without pride.

Isabel Preysler, in the meantime, who was married to Julio

at the time of the alleged affair with Maria Edite Santos says nothing on the subject whatsoever. But given Julio's expectations of her at that time – 'that I would be a completely faithful wife' – it seems unlikely that the paradox, for want of a better word, of a situation in which he was publicly accused by another woman would have escaped her. She is, as Julio says of her, a 'very intelligent woman'. But in certain situations – marriage to Julio being one of them – she was to discover that intelligence alone is simply not enough.

Chapter Eleven

Flash back to 8 March 1972. The occasion is the marriage of Isabel's close friend, Carmen Martinez-Bordiu Franco with aristocrat Alfonso de Bourbon Danpierre. Carmen, you will recall, is the granddaughter of General Franco and it is a mountainously high-society wedding. In the banqueting hall of the Palacio de Pardo – the residence of Franco himself – the crystal chandeliers sparkle and the white gloves of the waiters bearing canapé-laden trays glow. The exchange of gossip, the tinkling of laughter, the popping of champagne corks has reached dangerous decibel levels. Women, dressed for their inevitable appearance in that week's *Hola!* magazine, greet one another by bouncing off each other's cheekbones – lest their skin should be soiled with a lipstick-laden kiss. In a corner of the chamber, with her husband Julio, is Isabel Iglesias Preysler. In a dress of vivid silk, she stands by his side like an exotic bird of paradise.

Foolishly, but unsuspectingly, a photographer from *Vogue* who has an eye for a picture and who has spotted Mrs Iglesias – rare flower that she is – approaches and asks if he might have a picture of Isabel for the wedding montage the magazine is putting together for its society pages.

But for Julio the attention of this paparazzo was entirely unwelcome, and he flatly refused this apparently harmless request.

Was Julio jealous of attention being bestowed on his wife rather than him? Perhaps, a little. Was he uncomfortable in a situation in which he was not chief protagonist, in a place where he was not in charge. Possibly. For those who know him well often comment that Julio is most at home in his own house, finding the hospitality of others uncomfortable and difficult to deal with. But over and above all this, wasn't his reaction motivated by a constant need to insulate his wife from the outside world – an exotic flower in a glass case – whose beauty only he might gaze upon and whose fragrance only he might enjoy? Certainly, according to Isabel herself, it was something like that.

He was, as she puts it, 'exaggeratedly jealous and obsessed with the idea that I must never be unfaithful to him.' Indeed, it seems that the more unfaithful he was to her, hopping not just from country to country but from bed to bed, the more he insisted on his wife's fidelity.

Not that, at the beginning, Isabel was aware of her husband's infidelities. 'Well, how could I imagine that someone who was so concerned with my fidelity could be unfaithful to me? And his concern was so intense that I genuinely felt that he needed to get some help with it.

'I was not allowed to go to the movies with his brother Carlos, and I was not to be seen out and about with my friends in Madrid. I had to be protected from everything and from everyone. I could only see the people he wanted me to see. I could only speak to the people he wanted me to speak to. It came to a point where if we were at dinner and I smiled and said "Thank you" to the waiter serving me, he would get upset. If I said, "Well, I was just saying thank you," he would say, "Yes, but you didn't have to smile." The problem was that I am a person who usually smiles, who likes to smile, but maybe he thought that if I smiled then the person on the receiving end of the smile would think . . . I really don't know.

'Similarly, if I was shaking hands, I didn't have to shake the person's hand strongly, I had to shake it quickly and let go. So I got used to saying thank you seriously and with lowered eyes. I got used to letting go of hands immediately. It was just the way it had to be.'

For Isabel, the spectre of Julio's jealousy haunted their lives. 'Everything was a big deal . . . I needed to take my driving test in Spain and because the instructor was a man, that was a big deal. If I wanted to go and play tennis it was a big deal, too. If I wanted to go out for the night with a girlfriend in Madrid that was unthinkable.

'Very, very occasionally, we would go to parties, Julio and I – parties organized by members of my family. Julio rarely wanted to go to such things and when he did I would see him suffering. I would hold his hand and it would be perspiring and I could see in his face that he was thinking goodness knows what.'

While in Spain it is considered a compliment for a man to comment on the beauty of another man's wife, which often happened on these occasions, Julio would generally react badly to such observations, no matter how well intentioned.

'If someone said: "Julio, how lovely your wife looks tonight" he might reply, "No, she is not lovely, she is very faithful and also *muy solida*' – a phrase which has no equivalent in English, encompassing as it does not just solidity, but moral rectitude of the highest order.

In the early days – and, indeed, for the best part of the marriage – Isabel accepted her husband's hold on her life.

'Well, I understood him in a way. He was from a very

Catholic, very conservative family and when you're brought up like that it is difficult to have different ideas. Maybe now he is a different man, but I don't think so, because these things are very deep inside a person.

'Also, you see, I came from a very conservative, very Catholic family, too. So none of this was exactly alien to me – though Julio did seem a very extreme example of what one might expect, even coming from that background.'

There was also an inbred willingness on her part to make her husband happy. To be the good wife that he wanted her to be. 'So when my friends used to come to me and say, "Look, it's not normal. Why can't you come to the movies with us? Why can't we see you?" I used to say, "No, really, it's okay. I don't want to go to the movies. I'm perfectly happy to stay at home with my daughter. Really, I'm fine."

'Probably, if it had been desperately important for me to go out I would have gone – but it seemed more important to Julio that I did not and since I saw him suffering so much I thought "Why burden him by going against his wishes?"'

'Also, you know, I thought that in time Julio was going to get over it. I thought that this all came from a very deep insecurity that he had. He would say that I was the one that was mad and I would say, "Yes, Julio, you're right – let's go to the psychiatrist together." I would have done anything to help him.'

In 1974, perhaps the most telling and troubling example of Julio's control over her life occurred. Isabel had opted to be with her husband when he was performing in Mexico. She was in the early stages of pregnancy with her second child, Julio José, and unexpectedly began bleeding. She was having a threatened miscarriage.

'I needed to see a doctor immediately, but Julio insisted that I go to bed and wait until his father flew in to attend to me. On the one hand Julio's actions could have been motivated by a simple desire to ensure that his wife's medical care was left in the hands of the man who he trusted most. His father. On the other hand, and according to Isabel, it was motivated rather by a simple dismay at the idea that any other man might be allowed to gaze so intimately at his wife.

Life behind the closed shutters of the apartment at Calle de Professor Waksman – and later at the luxurious apartment that the couple bought in the Calle de San Francisco de Sales – had become weirdly claustrophobic. Yet the public perception of Julio at that time was of a happily married man, adoring father and faithful husband. Even before his marriage, in 1970, Spanish journalist Isidoro Penin Castillo had predicted for the young man that: 'One day, following the natural laws of life, Julio will form a Christian home and will become, without any doubt, a good husband and a good father.' It was an image Julio strove to foster.

Image, after all, and public perception, can never be underestimated in the battle to win the heart and minds of the record-buying public.

'We thought a great deal about what kind of image Julio should have at that time,' says Fraile. 'And though in each country that image was a little bit different, because each country wanted something a little different, I would say that certainly in those early days, while we wanted Julio's image to be romantic and lover like, we also wanted him to be seen as the kind of boy that every mother would have liked her daughter to marry. That every mother lamented that her daughter hadn't married.'

In other words, he was romantic but he was safe. He sang about love, but the message was meant for his wife. It was not the image fostered later, after the marriage breakdown, of the ultimate Latin Lover – a man with Valentino's looks and Don Juan's sexual appetite. No, in the seventies he was a normal guy, with a normal wife, and theirs was a stainless, blameless life.

As more children arrived on the scene, so the image of the loving family man grew. That he had been there to hold his wife's hand for only one of the births was irrelevant. He was busy, constantly touring, always on aeroplanes – and the missing of such events was simply a casualty of the war for international success. 'With Julio you had to get used to coping with things on your own,' says Isabel.

But, still, for all the image makers' efforts to convince the public otherwise, it was not a normal family life – and Julio was not a normal father.

'He did love his children, I can assure you of that,' says Isabel. 'But he loved them in his own way. He loved them, but you know, let's face it, Julio doesn't really *like* children. I can't say he was a bad father, but he never cared personally for them. That was my job. If they were sick, if they weren't sick . . . He never played with them either or took them out on Sundays. He wasn't that kind of father. He was nice with them, he was affectionate with them. He *did* love them. It was just his way of loving. He used to say, "When they get bigger, I'll like them more."

'I think he saw it as part of the housework. I never remember him saying, even once, "Let's take the children and do so and so." I'd always take them on my own. And, perhaps, that was one of the things which added to this idea that I was both mother and father. This feeling that I could survive on my own.'

Even before the catastrophic (for Isabel) discovery of Julio's infidelities, she had begun to shore up her own life and to see that she could survive, if need be, without him.

'You have to understand that in the beginning I was completely dependent on Julio. I came from my father's house, then my aunt's house, then I got married. I couldn't move without consulting him because that was the only way

I could feel safe and protected. But then occasions arose and I would think "I need Julio." And I turned around and he wasn't there. So you survive and then you think, "I did that alone, there is nothing that I can't do alone." And it makes you a very strong person.'

Despite her gathering strength, her sense of personal development, and a latent feeling that her marriage was not the fairy tale she had been promised, Isabel continued to love her husband and to believe in him and in the image of himself that he presented both to her and to the public. She denied her instincts, suspended her disbelief, ignored the evidence of her own ears and eyes and continuously gave her husband the benefit of the doubt in order to convince herself that, whatever the faults in their relationship, her husband was at least faithful to her.

There was one occasion in particular when she unexpectedly joined Julio while he was on tour in Mexico in the mid seventies. Inexplicably, there seemed to be rather a lot of fuss on her arrival – which she initially put down to some marital rumpus that was occurring between one of the other members of Julio's entourage and his wife. The wife had apparently discovered her husband sleeping around on the Latin American tour and intimated to Isabel that Julio, too, had been caught with his trousers down. She did not, however, have the full details and suggested to Isabel that she consult one of the other members of the tour who could certainly fill her in on what had been going on. Upset and confused, Isabel went swiftly to find this man – only to discover that he had mysteriously and indefinitely left the tour for unspecified personal reasons. Isabel's belief in her husband was so complete at this stage that she failed to read anything sinister into the event and dismissed the rumours of Julio's infidelity as malicious tittle tattle. 'Imagine,' she says, 'how completely stupid I was.'

*   *   *

See it from Julio's point of view. He was a highly-sexed man, away from his wife for long periods of time – a man who could charm the birds from the trees and who later claimed that he 'needed women like life itself.' He had been born into a family in which infidelity was the norm, raised in a society that gave its covert assent to it, and then immersed in a world in which it was encouraged, saluted and admired.

Temptation, too, was all around him. 'His mother would tell me stories about how Julio would go to his hotel room and find women in the cupboard – or under the bed,' says Gabi Fominaya. It is difficult to maintain a marriage under such circumstances.

On one famous occasion, for example, he returned to his hotel room after a concert and, exhausted, he went to bed. Once there he experienced a strange sensation in his back and, paranoid as he always was that his paralysis might return, he panicked and yelled for Alfredo Fraile who was in the adjoining suite. Fraile arrived and reassured his charge that he was imagining things, asked him to try to move his legs which, fortunately, still seemed to be in full working order and then returned again to his own quarters. Julio closed his eyes and attempted to sleep again – but felt once more a strange and unfamiliar sensation in his back. Fraile was hailed again and this time, on entering Julio's room, detected an odd shape beneath Julio's bedclothes and a female leg emerging from beneath the duvet. A naked fan emerged, grabbing clothes she had abandoned in the sitting room, and made for the door. Julio tells the story against himself and adds with a laugh that from that day to this he invariably looks beneath his bedclothes to check for unwanted visitors. But the tale has tragic undertones in terms of his marriage – for mostly the women who found their way into his bed were invited guests.

Of course, those years were crazy. Years in which his marriage disintegrated slowly, but his career built itself up

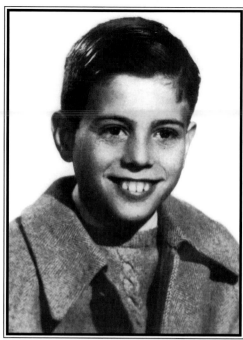

Julio in the summer of 1950, aged six. He rides a merry-go-round motorbike at the annual Madrid funfair. (Europa Press) *top left*

Smiling, toothy Julio, aged seven. Indomitable hair freshly combed and temporarily conquered for the photographer. (Efe) *top right*

An afternoon stroll in Madrid dressed in Sunday best. Julio aged eight holds Charo's arm. Carlos aged six walks with his father. Family politics were later to see the sons in reverse position to those pictured here. (Europa Press) *below*

Julio and the trio La-La-La at the 1970 Barcelona Song Festival, held at the Palacio de los Naciones in Monjuich. His song, 'Gwendoline', was selected to represent Spain in the Eurovision Song Contest of the same year. Vocally a winner, but 'a complete disaster' as far as image was concerned. (Europa Press) *above*

Goalkeeper Julio aged 17 (top left) with members of the Sagrados Corezones school football team. Girls from the neighbouring convent would attend matches to cheer for him. (Photograph courtesy of Ricardo Martinez, pictured bottom row, second right) *left*

Father and son in the summer of 1957. The two would often leave Charo and Carlos in Madrid while they visited relatives in Dr. Iglesias' home town of Orense in Galicia. (Europa Press) *left*

Julio dresses up as a city gent while recording his first album at the Decca Studios in London. The advertising slogan in the backdrop was strangely prophetic. In September 1983 he was named in the Guinness Book of Records as the highest selling recording artist of all time. (UPI) *facing page*

Wedding day, 21 January, 1971. Julio and Isabel were happy and in love. But the marriage fell apart seven years later. (Europa Press) *facing page, top left*

Maria Edite Santos and Javier, the son that she claims was fathered by Julio after a brief affair in the 1970s. Courts in Spain are still trying to establish the paternity issue. (Rex) *facing page, top right*

Julio and Virginia Sipl, known universally as La Flaca (the slim one). Their relationship was to last, on and off, for seven years. *facing page, centre right*

Julio, Isabel and the two eldest children, Chabeli and Julio Jose. Behind the happy family façade, the cracks in the marriage were beginning to show. (Alvaro Rodriguez) *facing page, bottom*

Julio with children, Chabeli, Julio Jose and Enrique during a brief holiday in Guadalmar on the Costa del Sol, where the family owned a holiday home. Pictured here at the stadium in nearby Tivoli where Julio was to give a performance the same evening. (Europa Press) *top left*

Girls, girls, girls. Julio pictured for the usual publicity purposes with beautiful young women. (Alvaro Rodriguez) *top right*

The Iglesias clan pictured in Miami in January 1982 - days after a joint military and police exercise had liberated Dr. Iglesias from his kidnap by Basque terrorists. Charo (top, second left) showed solidarity by posing for the picture, though her marriage to Dr. Iglesias had effectively been over for years. (UPI) *right*

Give us a J-U-L-I-O and it will spell success in any language. Five fans each wear a letter of Julio's name emblazoned on their hearts during the 1983 tour of Japan. (Alvaro Rodriguez) *left*

Julio and Diana Ross posing for publicity shots to accompany their duet, 'All of You', in 1984. Neither wanted to show their left profile to the camera. Julio won. (Alvaro Rodriguez) *facing page, top*

Julio with right-hand man Alfredo Fraile. Fraile was more than a manager, he was also a brother-in-arms and captain of their campaign for world domination. Pictured here shortly before their ultimate split in 1985. (Transworld) *right*

Julio plays to a packed Camp Neu football stadium in Barcelona in 1983. (Alvaro Rodriguez) *below*

riefs Encounter. Fans often profess undying love by hurling their underwear onto the stage dur-
ng performances. Julio's experiences have taught him to recognize one end of a pair of knick-
rs from the other. (Alvaro Rodriguez) *below*

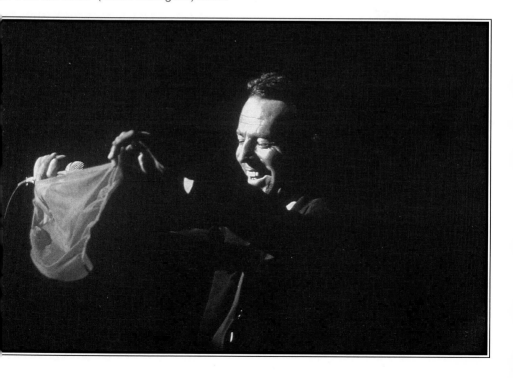

The legendary bedroom at Indian Creek, rumoured to have seen more conquests than the Spanish Armada. (Alvaro Rodriguez) *top left*

Julio pictured with Ramon Arcusa in 1990. Over the years their musical collaboration has rivalled that of George Martin and the Beatles. (Europa Press) *right*

Julio and current girlfriend, Miranda, pictured on tour in Shanghai with Dr. Iglesias in 1993. (Alvaro Rodriguez) *below*

like the Empire State Building. During that time, he released an album every year. He took part in festivals from Belgium to Japan. He toured Europe, Latin America, Asia, Africa, Canada, round and round in ever widening circles. In Chile in 1977, such was his stock in the international market that he filled the National Stadium at Santiago with more than 100,000 spectators. That same year he had sold a total of 35 million records worldwide. He was already being adored and fêted in almost every territory on earth – bar Britain and the US. If success went not just to his head, but to a certain other vital organ, then who could blame him?

There he was orbiting the globe like a mad bird in flight. But as Bassat explained, this was Julio at his most comfortable, 'reaching for the sky and touching the moon.' Marriage, children, fidelity and normal life all threatened to pull him back down to earth, to ground him, as it were. How could he cope with this? Perhaps Julio's answer to the problem was to divide his life in two. There could be his family life and there could be his career – each of them to be kept in separate compartments. He could live out two existences and what occurred in one had no bearing on the other. So if he slept with hundreds of women – well, that was part of one life, his life on the road. It was no bar to him going home at the end of a tour and playing the faithful husband. Maybe he could even believe in it himself. It was not he who had been unfaithful to Isabel, after all. It was the other Julio.

The infidelity was based on complex layers of feelings, circumstances, beliefs and insecurities. It had taken its roots in Julio's childhood, had been watered by the society in which he was raised and had been nurtured by a religion that liked to view women as either Madonnas or Jezabels.

'You have to know Julio to understand,' says Isabel. 'For him there is one woman and she is *La Nova Mas* [for which there is no precise translation in English since there is no expression which quite sums up the quality of a kind of sanctified Queen Bee]. And as for all the other women – well, Julio thinks, I can be with them, sleep with them and it doesn't matter because next to my wife, *La Nova Mas*, they are nothing. But there again, my wife, on the other hand, well she must be the Virgin Mary. That is the only way I can explain it to you.'

What Isabel is talking about, of course, lies at the very heart of Spanish sexual politics. What she is giving is a perfectly clear description of how millions of Spanish males have operated down the centuries. *La Vida Sigue Igual*, as Julio would say. And in this case life did go on in exactly the same way as it had always done.

The problem, however, for *La Nova Mas* in her glass case, on her pedestal, the flower among women, was also always the same. Her feelings were not part of the equation. 'Julio looked around, he saw the way that his father had lived, he saw the way things operated in the world that he was moving in. He saw how all the people around him were doing exactly the same thing. And it was accepted, so why wouldn't I accept it?'

Julio had seen his mother destroyed by his father's infidelities, but was drawn inexorably into the same pattern of behaviour. He had consciously chosen to marry a woman who he perceived to be at the other end of the scale from his mother, imagining perhaps that this would protect him from the sins of his father. But unconsciously, weren't all women like his mother, no matter how different they appeared to be? Without question, they were. The proof being that, ultimately, he was always to treat them exactly as his mother had been treated by his father, despite their superficial differences.

Fortunately, for Isabel, however, she was indeed sufficiently different from Charo to smash open her glass case and break free.

'Charo always told me that she wanted to leave Julio's father. But in Spain, you know, she would lose everything. But I thought to myself – look, I don't care if I lose everything. I really don't care. I'm young. I'm twenty-seven years old. I can definitely *salir adelante* [take my life forward]. I wasn't ugly, either. I knew many people. I was the wife of a famous singer who everybody used to call while he was away, and I was so faithful to him it wasn't funny. Men tried to go out with me all the time. And I would say no and be perfectly faithful . . . And this was Julio's response to me. When I finally learned the truth about what had been happening in our marriage, I had really had enough.'

The little girl who had married the famous singer was made of sterner stuff than anyone could possibly have imagined. Especially Julio.

Two years after the annulment of the Iglesias marriage, Julio released one of his best loved, best known and most successful singles – 'De Niña a Mujer' (From a Girl to a Woman). At the time, his daughter, Chaveli, was ten years old and much mileage was made out of the idea that Julio, witnessing his daughter on the brink of womanhood, had written the song for her. This was a cozy, sentimental idea, and a wonderful marketing ploy which gave rise to a rash of pictures of Julio and Chaveli together and record-breaking sales of both the single and the album of the same name. Yet, the truth was that 'De Niña a Mujer' was not written for or about Chaveli but, rather, was a song that took its roots from Julio's relationship with Isabel. It spoke of Isabel 'the girl of long silences' who had loved him so well – who had, when they first met, been simply 'playing' at being a woman. It spoke, too, of the world that had torn them asunder, of the success that neither of them had expected.

The song mirrored the fact that when Julio met Isabel she had been an innocent girl of nineteen and that when they parted eight years later she was a full-fledged woman.

While Julio toured, Isabel, imperceptibly to a husband who was rarely there, was busy growing and maturing. When the end finally came, no one was more surprised at how the girl had become a woman than Julio himself.

'Probably, he thought I was never, ever going to separate from him,' she says. 'He thought it wasn't possible. He thought, "I know her, she's a good girl. I mean, I practically brought her up. I've taken her from her parent's house and she's always been either with me or with her family. How can she manage without me?"'

Julio could not initially see that she had, in fact, been managing without him for years. The crunch point, the moment when worlds fall apart, when rose-tinted spectacles shatter into shards that pierce the eyes, the second when love dies and no amount of resuscitation can revive it, occurred in the early months of 1979.

In the latter part of the marriage, Isabel had become used to gossip column tittle tattle, linking her husband with glamorous groupies, nightclub divas. She had always treated it with the contempt she felt it deserved. She and she alone knew the truth, she told herself, that Julio was faithful to her. Then a well-meaning friend confided to Isabel that there was a Cuban woman (whose painful name Isabel has erased from her memory) who was claiming that she and Julio were long-time lovers, and that during Latin American tours he habitually visited her. Julio was due back that same evening from a tour. And with her friend's accusations still tormenting her like a fresh wound, she confronted him with it.

'I told him I knew about it and also I added that I knew about all the others too – though, in fact, at that time I didn't. I suppose I wanted to see how he would react. And he didn't deny any of it, which was rather devastating. He simply said,

"But you know you were always the only one that mattered, you were the only one that I ever really loved."'

The comment, meant to appease Isabel, simply left her in no doubt that her husband had been continuously unfaithful to her. Her response was swift and devastating to Julio.

'I said to him, "That's it, Julio. We're finished."' And, of course, they were.

Naturally, the breakdown of any marriage is an infinitely complex matter. But just as there is a rationale behind attraction, so there is a certain logic to the dissolution of a relationship. There is a certain $x+y+z=$ goodbye. And thus it was between Julio and Isabel.

Alredo Fraile, who was an intimate friend of them both, had his own perception of why the marriage had failed.

'In most cases the blame for a divorce is shared 50-50 by the two people involved,' he says. 'But in this case I think the majority of it was the fault of Julio. Julio and I were the same in this. Maybe, later, I took more care of my wife and my family. But in those days we didn't care too much.

'We thought that if we sent them money they didn't need anything more, and Julio knows now that this was not enough, he knows it was *his* fault. Isabel was a very good wife and a very good mother and he knew when they separated that he had made a mistake. Isabel looked at the equation of her life – the pluses and the minuses of her life with Julio – just as I did later, and she made her decision. And so it was that Julio lost the most important woman in his life.'

According to Fraile and others who know him well, Julio suffered from enormous guilt over his treatment of Isabel.

He gave various reasons for the wreckage. Isabel, he said, had come from an alien culture and was just too different from him. Thus it was that the exotic, mysterious quality that had first attracted him had become simply foreign. One of the very things that had lured him had helped to destroy the marriage.

He had forgotten the basic truth that, though his wife had lived in the Occident for many years, she was very much a product of the Orient, in which she had been born and raised for nearly twenty years. His steamy Latin temperament met her slightly chilly, 'pragmatic', controlled nature and the result was the formation of an iceberg between them.

In 1984, Julio lamented to journalist Gabrielle Donnelly: 'We didn't fight. No. No. You can't fight with her. You say something bad and you're waiting hours and days for her to answer. But she once said to me: "I don't know you." And I said to her, "I don't know you either." Can you imagine? You're married to someone for seven years and still you don't know them . . .'

Isabel accepts that blazing rows were not her forte, that when hurt she could be an uncommunicative person. Words, she says, at times did nothing but frustrate her. Also, to be reserved was in her nature and in her geography. She was a product of her culture. 'And, yes, perhaps I was a little on the quiet side, preferring not to talk about what was troubling – whereas Julio is the complete reverse. I never told anybody, for example, what was happening in my marriage. Even my very best friends were shocked when they saw we were getting separated.'

She was different from Julio and worse still she was, he said, indifferent to his career from the outset.

And it was this lack of interest in what was to Julio a *raison d'être* that seemed to him to lie at the heart of the ultimate marital rupture.

Sometimes in the early days, he says, she would come to his concerts 'but fleetingly and infrequently', always seeming 'disappointed and distant.' But then he had known from the start that she loved him for himself and not for his career. Had he not told reporters at his wedding that Isabel had fallen in love with a normal guy? With the ordinary Julio Iglesias rather than the singer. Had that not been what he wanted?

Obviously not. He had, rather, wanted Isabel to join the band of adoring females who constantly surrounded him. 'But I was Julio's wife and not his fan,' Isabel says. 'And you can be married to the King of England, but he's your husband and you don't look at him like the King of England. But Julio could never understand this. He thought that everybody – even the women who used to go to bed with him – saw him as the King, and so he couldn't understand how he could come home and I could be aloof to this, or sometimes maybe think that my things were more important than his. He could not see that I was preoccupied with my children and our home and my husband – the real Julio – and he could not forgive this.'

Even years after the breakup, he continued to see himself as the main protagonist of their marriage with Isabel as the bit player. His needs must come first and he had told her plainly that he could not brook no opposition to his career, that it was the most important aspect of his life, that it was crucial to him. She was well aware, he said in his autobiography, that the life carried with it certain disciplines, hardships, needs and responsibilities. Intelligent as she was, why could she not simply accept Julio's life for what it was.

He did not, however, when setting out the terms of the agreement, mention to her that she must also live with and accept his infidelity. For this, like Julio's mother Charo, would have been one quid pro quo that she would never have accepted.

He circles this point, alighting not on his infidelity but on his incessant travelling as being the factor which ultimately came between them. 'I travelled a lot – every day more,' he says. 'Every day more a slave to my life. And with my preoccupation, she became less and less preoccupied with me. And the abyss was forming between us.'

In sentiment it is almost a mirror image of Dr Iglesias talking about the effect of his infidelity on Julio's mother: 'Slowly, slowly the hurt was incubating inside her – until eventually she reached a point when she stopped loving me.'

La Vide Sigue Igual. Like father like son. It is a story as old as time.

After Julio's admission to Isabel that he had, indeed, been repeatedly unfaithful to her, he continued to swear that the other women meant nothing to him. 'Knowing Julio, I was prepared to believe that he wasn't lying about that. But for me that wasn't the point.' The point was that his infidelity to her constituted the one sin that she could not forgive him. She could not, as he had anticipated, simply accept it. Or 'indulge him a little' – as his father had expected Charo to indulge him. This was not Isabel Preysler's nature.

Instead, she agreed that she would not leave that night or even the next morning. 'But I told him that, as far as I was concerned, from that moment I was going to live my life and he would have to accept that. We didn't separate right away – basically because Julio refused to separate. So we had an arrangement whereby he was going to live his life and I was going to live mine. He never told me what he was going to do and I didn't tell him.'

There was, then, an uneasy truce – very uneasy as far as Julio was concerned. On one occasion his wife was snapped by a member of the Spanish paparazzi while she was out with her best girl friend, Carmen Franco. The headline the next day was of the 'Mrs Iglesias out on the town without Husband' variety, implying that all was not well in the marriage. It was not long, however, before a picture engineered by Julio appeared in the press conveying the impression of a couple still very much together.

'He wanted everyone to think that nothing was going on, that everything was normal. But it wasn't normal, obviously. The situation between us was definitely not normal.'

Isabel tolerated the charade for the sake of her husband and children, all the while believing that a formal separation was the only way forward. In March 1978, Julio returned to the apartment at the Calle de San Francisco De Sales from his latest tour. It was around midnight and he seemed tired and distracted. Isabel had been waiting for his arrival to discuss the matter of their separation once more. Julio once again brushed the proposal aside.

'But I told him that I had seen a lawyer and that I wanted the papers drawn up as quickly as possible. I wanted the world to know that, though I was going out, I was not cheating on my husband and I didn't want my children to grow up thinking I was *una fulana* [a tart]. I wanted everyone to know that I was out because we had separated and that we had both agreed to it.'

Julio continued to assert that he did not want to make the separation formal. 'He said, "I want you to continue to be my wife . . . everything that I have is yours."'

At this stage, Julio had already planned to make his exodus to the United States and had wanted his wife and family to be with him. 'But I said, "No, I don't want to go to the United States. I just want to stay here. The only thing I ask is for custody of the children – which I don't think you'll deny me – and the rest . . . whatever you think best."'

Julio, who has claimed to some journalists that the separation was his idea, has also claimed to others that it was Isabel's. Isabel herself remains firm in her assertion that the separation was always at her behest. Julio, she says, could see that, for her, there was to be no going back and agreed, albeit reluctantly, to a parting of the ways.

Before the separation was made official, however, he flew out for a meeting with Isabel's parents – which, says Isabel, was a rather 'sneaky' thing to do, since Isabel herself had not yet had a chance to discuss the matter with her own family.

'My parents' reaction was to think that I was a big, spoilt brat. My mother had always thought I was a spoilt brat anyway and so now she thought: "Oh, well, one more spoilt thing of my daughter's."'

Her mother confronted her. 'She said: "You have a husband who doesn't drink. He doesn't gamble. What else can you ask for?" And I said simply, "I'm just not in love with him."

'She couldn't understand that. My mother said, "If you think you have to be in love with the person you're married too . . ." But I interrupted her and said," Mama, I'm sorry but I just cannot live with someone that I don't love."'

On 12 July 1978, the couple issued a statement through their lawyers which appeared on the pages of *Hola!* magazine. Its contents were, roughly, as follows:

'To avoid possible speculation or scandalous news items that could arise from our personal situation, we both feel obliged to explain once and for all our decision, which has been arrived at by mutual consent and of our own free will, to legally separate. Above all, our chief concern, which is for our children, obliges us to resolve our personal situation in an amicable and legal fashion. The reasons for our separation being personal and intimate ones, will always remain private.'

Since divorce in Spain at that time was illegal and continued to be so until July 1981, Julio and Isabel moved for an annulment of their marriage. Strictly speaking, the usual grounds for an annulment were, firstly, non-consummation if one of the partners was physically unable to have intercourse. This was not true of Isabel and though it had been true of Julio after his spine operation the arrival of three children had more than proved that all was now well in this department. Another ground could be that either one of the couple had been under age at the time of the wedding or had not given their genuine consent to marriage. Neither of these get-out clauses applied to the marriage either.

However, it was common knowledge in Spain that those with sufficient money, fame or influence – which Julio already possessed in bountiful quantities – could buy their way into an annulment. The case of singer Sara Montiel, who had not one but two marriages annulled, was legendary. In 1971, after all, Pope Paul VI had granted certain diocese – some of whose ecclesiastical courts had rather more lax standards of evidence than the Spanish ones – the power to annul the marriages of expatriates.

A number of Spanish ecclesiastical lawyers had set up office in Brooklyn, for example, simply for the purpose of accrediting residence to wealthy Spanish couples seeking to have their marriages dissolved and needing someone to fight their corner in the more 'friendly' ecclesiastical courts of countries like the United States. Julio conveniently became, albeit temporarily, a 'resident' of New York.

The average sum of money exchanged for such an annulment – which was normally granted with few, if any, questions being asked – was around the 2,000,000 peseta mark (about £10,000). For Julio and Isabel it was, perhaps, a small price to pay. Julio himself made news of the annulment public in June 1979 while performing in Los Angeles. It was less than a year after the couple's formal separation. At this stage Isabel had not heard officially that her marriage was finished – since the decision, arrived at by the Brooklyn diocese, had still to be registered at the ecclesiastical tribunal of Madrid. But by August, while she holidayed at the couple's villa on the Costa del Sol, and while Julio performed in Buenes Aires, each announced that they now considered themselves 'single once more'.

Neither of them, by this stage, were in fact single in the strictest sense of the word. Julio had retreated into the arms of Virginia Sipl, a Venezuelan beauty who was to share his life, his love, his success and his sadness over the next five years. As for Isabel, she had embarked on a new relationship with Carlos Falco, the Marques de Grinon – who had recently split from his wife, Janine Girod, the mother of his two children.

Isabel declared that despite the annulment she 'continued to believe in marriage' and proved it by marrying Falco on 23 March 1980 – just nine months after the decision of the Brooklyn ecclesiastical court. This marriage also failed and in 1987 she married again. Her current husband is Miguel Boyer who has been a government finance minister and was at one time tipped to succeed Spanish premier Felipe Gonzalez. Isabel gave birth to two more children, one by Carlos Falco, Tamara, and the other, Ana, by Boyer.

In 1987, the year in which she married Boyer, there was fresh speculation that Julio and Isabel were getting back together again. Julio was even reported to have bought a villa on the island of Ibiza for Isabel and the children. Isabel, however, denies that, romantically, the flame was rekindled between them. It was, she says, simple speculation on the part of the Spanish press who had never fully stopped believing in the fairy tale of her marriage to Julio. They were, she says, like children hoping to be able to report a happy ending.

Over the years, in typical contradictory fashion, Julio was to claim variously that he still loved her and, then, that he did not. In 1980 he went on an Italian chat show to declare that 'the only woman I have ever loved [i.e. Isabel] did not love me'. And in 1988 he told British journalist Chrissey lley that, "I have not fully recovered from the breakup which was her [Isabel's] idea.'

On the other hand, he told journalist Gabrielle Donnelly

in 1984 that: 'It is better to be divorced than to be together when the woman loves you and you don't love her.'

As always, the smokescreen of contradictions hides the reality, that Julio 'in his own way' (Isabel's words) loved his wife. The tragedy was that he did not understand either the mechanics of love or the rules. He was devastated that while he was loved by millions of women who did not know him from Adam, the one woman who knew him deeply could no longer love him. He was shattered, too, by the loss of his children and by the dissolution of the romantic idyll he had created in his mind about how family life should be. His marriage had failed, just as his parents' marriage had failed.

Isabel and he remained, on the surface at least, 'good friends'. It was all very amicable and very civil. She kept the apartment in Madrid and the villa on the Costa del Sol – and until such time as she married Carlos Falco she also received a maintenance allowance for each of the children of 200,000 pesetas a month. The lines of communication, especially on the subject of the children, remained open and both were to reiterate time and time again that they felt nothing but love and friendship for one another. Accordingly, until now, Isabel has stayed silent about what specifically caused the breaking up of the marriage. In the mid eighties, to prove there were no hard feelings, she even travelled to Miami to interview Julio at home for *Hola!* magazine. That she would have done so is, perhaps, an indication of how little passion now existed between them.

After the split, Isabel hoped fervently to be left in peace. 'It was funny because Julio's father came to see me and, you know, he's always been a little bit eccentric, but we loved him, and he's always been one to say exactly what he thinks. He said to me: "Poor you, Isabel. Now you're not going to be appearing in the magazines any more and everybody is going to forget who you are." And really, he had no idea how I was dying to be left alone and not to have my pictures appearing in magazines. That was precisely what I wanted.'

Paradoxically, since the breakup with Julio, Isabel Preysler has rarely been left alone for a moment and it is a rare week indeed that does not feature her face in countless Spanish magazines, a rare day in which the minutiae of her existence is not discussed in the gossip columns and on the front pages of Spanish national newspapers. Like Julio, she continues to be an A-List celebrity. Unlike Julio, she says it is with reluctance.

'There is a myth about me that when I split with Julio I said to him, "Now I'm going to be even more famous than you." And this was complete nonsense. What I wanted was simply to get on with my life, to be with my children and to get over what had happened in our marriage. That the press continued to be fascinated by me was not my fault.'

She is, perhaps, as much a casualty of success as Julio. And though notoriety was his legacy to her, she does not regret their union. 'Though I'm glad that it is finished because, otherwise, by now I would be a completely frustrated human being,' she says. 'But also, without Julio I would not have had Chaveli, Julio José and Enrique – whom I love very much.' It was, she says, her destiny to bring them into the world.

Julio, also, for that matter does not regret his years with Isabel. The marriage, he has said on many occasions, was always for the good.

In marrying Isabel, the exotic creature with the cashmere-caramel skin, the velveteen hair and the mysterious almond eyes – and in siring these three children of mixed race – he had, he says, become, unconsciously, more universal. He had become a citizen of the world rather than a Spaniard.

Undoubtedly in many ways his horizons had become more

cosmopolitan, but when it came to his emotional life, he was and is a Spanish male in his thoughts, in his actions and in his very soul. Let that very marriage to Isabel stand as testimony.

Chapter Twelve

In each and every life there are events so shattering in their impact that the world seems to judder to a halt. When it begins to move again it seems to orbit on a different path entirely and nothing and no one are quite as they were before. Thus it was for Julio after the break-up of his marriage.

Of course there had been other defining moments in his existence – life-changing events, like the crash on the road from Majadahonda which Julio himself always cites as a moment of rebirth, seeming to imply that the old Julio died behind the wheel of the car while the new one limped towards his destiny. There was also another of Julio's favourite 'I was never to be the same again' moments when he won the Festival de la Canción at Benidorm in 1968. For this was the moment when Julio the Singer was born.

Certainly, both were important, both heaped with high drama and heroism, and yet, for all that, didn't the most revolutionizing of all the events in his life occur without either, in the late-night stillness of the apartment at San Francisco de Sales, while the three children that he was about to be separated from slept in their beds? That moment, after all, which occurred without fanfares or fuss, sirens or trumpets, was when Isabel, who seven years earlier had whispered, 'I do,' with tears in her eyes at the chapel in Ilescas, now whispered through tears again, 'I do not . . . love you any more.'

Wasn't it at that moment that Julio's world broke into so many pieces that when he attempted to pick them all up and glue them back together again he found that the shape of his existence had changed entirely?

On the day of the public announcement of his separation the newly formed Julio did not return to the apartment at San Francisco de Sales – indeed, that being part of his old self and his old life, he never slept there again. That night he stayed instead in a Madrid hotel, with his 'hermanager' Alfredo Fraile in an adjoining room, and the next morning the two men headed for Puerto Rico – not as part of a tour but simply to avoid the performance at home. 'Julio was devastated by the separation,' recalls Fraile. 'He could not face the press and the public – so we left to escape all the rumpus.'

Devastation, of course, swiftly gave way to the depression which tended to mark all the major crises in his life. This time its effects were to be catastrophic. He began to re-experience the feelings of paralysis which had laid him low after his operation, though now the symptoms were purely psychosomatic – just as they had been years before when Julio had called Fraile in the middle of the night with the panic-stricken news that he could not move his legs. This time, however, it was to take more than calm reassurances from Fraile to mend the problem and the condition began to spiral out of control.

His legs were numb and his arms, too, had lost all feeling. It took all his considerable strength and willpower to climb onto the stage and there were nights, indeed, when he simply could not face the spotlight. It seemed to follow him around the stage as though he were a caged animal.

On tour in Caracas four months after the separation, the situation became so critical that he was recommended to a psychiatrist. It was to be the first time he sought professional help for his personal problems but certainly not the last.

The psychiatrist listened long and hard to his patient and concluded that the problem lay not with Julio but with Julio's situation. He was a man in crisis – of this there was no doubt. But the problem was a simple, if overwhelming, domestic one – a family problem. Doubtless, the family he was referring to was Julio, Isabel and their three children, thought it might have been more astute to note the problems created in Julio's psyche by the family he had grown up in.

Having made his diagnosis, he prescribed that Julio should immerse himself in a non-stop programme of work. To work, more or less, until he dropped. He counselled Julio to fill his mind with work and work alone, to lose himself and his sorrow in his bid for international stardom.

He drove himself to the brink of madness attempting to forget the pain of his marriage breakup.

Back in the early days of his marriage he had toured incessantly, he said, out of a subconscious desire to impress his wife and to convince her of his enormous worth – and when they split, he worked that he might forget her, obliterating the memory of her. During his seven years with her, he says that Isabel had anchored and grounded him, had modified his tendency to be something of 'a mad bird' – a *pajaro loco*, which later, fittingly, became the name of his private Gulf Stream aircraft. Now freed from all the restraints of marriage, he says: 'I killed my pain on an aeroplane.' Which was a fitting place for someone who seeks to spend his time in the sky reaching for the stars and the moon. What had seemed in those early years like a non-stop journey on the fast lane to success, began now to look almost pedestrian by comparison.

Perhaps it was simple synchronicity – Julio's marriage broke down and Providence moved in to build up what was to be one of the most phenomenal careers that the world of popular music has ever known. It was almost as though his career rose Phoenix-like from the ashes of his marriage and took flight. Julio had screwed up big time on the personal happiness front, but professionally his dreams remained intact and chief among these was to conquer the hearts and minds of America.

Love had died but the war, as Alfredo Fraile continued to refer to it, went on as never before.

America – land of dreams. Especially for Julio. Even during his marriage to Isabel he had set his heart on success in the United States. In 1976, indeed, he and Isabel had even looked at properties in San Francisco with emigration in mind. When the marriage ended, it strengthened his resolve to uproot and head for the land of opportunity. 'Part of the effect of the breakup was that Julio took the decision to get as far away from Spain as possible,' says Fraile. 'He was determined that he would make it on his own without Isabel's help. He felt that he was alone in the war.'

Not quite, of course, for there was Fraile himself – commander-in-chief of the struggle. Fraile had set out to build on the success of the May 1975 Carnegie Hall concert and in 1976, before the split with Isabel, Julio was to headline at the world-famous Madison Square Garden on New York's Seventh Avenue. Unlike the relative intimacy of the Carnegie Hall with its 2,800 seats, Madison Square Garden could hold a 20,000-strong crowd. Could Julio attract a crowd of this size in unfriendly US territory? It was to be the biggest and most decisive test of his career so far.

The occasion was doubly momentous because Fraile, without prior consultation with Julio, had taken it upon himself to invite the heads of all the major American record companies.

While the arrangement with the Spanish wing of Columbia had been progressing happily – Julio's contract having been renewed with them in 1972 – it was clear that to penetrate America, Julio needed the backing of a US-based international company. 'So I sent them all complimentary tickets for the first row,' recalls Fraile.

But when Julio arrived for rehearsals two hours before the show, he was unnerved by Fraile's actions and 'also he began with his usual, "I don't like this and I don't like that", about the way that things had been organized.'

Fraile, who had arrived several days earlier to ensure the smooth running of the show, was furious. 'I'd been at Madison Square Garden for two days solid without any sleep and I wasn't happy when he arrived two hours before the show complaining about everything.'

A legendary fight ensued – one of the many that character-ized a volatile relationship that was loving and livid by turns. 'I took Julio by the shirt collar and I said, "I'm going to kill you, Julio. Your job is to sing. That's all you do. Sing. That is it." I was sick of hearing his complaints about everything.'

Julio, pent up with the challenge ahead of him, furious with Fraile for adding to his worries by inviting record company chiefs, and for standing up to him in front of other members of the tour, responded by sacking his manager on the spot – a not uncommon event. 'He said: "I don't want to see you again! That's it!" And I said: "That's fine. But today you sing. Just sing. Okay? That's the most important thing. And tomorrow I'll go."'

In the event, Fraile did not leave the next day, or for many years to come. Julio had filled Madison Square Garden easily, breaking all previous box office records, and received a rapturous welcome from his audience. Despite the fact that the critics again sour-pussed his performance. *Variety*, for example, noted that non fans might find his 'laid back, non energetic show, boring'. The audience, as usual, failed to agree, as did the record chiefs who flocked to Julio's dressing room after the show to offer the star their congratulations.

Any one of them, says Fraile, would have been prepared to steal Julio from Columbia. But it was Dick Asher from CBS records who most impressed Julio and his manager.

'With Dick Asher you could tell that he really believed in Julio and that he was a very positive person. I thought we could do business with Asher. He was the right man.'

Asher was both an astute businessman and, says Fraile, a man of vision. Not that it took too much vision, at this stage, to intuit that Julio was the goose who could lay the golden egg for CBS records. While Asher flirted with the idea of taking Julio on board, Julio's album *El Amor* ('Love') was number one throughout Europe and all the usual Julio-friendly territories.

Early in 1978, Asher began the serious business of courting Julio and his management. Fraile, despite sensing that they were on the brink of sealing the deal of a lifetime, maintained his usual poker face. They were about to play with the big boys and Fraile shrewdly recognized his own limitations. He headed for New York's Park Avenue and the Pan Am building – the plush headquarters of a firm of show business lawyers. There is, he says, a time in every war to bring in the big guns.

'I met with the lawyers and I said to them, "I'm the manager of one singer and believe me, we are going to be a big success. We are going to sing in different languages and we are going to take America by storm." I explained that we already had a contract with Columbia but that now we were going to make a new contract with another company and I asked them to negotiate this contract for us.'

In the months prior to the Madison Square Garden appearance, a successful Latin American tour had earned Julio around $100,000 dollars. 'This,' says Fraile, 'was all the money we had – and, by coincidence, that was exactly what it cost for these lawyers to represent Julio.'

Julio, however, was neither amused nor impressed. Not for the first time he threatened to kill his manager. 'Well, I had spent everything that we had and Julio thought I had gone completely crazy. But I felt calm about it. And I said to him: "Julio, listen to me. This contract is going to save you millions of dollars and to make you millions of dollars."' And history would prove Fraile right.

The contract signed between Julio and CBS in 1978 was, without question, one of the most inspired agreements ever witnessed in the world of popular music.

'The most important feature of the contract was the royalties deal,' Fraile recalls. 'They initially said they would give us a maximum of 10 per cent, no matter how many records we sold. But we negotiated a deal whereby Julio would earn 10 per cent on the first million that he sold, then, if the sales went up from one to two million, he would be entitled to 12 per cent, two to three million would earn him 13 per cent and so on.'

The record company had felt it safe to agree to the terms, never believing back in 1978 that Julio would sell beyond a million records on any one album or single.

'But we knew that Julio would sell more and we believed completely in this. And those who did not believe? Well, they had to pay. Eventually, Dick Asher started calling me and saying, "Alfredo, I just can't pay you this money." Because by this stage Julio was regularly selling upwards of eight million records every time he released an album.'

The singer was now earning an eighteen per cent royalty – which was unheard of in the record business and, said Asher, was crippling his company. Ultimately a new contract was renegotiated – but, by this stage Julio was already a very, very rich man indeed.

*   *   *

He would not have made it quite so big had it not been for Ramon Arcusa, who joined the battle campaign shortly after Julio signed with CBS. Arcusa and Manolo de la Calva had formed the legendary Duo Dinamico – a popular music twosome that had enjoyed enormous success during the fifties and sixties in Spain. Though he was only five years older than Julio, Fraile had spent his teenage years listening to and dancing to the Duo Dinamico. 'Ramon and Manolo were my first music teachers. I'd almost say that I learned to dance with them.'

Like Alfredo Fraile, Arcusa's collaboration was to be central to Julio's success. 'I would say that I owe 100 per cent of what I achieved to Ramon,' he says. This is perhaps to overestimate Arcusa's part, but there is no question that theirs was one of the most important collaborations in the history of popular music, rivalling that of George Martin and The Beatles. Arcusa had come from the Duo Dinamico and formed an even more dynamic partnership with Julio. The fact that he was to remain in the shadows, the unsung hero of the campaign, did not bother him in the least. He and Manolo de la Calva had, after all, said goodbye to their own performing days back in the early seventies.

'I'd had many hits with my partner but when The Beatles and The Rolling Stones came along we felt that our music was too old and we retired,' Arcusa has said. Having quit, he became EMI's A&R director for Spain and also a record producer and it was in this capacity, at the 1976 Viña del Mar Festival, that he met Julio. 'He liked the productions I'd done and wanted me to work with him,' Arcusa recalls. In 1978, after the legendary signing of the CBS contract, he got his chance and the two collaborated on *A Mis 33 Años* (At 33 Years Old). The album went on to occupy the number one position in Latin America, Europe, Canada, Africa and the Middle East. It also sealed the relationship between Arcusa and Julio.

Ramon himself was thirty-eight at the time, still relatively young but nonetheless a veteran of the music world. Having grown up as a performer, his intricate knowledge of music, song writing and production were to make him an invaluable ally and his contribution to Julio's success is incalculable.

After the success of *A Mis 33 Años*, he went on to produce or co-produce every one of Julio's albums. It was also at his suggestion that, for maximum efficiency and to reach as many markets as possible with the minimum of effort, Julio's albums would be recorded in Spanish then overdubbed in Italian, French, Portuguese, German and Japanese when Julio had the time and the inclination to do so. It was to be one of the key strategies in the battle campaign for world domination. And in the first year of their collaboration Julio recorded his debut album in French, *Aimer la Vie* (Love Life), and in Italian, *Sono un Pirate, Sono un Signore* (I Am a Pirate, I Am a Man).

Arcusa, who had himself at one time faced the spotlight, was now more than happy to step into another's shadow. He recognized, as Fraile had before him, that Julio was blessed by that special something. And given the right management, the possibilities were endless.

It was to be a mutually beneficial relationship – a relationship that worked with the slick precision of a Torvill and Dean. Arcusa was to supply the know-how, the knowledge of music and of sound engineering, while Julio would bring the charisma, the ability to communicate the songs and the commercial instinct for what the people want.

What differences they had were of the complementary rather than the combative variety, which was largely due to Arcusa's willingness to cede to Julio – 'to bend over backwards' as Julio puts it – even when his instinct and experience told him Julio was in the wrong. The rangy Arcusa, who is a good six inches taller than Iglesias, adopted a gently-gently approach, smiling goodnaturedly in the face of Julio's frequent obstinacy and intransigence. He learned early that it is infinitely more productive to appease Julio than to confront him head on. In time, Julio would often arrive at the opinion that Arcusa had expressed to him hours earlier – at which point it would have become his own idea. He knew what Gabriel Gonzalez also detected, that: 'Julio does not respond too well to criticism or to opposition. He doesn't want to listen.'

Arcusa had wisdom, as well as experience, beyond his years. He also genuinely liked the often impossible singer. In the early eighties Julio admitted that Ramon was far more than simply a colleague. He was also advisor, confidant, older brother and late night companion during the bleak times. In other words, he was to become more than his producer. He was also one of his very best friends.

Apart from their differences in personality and in approach, they did also have many other things in common. Chief among these was a relentless perfectionism that characterized their work together from the very beginning. While working on *A Mis 33 Años*, which was recorded at CBS's New York Studios, the two of them would spend hours discussing the music, experimenting with it, tinkering around with the score on a piano or on a guitar before even entering the recording studio – a habit which persists to this day. Invariably they would enter the studio as dusk was falling, Julio preferring to stay outside in the sunlight for as long as he can. 'The studio is like a crypt,' he once remarked. But once inside his crypt he would become a truly nocturnal creature, working all night long, only emerging again when the sun had risen the next morning. Each note was honed and polished, each musician required to play again and again until Julio and Ramon would finally give a nod of approval. Quite simply, they would record and re-record until both were satisfied that they had created the perfect product.

It was a *modus operandi* that needed to be understood by

all those who became part of the production team. Or else. The team would be made up of a couple of sound engineers, a language coach if a foreign-language album was being recorded, and a small band of musicians – a rhythm section, drums, a bass guitar and a piano. The orchestra and backing singers would be recorded later under Ramon's supervision, often back in Madrid, though the mixing of tracks was always overseen by the two men in collaboration. 'I am not one of those artists who sings and then leaves all the work to his producer,' says Julio. 'That is not my style.'

Far from it. In the studio, Julio is hands-on to the point of obsessiveness. Once inside, be it at Westlake in Los Angeles or Compass Point Studios in Nassau or near his home at Criteria Recording Studios in Miami, his routine would be the same. Before entering he would talk to Ramon, either in person or on the telephone. They would discuss whatever song was on the agenda for that particular session. Bombarded with material, Julio needs to hear a song again and again and again before he, and Ramon, can be convinced that it is the right one to record. They will discuss the arrangements, the feel, the vocal phrasing, the very essence of the song and what they want to do with it. At work in the studio at night, the perfectionist will refuse any alcohol (his fondness for a glass or two of wine is strictly for a non-working environment). Instead, at hand ready to soothe the maestro's throat, will be gallons of freshly-squeezed orange juice and mineral water.

'I am like a natural amphetamine,' Julio was to tell America's *Interview* magazine in 1992. 'I can be sitting in the recording studio for ten hours without making wee wee. Forgetting that I have to make wee wee. And even though I am not a young guy, I am able to put all the engineers to sleep. I am able to put *everybody* out.'

Later, it was not unusual for albums to take anything up to three years to produce, as was the case with 1988's *Non Stop* and 1990's *Starry Night*. Julio and Ramon's mantra became 'it's impossible to produce a good album in two weeks', to be chanted when anyone became exasperated by the excessive perfectionism – though such people rarely lasted. No album was to be released to the public without each note of each track having been meticulously considered, crafted, delivered and recorded – and anyone who was unequal to the task found themselves swiftly dispatched from the team.

In the hands of a less capable artist the end product might have seemed over manufactured, worried to death, starved of all spontaneity. Perhaps Julio's greatest ability was, like a champion skater, the illusion of ease. Intricately-layered arrangements seem unforced, relaxed and entirely natural. The final version of a song may have sounded like Julio had popped into a studio, sipped an orange juice, and delivered his soul onto vinyl in one seamless take. In reality, of course, he had cut and polished his gem again and again until it shone diamond-bright.

As Fraile said, the lyrics of Julio's songs relate to ordinary people: tales of lost love, of dashed hopes, of yearnings for that special someone that you may never find. Like all of the very best of popular music, from The Beatles to The Beach Boys, Julio's songs, says Fraile, were understood by his fans immediately, they made them a part of themselves. For his audience, of course, Julio's material is exactly right. But that doesn't make it easy. 'The songs look simple . . . but maybe they're not so simple after all.'

And the same was every bit as true for the records themselves. Easy listening they may have been. But easy to produce? Never.

The Iglesias-Arcusa collaboration honed what had previously been an instinctual style into a carefully considered science. Yet, for all its painstaking creation, it could still speak to audiences with what appeared to be an artless innocence. By the time it reached the ears of fans it 'shimmered in the mind like the memory of a Mediterranean sunset', according to *Newsweek* in July 1983. Julio, they added, 'could strike a melody with legato tenderness or let a note curl and break like a wave on the beach. In one carefully turned phrase he can register elation, hope, despair.'

The last, in particular, spoke to audiences – and had done ever since the breakup of Julio's marriage. Even before the split, the songs had sung of lost love, goodbyes and the bitter-sweet relationships between men and women. But afterwards these sentiments took on a new dimension and depth – for the simple reason that Julio had genuinely experienced the pain of which he sung. And the audience knew it. His songs now had something more – something that no amount of technical wizardry or sound engineering know-how could provide him with. They had sincerity.

Julio was aware of it, too, and suffered, for the first time, the uncomfortable realization that a good artist uses pain to improve his art. He was aware that he was benefiting from it, both artistically and economically. Every cloud has a silver lining or, considering the amount of money that his pain would earn him, a gold one. It was, however, simply the happy side effect of a very unhappy set of circumstances and the audience lapped Julio's sorrow up.

'People were convinced that every song that Julio sang was about his marriage breakup,' comments Fraile. 'And it wasn't always the case. What happened was that people saw it that way. There were songs that weren't even written by Julio, that had been composed long before his separation from Isabel. But when you're determined to see something in a certain way that's the way you end up seeing it. People saw what didn't really exist.'

There was an example 'Me Olvide de Vivir' (I Forgot To Live) which was released on the appropriately-named *Emociones* (Emotions) album of 1979. The song seemed to speak of Julio's regrets about his marriage – and the public clung to the idea. In fact it was a French song written by someone else and adapted for the Spanish market by Julio and, though it may have reflected Julio's feelings, it had not been created as a result of them and had no bearing on his own private life. 'But we did not make any effort to put people right on this score,' says Fraile. 'We thought that if people liked this, then why should we disillusion them.'

Why indeed? What the campaign leaders saw – Fraile especially – was that Julio's pain was a marketable commodity. Image-wise, where he had once been the happily married, faithful husband, he now became the soul in torment, constantly seeking and never finding solace. A man on the run from his own pain.

Meanwhile every woman in the audience fantasized that she would be the one into whose arms he would fall. That she alone could bring Julio the comfort he needed, provide the soft bosom on which to rest his aching head.

There is no question that Julio was genuinely devastated by his separation. 'He definitely went through hell,' asserts Gabriel Gonzalez. But in marketing terms, his broken heart was manna from heaven. It was money in the bank.

The darkly brooding peddler of pain was, however, only one part of the newly formed, post-marital image of Julio. There was more. In 1976 the press had already begun to call him the New Valentino but, while still married, it was not possible to play the role to the full. A Valentino – perceived in the Don Juan mould of great Latin Lovers – should be free to play the field, and while Isabel remained his wife it was not possible to do so, in public at least. Relieved from these restraints, Julio now became a self-proclaimed connoisseur of women, a man who could savour a woman's body as though it were a fine wine, who could caress her with his voice and undress her with hands that fondled the microphone so suggestively that it should probably have been wearing a condom. He was the ultimate in the satin-smooth Latin lover. The combination of vulnerability and sexual ability was mesmerizing. Women were not just buying his records, they were buying the fantasy. And Julio knew it.

Chapter Thirteen

It was early in 1979 that the newly-formed, the reconstructed Julio determined to leave the old country for good and put down his roots where his heart and his ambition now lay – in America. It was to be a farewell to the past and an embracing of the future. It was to be an entirely new chapter in his existence – one that would see him transformed from a successful but restricted Latin crooner into a major pop industry colossus.

A new chapter, of course, required a new woman and in April 1978, three months before his separation from Isabel had been officially announced, he met the beauty who would be required to live in his shadow on and off for the next five years, Virginia Sipl.

'Virginia was an important woman in Julio's life,' asserts Alfredo Fraile. 'She was a woman who shared the good times and the bad times with Julio. She was a very natural girl, very spontaneous. Someone who loved Julio a lot.'

Physically, she was more traditionally Julio's type than Isabel had been. Blonde, blue-eyed, Scandinavian in appearance. Like Gwendoline, and like his own mother, she was descended from aristocracy. Her great-grandmother had been the Baroness von Pfeifer and had lived in the court of the Russian Tsars. Her parents had emigrated to Venezuela from Yugoslavia. Growing up in Caracas, her cool blonde looks had singled her out from the crowd and in her teens she had become a celebrated beauty queen and photographic model.

It was during Julio's 1978 tour of Latin America that he met her at the Caracas Hilton, where he and the rest of the tour members were staying. That day she had been on an assignment at the beach with a photographer friend. When the session was over he suggested that she might like to come with him to meet 'a friend'. Unbeknown to Virginia, the friend was Julio Iglesias.

The first meeting did not go well. When Julio clapped eyes on her, she recalls that he rose from his seat and began twirling her round while complimenting her on her stunning figure. Later, he was to christen her 'La Flaca' – 'the slim one' – a monicker that came to replace her real name and by which she became known not just by Julio, who would at times of intimacy call her Flacita, but by the press and public. Even today, more than ten years after the relationship ended, she is seen frequently in Spanish magazines and still always referred to as La Flaca. 'I came to love the name that Julio had given me,' she says.

Back in April 1978, however, La Flaca was not impressed at being manhandled by Julio and walked out of his luxury suite in a huff. Given Julio's psychology, her departure was probably the biggest come-on that she could have invented – though this, of course, she was not to know. Although his tour was leaving Caracas the next day for Brazil, then Argentina, he plagued her en route with phone calls, apologies and flowers and her resolve began to crumble. By the time he returned to Caracas several weeks later, Julio had secured a dinner date with his new destiny.

That evening, Julio arrived for her in an anonymous taxi

so as not to draw attention to her. They went to the El Alamo restaurant where they sat in a booth away from the prying eyes of fellow diners.

In the restaurant, whose name must have reminded him of the song that he had written for Isabel, 'Como el Alamo al Camino', he spoke to Virginia of his failing marriage and of his fears for his children – particularly Chaveli, who was devastated by her parents' imminent split.

'I was discovering the other face of the famous man,' she recalls in her 12-part memoirs published in *Semana* magazine. 'Someone who laughed and looked happy in front of the public. But privately I was looking at the face of a man with serious emotional problems.'

The conversation, which could be interpreted by cynics as being a classic of the 'my wife doesn't understand me' variety, was, in fact, much more than this. It was Julio doing something that he never did with any of the more insignificant women that he slept with. It was Julio letting Virginia Sipl into his life.

Julio walked her home and kissed her good night like a teenage lover after a school dance. Virginia sensed in her gut, she says, that Julio was to be the great love of her life, 'but, also that he would make me cry more tears than all my other boyfriends put together.'

Not that these numbered too many. Like Isabel, the then twenty-one-year-old Virginia had been a convent-raised girl who at one time had believed her future was as a nun. She had been chaperoned by her brother for all her teenage years. By the time Julio met her she had known one or two men – but not enough, in Julio's eyes, to have fallen from grace. She was pure enough for Julio to covet her and to wish to make her his very own.

He invited her to join him in Miami the following Friday, where he was giving a performance at the Orange Bowl. She agreed but unlike the other, unimportant women in Julio's life – models and good-looking good-time girls who would be there either to promote themselves or to promote Julio by being photographed with him – she and Julio went to extraordinary lengths to keep their burgeoning relationship from the attention of the press. Another indication that she was to be an important addition to his life.

They travelled to the airport separately and when Virginia met an inquisitive journalist friend in the departure lounge who suspected a liaison, she denied all knowledge of Julio. 'Is it my fault,' she said, 'that this singer is on the same flight as me?' Subterfuge was to become second nature and she was off to a brilliant start. For it was a rule of thumb in Julio's love life that the more a relationship was publicly trumpeted, the less significance it had. Thus it was that Virginia Sipl became part of the reality rather than the myth – though, for her, it was to be at times an extremely harsh reality.

In Miami, the tour members booked into the Maituny Hotel. Again to avert suspicion, Virginia was checked in to share a room and even a king-size bed with Julio's faithful secretary Adriana. That evening, she went to the performance and noted how 'young women and not so young were pushing desperately, trying to get close to Julio. They wanted to touch him, kiss him, eat him alive.' It was the first indication she had of how very difficult it might be to keep Julio for herself alone.

She opted at that point not to attempt to compete for Julio's attention and went back to the hotel without him to await his return. Julio, on not finding her in his dressing room, became incandescent with rage and on returning to the hotel stormed that she was never again to leave his side without prior consultation.

'I should have known then that this over-protection of Julio's would underpin our relationship as he over-protects everything that he owns. And even more the woman that he loves. This woman must forget her own personality and live in his shadow, because that's how he is and that's how you have to take him . . . Or leave him.' It could have been Isabel herself speaking.

That night, however, all was forgiven before she retired with Adriana. In the middle of the night, when the secretary rose from the bed, Virginia, who was still half asleep, assumed she was simply going to the bathroom. Moments later something, or more specifically someone, landed with a bounce and a thump on the bed. Looking up from her sleep she saw a smiling, mischievous Julio who had dispatched Adriana to his own suite. 'Are you cross?' he smiled at her.

'This,' she says, 'was the Julio Iglesias that I loved – romantic, warm and funny.'

'Yes . . .' she responded.

The inevitable first night of passion was, she says, unforgettable. 'Julio,' she confides, 'is a marvellous lover. Warm, sweet, very normal. He is a very romantic man, seductive, giving the maximum respect to the woman he loves, never forgetting to whisper loving words to her . . .'

Even when the relationship had begun to sour between them, the sex remained good. 'I confess that what I liked most about Julio was precisely this – the way that he used to make love to me. He was so tender and loving . . . I died for him.'

The man she died for in bed also required the slaughter of her independence. 'He conquered me completely and I gave him my liberty,' she says. In time the possessiveness and the jealousy were to overtake Virginia's life just as they had overtaken Isabel's. But his profound failings were always balanced for her by the exceptional qualities that were also a deep part of his nature.

Julio was *un moro*, she says (a Spanish expression that means literally a Moor or a Mohammedan – someone whose attitudes stem from the Islamic tenets of male superiority and ownership of women). 'He was *un moro*. Macho and jealous.

A good Spaniard,' she asserts. 'But also he was romantic and generous, funny and cultured . . .' Otherwise how could she have remained with him for five years?

Why, indeed, considering his numerous infidelities to her – many of which, unlike Isabel, she was aware of from the start. Julio had always been a womanizer, but he was about to turn his failing into a virtue – to publicly enter his Girls, Girls, Girls phase. It must have been excruciatingly difficult for the woman he left behind at home. For Virginia Sipl, that is.

'I remained in the shadow – the anonymous woman in his life. Julio was seen everywhere accompanied by girls of all races and colours. While I stayed in the shadows,' she says. 'That, I suppose, was my biggest sacrifice.'

The gilded cage which held her and from which she watched her man constantly taking flight – reaching as usual for the stars and the moon – was to be at the millionaire's enclave of Indian Creek in Miami. They had searched for exactly the right place for months, combing the exclusive coastline, often imagining they would never find what they were looking for and finally stumbling on a ramshackle single story hacienda gazing out onto the Biscayne Bay. The house, with its own jetty and mooring point, was set in a beautiful tropical garden. It had been owned by an old lady who'd had neither the funds nor the enthusiasm in her latter days to do the property justice. She handed it over to Julio at a bargain price – though over the next two years he was to spend around $3 million on its obsessive refurbishment. The house was to take on a metaphorical significance. Julio's marriage had broken down and emotionally he was dispossessed. So why not compensate by possessing what money *could* buy him – why not pour millions into the house of his dreams at Indian Creek? His marriage had been built on sand and crumbled in the whirlwind of fame, fickleness and infidelity. So he would shore up his life with an unshakeable monument to his own success. A tribute to his triumph. A millionaire's refuge.

The site was hand picked for its exclusivity and its Waspishness. It was a place where your chauffeur and those of other self-respecting milionaires could compare notes about their bosses' latest Rolls Royces, where on a clear day (which, the sun-loving Julio noted joyfully, was just about every day) your servants could wave to other people's servants while putting out the rubbish.

To own one of these houses you needed a bank balance in excess of the gross national income of certain third world countries. (And certainly by 1990 Julio's accounts were said to total more than Nicaragua's.) To be permitted entrance as a visitor you must cross a bridge and report to burly, armed guards.

From the vantage point of the overhead helicopters, whose passengers tend to be members of the paparazzi pointing kalasnikov-sized lenses at the famous prey beneath, the millionaire's paradise with its own country club and town hall (the Municipality of Mega Bucks) appears to be lying on its back like a rich curvaceous beauty. Indian Creek forms a mesmerizing aerial landscape – undulating golf courses, manicured hedges, each house gleaming like a pearly-white tooth, each azure swimming pool glinting like a shimmering sapphire in a necklace that adorns a soft, rich throat.

No wonder that the moment he clapped eyes on Indian Creek, Julio was drawn to its wanton glamour as though it were the landscape equivalent of the beauty queen who now shared his bed. As Julio began supervizing plans for the creation of his house, he determined that it, too, would be a physical masterpiece. It was as though Julio was striving for the perfection in his house that he consistently failed to see in himself and always looked for in his women, in his friendships, in his recording career and in his life. The house would make up for everything.

It must, then, be a house of phenomenal grace and beauty – a Kubla Khan affair. It was to have the charm of a South Seas hideaway and the grandeur of a rococo palace. The roof was to be constructed of Polynesian thatch while the halls and walkways were to be of solid, beige Italian marble. There were to be exercise rooms with state of the art equipment, guest rooms with fantastical beds. There was to be a dining room where white-gloved servants – at one time reputedly fifteen of them – could attend Julio and his intimates in grand tradition. There were to be works of art on the walls and exquisite furniture hand picked either by Julio himself or by Virginia, whose taste in such matters Julio considered to be impeccable.

They pored over plans and brought in teams of workmen. Walls were to be knocked down and others built. Chimneys were to be constructed, as was a huge glass conservatory that would look out to sea. At Virginia's insistence, a large jacuzzi was to be built in a room overlooking the garden and the bay – 'and this was where we most liked to make love,' she recalled. Failing that, there was the couple's enormous, king-size bed which they chose together, sampling the mattress like newlyweds in the showroom of one of Miami's most exclusive furniture shops.

At times, the creation of Julio's dream house took on nightmare proportions – particularly for Virginia, who was left to oversee the work while Julio went touring. The builders, in traditional fashion, were unreliable, expensive, constantly creaming off funds from a man whose wealth was already perceived as being astronomical. Julio, says Virginia, was constantly being taken advantage of by builders who dragged their heels, never did something cheaply when it could be done expensively, often building things in a way that they knew would be unacceptable simply so they'd have to start again. Julio was the client from heaven. An inexhaustible font of finance. 'Sometimes it seemed that he was earning money simply for other people,' Virginia noted, a sentiment which is heartily supported by Julio's father, who constantly complains to his son that those around him are taking advantage of his wealth. 'Julio is the one who gets to enjoy his own money the least,' he says. Such are the lives of the wealthy.

During the construction of Indian Creek there were to be classic examples of the too much money and too little sense variety. At one point all the windows were replaced with wrought iron balustrading – partly for security reasons and partly because the effect appealed, initially, to Julio. Virginia had been home in Caracas and was stunned on her return at the appearance this had created. She informed him instantly that the place looked like Sing Sing prison (appropriate, perhaps, considering Julio's occupation) and his wounded response was to have all the barred windows removed immediately and reconstructed with simple glass. A hugely expensive process which had the builders rubbing their hands with glee . . . as did the various swimming pool disasters.

Julio had fantasized about building an indoor pool adjoining the suite of bedrooms, his own and those of visiting guests. Specifically, he wanted his children, when staying with him, to be able to step straight out of their bedrooms and into the pool. He set out his instructions for the builders.

On returning from tour, however, the pool did not meet with his approval – it was too small. 'It was laughable – practically the size of a large bath,' Sipl recalls. 'The whole project had to begin again and an entirely new pool constructed.'

Even worse problems followed with the construction of the outdoor pool. Julio, who swims each morning for two hours as part of his back-strengthening physiotherapy, was, according to Fernan Martinez, 'fanatical about it, you know. In the end, he had the thing built in five different positions until he was finally happy with it. But that is the way Julio is. He is a perfectionist. When the building was going on he was pretty obsessed by it. But then Julio is always obsessed by whatever project occupies him at that moment. That's his nature.'

When the house was well underway, Julio turned his obsessive gaze upon his beachfront garden. He would tame it, recreate it, bend it to his will and possess it. Lawns were planted and clipped with the fanaticism of a mad geometrist. A multi-coloured display of flowers arrived and was planted but failed to please. Julio wanted every flower in the garden to be blue – blue like the sea, blue like the sky, blue like the pool and like the colour of Virginia's eyes. The offending flowers with their impudent array of colours were wrenched from the ground and replaced at a cost of £4,000 on the very same day. Julio was happy.

Happy with the flowers – but not with the trees. Trees had a special significance for Julio and had done since the days when, recuperating from his spinal operation, he would walk falteringly in Madrid's Casa de Campo and gaze up at their indomitable magnificence. He loved trees, sang songs about them, and wanted several fine examples of them in his garden.

On one occasion, while driving through the rich suburbs of Miami with Fernan Martinez at the wheel, he spied one such tree in someone's front garden and determined to have it. 'Julio asked me to pull over and to go knock on the door to see if the owners would sell it to him. The woman who opened the door thought I was mad. She said that the tree wasn't for sale. But Julio just wouldn't accept it. When I went back to him he said, "Offer her $15,000 for it." And sure enough, she sold it to him.'

There were to be other trees, too, that would turn Indian Creek into a veritable Garden of Eden. Trees groaning with oranges, plump avocados and coconuts. Coconuts, especially, were important.

'He wanted coconut trees real bad,' recalls Martinez. 'But he didn't want to wait for them to grow so he had fully-grown trees shipped in. Then he complained because the trees arrived and they didn't have coconuts on them. It was explained to him that you can't move a tree when it has coconuts on it – because it's like a mother with her baby. But he wouldn't have it. He had to get rid of the trees and have others with coconuts brought in.'

Twenty-five of them arrived at a cost of £80,000, fronds waving 'hello' absurdly at their new owner, coconuts jangling and rattling as the lorry approached. Well, if he could uproot himself then why not a coconut tree?

Julio was not the only one to have uprooted himself. With him came Virginia and also, of course, Alfredo Fraile. Fraile and his wife, Maria Eugenia, plus their growing family, all exiled themselves from Spain, as did Ramon Arcusa and his English-born wife Shura. Julio's battle front was now America and he needed his generals with him.

Brothers in arms, Julio's right-hand men swiftly found properties close to Indian Creek and to the Criteria Studios where so many of the star's most successful albums would be recorded.

Then, in the spring of 1979, Julio began to talk about the possibility of bringing his brother Carlos to Miami to oversee his financial affairs. There was talk, too, of Julio's mother Charo joining them. One big happy family again.

'On a personal level and on a professional level, Julio's life was going through unchartered waters,' Virginia Sipl asserts. 'I think he missed family warmth.'

Family warmth, however, particularly from his mother, was not something he had enjoyed for years and relations with his brother, though underpinned with love, had lost none of what Alfredo Fraile refers to as that 'bad thing that existed between them.'

'But,' Fraile adds, 'I think Julio had this idea that he would try to be part of one big happy family because he believed in the idea of family. He wanted also to create a picture of a happy smiling family, not just for the world but for himself. But his family was *not* a happy, smiling family.'

Indeed not. Nor had it ever been. Yet, undeterred, Julio proposed to Carlos that he quit his job in Madrid's top hospital, where he was senior consultant in the field of breast cancer, and head for Miami instead. Though he was not renowned for his knowledge of show business or for his business acumen, he agreed to his brother's request, much to the amazement of colleagues and friends.

'Carlos was a great doctor – really he was quite famous in his own right,' comments Gabriel Gonzalez, who had remained friends with the family, despite the end of his professional relationship with Julio after the signing of the CBS contract. 'But he saw that the life of a doctor was maybe not as glamorous as the life of an artist. He was a good-looking guy, with brains and a lot going for him and maybe he thought, "Why shouldn't I have a piece of it?" He looked at Julio's lifestyle – the women, the aeroplanes, the first-class hotels and the travel – and it attracted him. Of course it did.'

In the summer of 1979, Carlos arrived in Miami with his wife, Mamen, and his children, Carlitos, Jorge and Martita. With them came not just Charo, but the pent-up sadness and grief of her helpless marriage, which she bore on her shoulders like a cross. 'She was definitely marked by the failure of her marriage,' Virginia Sipl recalls.

Over the years, the drip, drip of disappointment had distilled itself into an acid bitterness that, according to Fraile, tended to affect the lives of all those around her. 'When you have a problem with your marriage you either stay together or you divorce,' he asserts. 'But to make problems between people is no good.'

Though she transferred her life to Miami, it seems most likely that she did so for Carlos, rather than for Julio. Carlos, Fraile concurs with Isabel, was certainly her favourite son.

Her bias, he says, also extended to Julio's children. Though, in time, Julio would negotiate custody of them and they would transfer to Miami, living indeed with their grandmother while Julio toured, Fraile insists that 'she never loved them in the way that she loved Carlos's children. She never liked Isabel and when Julio's children were born she would always refer to them as Isabel's daughter or Isabel's son.' The warring teams had transferred from Calle de Benito Gutierrez to Miami. But the fight had lost none of its force. *La Vida Sigue Igual.*

Virginia Sipl observed Charo's lonely figure in the autumn years of her life. She had left the familiar territory of Madrid to be with her sons, or at least one of them. She was in the land of bright futures – especially Julio's – with no conviction or optimism about her own. She was bowing to the whims of a world that she had rejected from the moment she had learned with tears that her son had won the Benidorm Festival. Unlike Julio's father, she continued to distance herself from it as much as was possible, never giving an interview about her famous son or visibly puffing up with pride at the mention of his achievements. Quite the reverse.

In the mid eighties, after the arrival in Miami of his children, Julio was to buy his mother a fabulous house of her own. But in the early years she stayed at Indian Creek. Often, recounts Virginia Sipl, while Julio was away, the two women would rattle round the enormous mansion like two discarded crumbs in a golden biscuit tin. They would frequently share the king-size bed – driven together by sheer loneliness.

Charo would spend her days doing crosswords or playing solitaire. In the Godless America, she remained obsessed with her religion. Though there had, clearly, never been any love lost between Isabel and herself, she admonished her son that the annulment, which had amounted to a divorce, had been a sin, as was his sharing a bed with Virginia, to whom he was not married.

Although she and Dr Iglesias had obviously lived separate lives for years, she had always remained faithful to her marriage vows, which her husband never had. Despite this, Julio, according to Virginia, unsurprisingly sided with his father who had been having an affair with the Madrid socialite, Begona, for years. Happiness, he said, was something that his father deserved. 'But,' she adds, 'I don't think he would ever have tolerated the idea of his mother and another man.' Naturally not.

Even when divorce became legal in Spain in 1980, Charo refused to agree to an official separation on the grounds of her religious beliefs. 'People used to tell me it was because she was still in love with me,' says Dr Iglesias. And pigs will fly.

When Carlos and Charo arrived in the summer of 1979, the Indian Creek refurbishment fiasco was in full swing. Julio, therefore, rented a large and elegant property on another of Miami's millionaire enclaves, Bel Point. The house was big enough to accommodate all the newcomers, plus Virginia, himself and his children who arrived for the annual sojourn in Miami that had been part of the custody agreement.

Once the summer was over, however, Julio and his brother rented neighbouring apartments in an exclusive block at Mar de Plata. Later Carlos was to buy himself a fabulous property at La Gorce, which is ten minutes' drive from Indian Creek. Julio's father continued to arrive on the scene whenever his work commitments allowed. The family that had done nothing but fall apart from the beginning continued to put up its façade of solidarity.

Though, like Julio, a Madrileno to his core, Carlos adapted well to Miami waterfront life. He ran Julio's business affairs to the best of his ability and lapped up the lifestyle that had lured him to Miami in the first place. There was the expensive house and the yacht moored to his own private jetty. There were the long afternoons when Carlos – an astoundingly good water skier – would pick up the more than competent Virginia in his boat and they would spend hours ploughing through the ripples of the bay. Meanwhile the ripples created by Julio and Carlos's family background continued to have a profound effect on their lives and on the lives of those who came in contact with them.

Though they were in a new land, the old problems remained. They had been brought from Madrid and transplanted in Miami, where they grew with fresh vigour.

'It was the same family problem all over again,' says Fraile. 'It wasn't Julio's fault and it wasn't Carlos's fault. It was just the split family thing, once more. Julio remained connected to the father and Carlos to the mother and so the fighting and the bitterness continued.'

Fraile understood the problem, knew it from old. But, he says, it was a difficult problem to work around. After all, despite the monumental fights which were a constant in Fraile's relationship with Julio, there was always a common purpose – Julio's success. Carlos's position, as a newly-commissioned general, was, however, infinitely more complex.

'For me to be Julio's manager and also to be in Julio's shadow was completely normal,' says Fraile. 'But for Carlos, it was difficult. It was hard to be Julio's brother and to think, "Well, I'm more clever than my brother and I'm more handsome than my brother. So why is he more successful than me?" It was impossible for Carlos to work happily with Julio. He loved his brother – for sure. But there was something inside the relationship that was very bad.'

It was, according to Fraile, an enormously difficult and divisive situation. 'I didn't like being between the two brothers. But Julio insisted that his brother would take care of him, that he would save us money. And it was true that, at that point, we were travelling so much that I didn't have time to look after the money side of things.

'But I also thought it was a mistake to bring Carlos in because he didn't know anything about show business – he did not know his left from his right as far as show business was concerned. And because of this, even though he was Julio's brother, we had lots of fights. I used to say to him, "Carlos you should have continued with your own career." Because that was something he did know about.'

Carlos, Fraile concurs with Gabriel Gonzalez, was seduced by the lifestyle without properly understanding that it came with certain quid pro quos. 'Most important was that you had to know how to be around Julio, and Carlos did not. You must accept that you are one of the courtiers and that Julio is the king. This you must never forget.'

The professional relationship between Carlos and Julio was to last eight years before their differences were to force a parting of the ways. The personal relationship and its repercussions, of course, will go on forever.

With Carlos controlling the purse strings and overseeing the refurbishment of Indian Creek, Julio and Fraile took off again on the campaign trail. Since signing the CBS contract, Julio's international career was going from strength to strength and by the time 1979 ended he was already one of the five top-selling artists in the world.

It was in 1979, for example, that he had released *Emociones* (Emotions) with the fabled 'Me Olvide De Vivir' (I Forgot to Live) as the opening track. It also featured the song 'Spanish Girl', which he privately dedicated to Virginia Sipl. The record, under the superb production once again of Arcusa, outsold every one of Julio's previous albums and sparked the most comprehensive and successful world tour to date.

His international following was burgeoning, as was his list of influential contacts. Early in 1980 he travelled to Egypt at the behest of President Anwar Sadat to give a concert in the shadow of the pyramids. Sadat subsequently became a close friend – one of Julio's many allies in high places, including the Spanish and the Monegasque Royal families, who gave credibility to the singer and to his career.

As for the humble fans, they simply kept on buying Julio's records. In 1980, *Hey* topped the album charts in eighty countries and surpassed even the sales of *Emociones*.

Track two of the album was 'Amantes' (Friends). It was about the secret love of two people – 'to the world we're simply friends.' For Virginia Sipl, the woman in the shadows of Julio's life, it was very much a song about their relationship. For while the world's press – manipulated by Julio's own management – began to link him with every model, actress, and tight-bellied glamour girl who came within fifty feet of him, Virginia Sipl was the untrumpeted, long-suffering, newly elected *Nova Mas*, that Julio went home to. Eventually.

Chapter Fourteen

In Lebanon, in the ancient ruins of Baalbek, Julio holds a beautiful blonde in his arms and kisses her on the lips. Julio is dressed as Rudolph Valentino in the silent movie *Sheik*. Full desert costume. Smouldering brown eyes. The woman in his arms is actress Sydne Rome, dressed as the abducted heroine Agnes Ayres in the 1921 film. She too wears the costume of a Bedouin.

It is a publicity stunt, of course. A way of consolidating the view of Julio as the New Valentino – always with a girl who falls in love with him, despite herself. But it is also, according to Julio later, a genuine love affair between himself and Sydne Rome.

He had met her in Paris in 1980 while recording a programme for French TV and had instantly been drawn to her beautiful eyes and her way of 'spreading happiness all about her'. Raised in Italy by American parents, Julio later recalled that she spoke like an American, but thought like an Italian. He was besotted by her from the outset.

After another chance encounter at a dinner in Rome, they had swiftly become lovers, meeting, Julio says, in every corner of the world. They would speak long distance on the telephone and fly off to be together whenever the opportunity arose. It was, according to Julio, 'a beautiful love story.'

The meeting at Baalbek was another of those snatched reunions taking place in the summer of 1980, just as war was breaking out in the Lebanon. Sydne, a Jewess, apparently had to disguise herself as a mechanic and travel in a lorry for hundreds of miles from Beirut to Balbeek for her 'secret' assignation with Julio – risking her life, he says, to be with him for just a few hours. Such was her love for him.

Despite this, the glamorous whirlwind affair blew over after a year. Distance and career differences finally separated them. She bequeathed Julio a dog, which still lives with him, a black-and-white pointer that he called Hey, after his 1980 album success. Julio, rather eccentrically, took it home from Paris to Miami on a first-class seat next to his on Concorde and in 1990 dedicated the album *Starry Night* to his loyal canine companion.

Aside from the dog, Sydne also bequeathed him the mocked-up Valentino pictures which a photographer had, of course, just happened to take at Baalbek after the two of them had made love and then donned their costumes in time for the camera to capture their romance.

That summer of 1980, the pictures appeared in all the countries Julio had already conquered, including Spain. Virginia Sipl, on holiday in Majorca with Julio's children, was awaiting the return of her man when she picked up a newspaper and saw him entwined with Sydne Rome.

The jealousy and paranoia that had shown themselves in his marriage with Isabel were re-emerging in his relationship with Virginia. All the time that his affair continued with Sydne Rome, and indeed with any number of paramours, he remained 'super jealous and *moroismo*' towards Virginia.

'I was required to do my shirts up to the very top button – even in the height of summer,' she says, echoing again the obsession with such matters that Isabel had also mentioned. 'I would say to him, "If you like I could wear a hood and cloak too". Just as well I didn't suggest it twice.'

'Plunging necklines? Practically forbidden. Tight trousers? 'Only if I was going out somewhere with him and as for bikinis, he didn't like that at all.'

The paradox of her situation was not lost on Virginia – and this despite promises and pleas from Julio, who returned unannounced, breaking his tour schedule to pacify Virginia over the pictures. He assured her that what was between him and Sydne was a publicity stunt that was beneficial to both of them – and that was all.

Not for the first time, nor the last, Virginia was to note that 'I never did get used to this kind of *publicity.*'

The more high profile the potential partner, the more mileage Julio's publicity machine tended to make out of it. During Julio's career there have been endless links with some of the world's most famous and beautiful women: Bianca Jagger; former Miss UK Caroline Seaward; *Fall Guy* star Heather Thomas; Brooke Shields (whom Julio was supposed to be on the point of marrying); model Giannina Facio (who was Phillipe Junot's former lover). None of them, in fact, were ever serious contenders for Julio's love.

A classic of the genre was to be Diana Ross. Though much was made of the rumoured 'affair' between them, the relationship was never anything other than one of mutual convenience. They had recorded a duet, 'All of You', for Julio's 1984 album, *1100 Bel Air Place,* and it seemed appropriate to promote the idea that the sentiments expressed in the song were echoed in real life. Which they never were. Their coming together was rather a mating of two massive egos, each determined to prosper from and prevail over the other. During a picture session in which a tuxedoed Julio entwined himself around Diana, clad in a dress that exposed her long legs and enclosed her body like a golden sheath, there were, according to one source, for example, arguments over which of the two stars would be the one to show their 'wrong' side to the camera. Both insisted that they did not want the left side of their faces photographed – which would have meant them gazing in the same direction, instead of into each other's eyes. Julio, naturally, won.

Relations between them were, at best, a little strained. Yet in the press it was claimed that Diana was madly in love with Julio. Julio himself dismissed the rumours with the words, 'Diana and I are just good friends and business associates.' But the twinkle in his eyes and the smile said something different. Let people believe all the rumours, it was good for business.

According to one report, however, Diana was not happy with the situation. She was said to have ended her professional partnership with the words: 'Go away. I don't want you to touch me anymore.' A statement which is open to some fairly wild interpretation. Probably, however, the precise meaning of it was: 'I am tired of you putting your arm around me in public to promote your image as the world's most successful lover.' Only guessing, of course.

There again, it was not a dissimilar situation to the one that existed between Julio and Priscilla Presley, at a time when Julio was, in reality, Virginia Sipl's man. They had met at Viña del Mar in February 1980 when Julio invited Priscilla to take part in a nightly show he was presenting during the annual festival.

Julio recalls in his memoirs how he tried to woo Priscilla. He went riding with her to the foot of the Andes dressed, for some unfathomable reason, in a peasant style poncho. He wined and dined her and attempted in various ways to sweep her off her feet. He asserts that when they parted it was with a certain sadness and that they continued often in the aftermath to send each other flowers. He concluded that the two of them would end up together if destiny decreed it.

According to Priscilla however, it was, not so much destiny that intended them to be together, but Julio's marketing team. In an interview with R.L. Torrente-Legazpi, for the Spanish news agency EFE, she declared that she felt herself 'used' by Julio.

'With Julio you never know when he's acting for himself or for the people who manage his career,' she said. Adding that by this she did not mean Alfredo Fraile, but rather the team of what she called 'Cubans' who surrounded him. 'And in Miami they all live as though in Cuba. It's the other Cuba,' she said.

These people – members of Julio's growing entourage – were, she said, 'a team of workers' who look after everything. 'He has journalists and photographers on the payroll. He wanted to give the impression in all the papers that he had something going with Bianca Jagger so he had a Spanish photographer take a picture of the two of them together. A journalist on the payroll wrote his autobiography *Between Heaven and Hell*.

'Wherever we were together, photographers appeared, often in the most unexpected places. Sometimes you'd see the same old faces in different countries. This made me suspect they'd been tipped off by his father or by his brother or by a whole set of Cubans that he always brought with him.'

The relationship, she said, was more a friendship than the heady romance that the press spoke of. Julio, she said, was charming and educated and it was a real pleasure to go with him as she did to Montevideo, Miami and Rio. 'It was fantastic and unforgettable,' she says. 'But I would have had as good a time with someone else and I thought of him, above all, as a friend.'

Therefore, she was none too delighted at reports that she was desperate to marry Julio, that she 'waited like a dog for him at airports' and that she had to fight against fans who wanted to take him away from her. 'Lots of things have been invented,' she said. She had been used, she felt, to bolster Julio's image as the Latin Lover – an image which she, personally, found contemptible and 'a nonsense.'

'What we want is for a man to treat us like a woman, to make us happy as women, but also to be our friend. We want emotion. We don't want to be treated like something out of a market. We're not something that's for sale in a shop.'

Everyone, she concluded, has their own strategies for achieving fame. 'But being a singer who's made millions in the Spanish-speaking countries, who's got CBS behind him, who's sold 70 million records, doesn't mean he has the right to use people.'

In her view, Julio was a man who was 'desperate to impress me with his power and popularity – with the thousands of girls who fainted outside the door of his dressing room.' But who was, nonetheless, a man completely alone. He was also, she said, a man still totally in love with his first wife, Isabel Preysler. 'How curious that our surnames should be so similar,' she said. Others hinted at further parallels between her relationships with Julio and Elvis. These she denied. She also refuted a story which appeared in the press claiming that she had sent Julio an emotional farewell letter. In it she was reputed to have said that she could never be with him because she didn't want to suffer again what she had suffered with Elvis.

Of all the stories that appeared in relation to her and Julio, it was perhaps the one that should have been true.

That Julio had many lovers was not, however, a matter of flim-flam. Even as late as 1995, a member of the singer's entourage illustrated the pattern of Julio's love life to *Independent on Sunday* journalist, Ian Parker, by drawing a symbolic triangle.

'Here at the top,' the man said, 'is Julio's current girlfriend and here below are the girls he sees quite a lot of, a few times a year, and, here, at this level, are the girls he has met once before, and here – at the bottom – are the new girls brought in for Julio to meet.'

The entourage member here reiterated Feliciano Fidalgo's contention that Julio liked the girls to be young, 'so he can mould them', and added that Julio encouraged fooling around among his employees 'because it makes him feel less guilty. Especially if a married guy has girls. Makes him feel much better. But you'd better not think of going after his girls. No way. Never. People have got into big trouble for that. When I first joined him I was clearly told to stay away from his women.'

Fernan Martinez concurs that Julio is a jealous man, 'but work comes first.' 'If someone he's involved with professionally screws one of his girlfriends, he'll find that difficult to forgive. But if that guy comes to him with a song and it's a good song, he'll say, "You're a son of a bitch, but the song is good." And he'll record the song and let bygones be bygones because work always comes first.'

Women were thus reduced to playing second fiddle but remained vital to Julio. It was little consolation for Victoria Sipl that she occupied prime position in the pyramid of paramours for she was all too painfully aware of those who occupied the lower echelons. If it had only been the famous 'loves' Virginia might have been able to deal with it, knowing as she did that this was, indeed, part of Julio's publicity. But it was the unknown, faceless threat of the air hostesses, models, small-town beauty queens, and dancers that undermined her relationship with Julio – just as they had done with Isabel. She was to leave Julio time and time again over his myriad infidelities.

There was, for example, a woman referred to only as Pit, in Sipl's memoirs. She had been an air hostess and an ex-lover of Julio's and was then imported to Indian Creek to be his 'nurse'. There was a regular lover in Puerto Rico, affairs with a model called Dani, a Canadian beauty queen, and with the dancer Vaitiare Hirshon, a seventeen-year-old Tahitian, who was to crop up periodically to cast a shadow over Virginia Sipl's life. And this was, as Julio later intimated to her, simply the tip of the iceberg.

Julio, had been known to sneak out to make phone calls to his latest loves, and farcically on several occasions in Virginia's presence conducted placatory conversations with Vaitiare's mother in the aftermath of that relationship. Virginia understood that this was a man who was 'unfaithful by nature' and loved him all the same. Though when his memoirs were published in 1981, detailing the beautiful relationships he had enjoyed with any number of women while he had been living with her, it understandably stuck in her craw.

She was outraged, she said, that Julio had mentioned her in the memoirs when she had expressly asked him not to do so. She had constantly denied her liaison, at Julio's own behest, to friends that she had in the Venezuelan media. It was, she said, unforgivable.

But rather more unforgivable was the fact that he mentioned her so little and damned her with such faint praise. 'She adores me in a completely unselfish way and sometimes I think that she must tire of loving me so much in exchange for so little,' Julio said. In other words, she was the perfect partner for him.

Adoring Julio as she did, she was left to guess which of the women in his infamous address book had spent the night with him. Paradoxically, it was never the girls brought in for effect to pose around him in newspaper pictures. These were merely photographic props, bolsters for the image. In fact, it became a constant that whenever he was seen in public there would always be beautiful girls around him. More often than not the girls were paid for. Julio's management would drop into town, call the biggest and the best model agency and have the girls shipped in to wherever Julio was dining that evening. Caroline Seaward, who had once been linked with Prince Andrew, claims that there were reports of a romance between her and Julio after she was 'summoned to his dinner table'.

In London, after Julio made his breakthrough into the 'Anglo-Saxon market', it was the Laraine Ashton agency who got the business. 'Last time they invited three girls down to Monte Carlo just to sit with Julio at dinner,' grumbled Ashton's assistant, Dick Kries, in 1982, when Julio was on tour in Britain. 'They just sat there and looked pretty. But we didn't send anyone this time. The girls aren't interested. They're models not tarts,' he added. Not that Julio ever had need of tarts. Indeed, he has gone on record to say that he has never had to pay a woman for sex. But the paying of women to complement the image was another matter.

Wherever Julio was performing, tour managers were warned to lay on the girls. Julio, of course, protested ingenuously that 'everywhere I go people put a pretty girl on my arm and take pictures. Then I read that this is Julio's latest love. It's crazy.' But if so, it was a madness whose method was devised by Julio himself and by the people who sought to promote him.

Don't let us forget that Julio was not now to be just the Latin crooner – he was also the ultimate Latin Lover. It was the bedrock of his mythology. Put a tape recorder in front of him, send in a camera crew, invite him to share his memoirs and he would arrive with the appropriate Latin Lover script.

He would claim to be 'intensely erotic' and add that sex for him was as vital as sleep. In the early eighties he claimed that he had made love everyday of his life for the last 15 years – 'through desire, through necessity, but always with joy'.

He was also, he said, a very creative lover, savouring the experience as though it were a work of art. But then he loved women, needed them, and desired them. Didn't he? They were, he said, magical exquisite creatures.

He was not the type of lover to give his lady the cold shoulder after making love, or to brutally show her the door. 'I don't despise a woman immediately after having sex with her,' he would say. 'In fact the 8 a.m. kiss, the long sleepy embrace that starts the day without shutting out the night, gives me particular pleasure.'

What woman, apart from perhaps his wife, who knew his complicated nature better, and whose trust had been constantly betrayed by a sexually compulsive husband, could not love such an adorable, passionate man? He was, as in the title of his 1977 song both 'Un Truhan' (a rascal) and 'Un Señor' (a gentleman) – a wicked and heady sexual cocktail. He was a rogue, but a lover of women. 'I am always in love, even if it lasts only a second. When I say I love you, however fleeting it may be, I mean it with all my heart. I am sincere. That is me. I cannot be otherwise.' No wonder women from around the world flocked to his bed – as many as 3,000 according to Julio myth. The number, Fernan Martinez said, had been arrived at by Julio – 'probably on the basis that at that time he'd had 7,000 nights as an adult and that nearly half of them had been spent sleeping with women. I don't know how accurate the figure was,' he adds, 'but I do know that I almost never knew Julio to sleep on his own.' For all that, in 1991 he told journalist Kitty Bean Yancey from *USA Today* that his claim had been 'completely a lie.' Before adding with a smile: 'But the best promotion I had in my life, actually.'

Whatever the truth, there was certain madness in all the frantic promotion of Julio as a sexual superman. Particularly as this was not, indeed, how Julio felt about himself. Quite the reverse. Thus it was that in between trumpeting his sexual prowess, he would descend at times into abject self-loathing. 'I'm just a skinny guy in a pair of jogging pants' became a mantra that was recited to every journalist in every territory of the world.

In the end, Julio's image created profound problems for someone who, as Enrique Bassat put it, 'is beneath it all, a little Spanish man with no self-confidence.' A man who had been hung up about his looks since the day that his brother Carlos was born. A guy who could never really believe that any woman wanted him simply for himself.

'I know, my friend, what most of them (women) love,' he told Donald McLachlan in 1982. 'It's three things. Fame, success and money. Eh? I think so. How do you know what goes on in another person's head? If they met me in a café in Spain, if I'd not become a famous singer, maybe if I'd been a small town lawyer, do you think they would say, "Aahh, that man! I want to marry him and live with him and have his children." I don't think so. I don't think they would have looked at me two times.'

He did not trust the love of women, but he continued to need it and the more the better. To that end the female audience who screamed and cried and died for him at his concerts were all grist to the mill. They became like one large amorphous and unassailable lover – that no one woman could fully compete with.

'Maybe it is too honest to say, but there is nothing, no woman, who can compare with singing onstage,' he told Nina Myskow in 1984. 'I find so much more onstage. The lights go down and there are 10,000 people loving you. The lights go up and you leave the stage. Maybe you find a girl. Maybe not. But after such a strong feeling, such a strong excitement, every nerve in your body is alive. How can you find a woman who can give you the same?'

It was Sydne Rome who made a similar observation about Julio. 'He would,' she said, 'never remarry because he was already married to the millions of fans who applauded him.'

By the end of 1981, he was about to add thousands of them to the collection – fans of the most precious kind to Julio. He was about to 'Begin the Beguine' in Britain, the first Anglo-Saxon territory to fall. He was about to conquer the most unconquerable market in the world – the English-speaking nations. And, of course, winning the fans' love in this hostile land meant all the more to him. For if there's one thing that Julio adores, it's those who play hard to get.

Chapter Fifteen

It was on 19 November 1981, that Julio first appeared on BBC 1's *Top of the Pops*. Sun-tanned, suave – every British woman's image of a potential Spanish holiday romance – the female viewers received him rapturously with their hearts and with their hormones. After his appearance, the BBC switchboard was jammed with Shirley Valentine types demanding to know how to contact the singer. To Julio's delight, and that of CBS International, Britain appeared to be falling without resistance.

It had helped, of course, to have Radio 2, the housewives' favourite radio station, on his side. In the weeks before Julio's *Top of the Pops* appearance, his single – an adapted version of Cole Porter's 'Begin the Beguine' – had been given more air time than a decade's worth of shipping forecasts. By the time he hit the screen on 19 November, it already occupied the number one slot in the UK pop charts.

It featured just one line of English – 'When You Begin the Beguine' – but it was enough to begin an avalanche of record sales. By December 1981, the song had sold over 500,000 copies and earned Julio yet another gold disc. A compilation album, featuring some of Julio's best songs – 'Hey', '33 Años', 'Me Olvide de Vivir', was also released under the same title. With sales topping 100,000, it too went gold.

There was without question a market for Julio and for his music – as later success also proved. In March 1982, he released 'Yours' which rose to number three in the charts and earned him a gold disc for sales of over 250,000. By the end of 1982, he was ready for a full-blown tour of the British Isles, taking in Dublin, Manchester, Coventry, Brighton, Edinburgh and London, where he sold out for five nights at the Royal Albert Hall. Whatever it was that Julio had, the public – even the British public – wanted it. They screamed and screamed for more.

The irony was that in the beginning, Britain was only ever intended to be a testing ground for the bigger prize, the US, and 'Begin the Beguine' was to be a Britain-only release. It was to be an experiment that would tell Julio and his people whether ears that were used to listening to songs written and sung in English could respond to Latin sounds and words. If they could in Britain, then the likelihood was that the US could fall too.

In the event, success in Britain was to exceed wildest expectations, making it an important market in its own right. After the initial success, Julio began to shore up his triumph in the usual ways. There were the ubiquitous press interviews and the *Mail On Sunday* used him on the cover of their launching issue of *YOU* magazine. On top of this there was the standard media bun fight at Old Trafford when Julio arrived with a coachload of journalists to stand between Manchester United's hallowed goalposts in a pose reminiscent of his days at Real Madrid.

As ever, Julio understood the importance of publicity – any kind of publicity – and he began the serious business of courting British journalists.

'We made it a policy whenever we went to any new

territories to contact a few key journalists and to make them part of the team,' Fraile admits. 'It was always a good idea to have some friendly journalists who would write positive things about Julio and his music. A star needs the press.'

The chosen ones would usually be wined and dined and sometimes flown out to Miami to stay at Indian Creek. They would, at any rate, be exposed to Julio's charm and his undeniably winning ways. They would arrive determined to dislike him and leave believing Julio was their best buddy. 'Even some of the toughest journalists in the world, who had been sent to destroy Julio, ended up liking him,' Fernan Martinez asserts. Whether he genuinely liked such journalists or simply liked what they might be able to do for him is another matter. On the question of whether Julio considered any of them his real friends, Alfredo Fraile smiles and shrugs. 'Perhaps,' he says.

Or perhaps not. In any case, the British press was, and is, among the most resistant in the world to Julio. And regardless of what any individual journalist thought of Julio, the brief from features editors remained the same – crucify him. Indeed, only his native Spain, which still smarts over the singer's desertion from their shores, gives Julio a harder time.

It is perhaps a little odd, but while the French, for example, have always eulogized Julio, the British press have remained aloof, xenophobic and determined not to like him. Never mind the British fans who form a body of Julio's staunchest supporters – they were to be dismissed as menopausal, MFI shoppers with shell-suit-wearing husbands. And as for Julio himself, his image was always to be bracketed in the Barry Manilow or David Copperfield genre – foreign upstarts who, despite their otherwise global appeal, would never find acceptance in the UK.

Right from the beginning the media strove to cut the conquering hero down to size, much as if he represented a fresh onslaught from the Spanish Armada itself. There were jokes and jibes about the singer's name. Julio Iglesias, they laughed, translated into Jo Churches (which it does not – Julio, is simply, July or the Spanish equivalent of Julius). Julio smiled, took it on the chin and, for one seeking street credibility, made the fatal error of appearing on the *Des O'Connor Show* whenever he was in Britain.

It was perhaps unfortunate for Julio that Brits tend to have a ready-made caricature of every Spanish male – just as they have one for the French, for the Germans and so on. Julio thus became Mr Garlic Chomper, with olive oil charm, Mr Snake – hipped Suntan Man. A jumped up version of the Spanish waiter who attempts to fondle your girlfriend on a beach in Benidorm.

Julio's Latin Lover promotion of himself did not help the cause. An endless stream of nubile Fleet Street feature writers would be dispatched to his hotel suite at the behest of male features editors to stitch the poor guy up.

They would report back to the public about his tendency to squeeze the interviewer's knees and to put his arms around them. They would comment cruelly on his over-bronzed face, which struck them as being the colour of American Tan tights. They would quote him verbatim while he talked about Es-Spain, conjugated his sentences incorrectly, and pronounced all his J's as H's. The effect was to make him come across as a kind of semi-witted Manuel – which was to do his rather profound smartness a terrible disservice. That he'd had the courtesy to speak in a language that was not his own to journalists who, generally, could not speak a word of Spanish themselves, went unremarked upon. Julio's role was to be pilloried.

Not that he seemed to care too terribly. He continued to give interviews, regardless of the write-ups he received. He was not, he admitted, keen on criticism. But it was better than nothing, and provided his picture was in the paper, why should he worry? He loved publicity – the more of it the better. 'If I'm going to be in the paper then I'd rather appear on the front page than on the back,' he would repeat with constancy. And it was a philosophy that he lived by.

He and his team understood, too, that being boring never earned anyone column inches. Thus, he became what journalists call 'good copy'. At various times he would claim to one that he had slept with 3,000 women and to another that he was completely celibate or 'performing very badly below the belt'. Sometimes he would discuss trips to his psychiatrist with one journalist and at other times claim that he was his own physician. He would show angst on any number of subjects from his marital breakup to his spinal tumour.

Journalists would leave his suite, their tape recorders hot from his revelations, initially unaware that Julio was playing cat and mouse with his interviewers. He appeared to tell them everything but actually told them nothing of any real importance. The stuff that mattered he fanatically kept to himself.

If the papers wanted stories, then Julio was their man. No point in being happy or just a regular guy. Legends are not made of such stuff. Legends are, rather, tortured, complex, eccentric fellows. Julio would display for the world that he was all the above and more.

You want eccentric, then how about the incident in 1984 when Julio was said to have dipped his toe in his Miami swimming pool, declared the water too warm and ordered three tons of ice to cool the thing down. 'I arrived at his place and the pool looked like a f—ing Tom Collins,' former press supremo Fernan Martinez recalls, before launching into another series of anecdotes.

There was the one about a flight from JFK to Chicago in which Julio discovered that there was no tomato ketchup for the hamburgers that had been prepared on board his $8 million dollar Gulf Stream jet. Without more ado, the pilot was ordered to turn round and head back to JFK, where one of the ever-growing entourage – reputedly numbering fifty by 1988 – was sent in search of the essential condiment.

There was the story, too, about the time that Julio found himself delayed at Barajas Airport for five hours during an air traffic control dispute. He could not, he said, contemplate such a wait without having several bottles of his own vintage wine – being stored in preparation for takeoff in the aircraft hold – brought to him and his friends in the VIP lounge. 'He wouldn't take no for an answer,' recalls Martinez. 'Eventually, security guards had to go out onto the tarmac to get the bottles out of the hold. Julio was used to getting his own way.'

On and on the stories go. There were tales about how Julio, keen to look his best for his first appearance on the Johnny Carson show in 1983, had sent his secretary from Los Angeles to Miami to bring back five gallons of water. The reason was that he simply couldn't do a thing with his hair after washing it in LA's H_2O. And there was the story about the chambermaid who found a $100 bill in Julio's shirt pocket and returned it to the star. So impressed was he by her honesty that he had his secretary write her a cheque for $1,000.

Then, of course, there was the shoeshine man who refused to take money for his services on the basis that my wife would never forgive me if I'd taken money from Julio Iglesias.' Julio removed his gold Cartier, worth a cool £10,000, and gave it to the man instead. This is the stuff that legends are made of.

There were other Cartier stories too. Fernan Martinez recalls how, all in all, his boss gave him five of them in succession – but they were never meant for him to keep. 'If someone was good to Julio – maybe a journalist who'd written something nice or who'd impressed Julio – he would say, "Fernan give them your watch." I never expected to keep one permanently.'

Tales of gargantuan generosity and of big-time kookiness all added interest to the legend. It was said that when Julio had bad news he used to burn all his clothes and leap into the bath.

He was wildly superstitious. He would not, for example, they said, accept salt from another person's hand, and if someone spilt salt he would leave the room. Nor would he allow whistling in his presence or stay on the thirteenth floor of a hotel. It would simply be out of the question.

Julio was also said to observe all kinds of rituals before going onstage. He always wore an off-white shirt to remind him of his first appearence at Viña del Mar when the chambermaid lost his laundry and he had to borrow the used shirt of another singer. He always did the shirt up from bottom to top and insisted on buttons at the cuffs rather than cufflinks. His trousers must be precisely two centimeters above his shoes just as they had been on the night he took to the stage in Benidorm in 1968. His underwear must always be black silk. His fly must be double stitched to avoid the possible embarrassment of its bursting open. His waistcoat must hug him like a corset to support his spine and his shoes must have paper thin soles to allow him to grip the ground. He must never wear yellow because this was the colour he was wearing on the night of the Majadahonda accident.

He must drink no alcohol before going onstage, but lubricate his tonsils with a mixture of tea, lemon and honey. He must never have sex before a performance, reserving his sexual energy for the fans. Before leaving the dressing room he must wash his hands five times – for no particular reason. In the wings, as the orchestra warms up, he must yodel to loosen up his voice.

It was all a lot more interesting than someone who just turns up, gets dressed and sings. But then he was not just a singer, he was a matador in the moments before entering the ring, a Conquistador about to go into battle. He was larger than life. A man reputed to employ twenty-two body-guards and to shoulder an annual staff bill in the region of a million pounds, a person who thought nothing of opening an $8,000 bottle of vintage wine to share with friends. 'If I want

something then I just have it,' he told the *News of the World*
in 1985. And that was about the size of it.

Let them accuse him of what they liked as long as it wasn't
dullness – which is precisely why stories of Julio's quirks
were deliberately filtered to the press, more often than not
by Fernan Martinez who, even years after departing from
Julio's service, continues to tell tales of Julio's extravagances
and eccentricities. Martinez himself had been a top-flight
Colombian journalist who had interviewed Julio back in the
seventies and had so impressed the interviewee that four
years later he offered him a job. Martinez knew a good story
– knew what the papers wanted. So just how much of the
above was manufactured for the press? Probably most of it.

The truth was, rather, that Julio was actually pretty normal.
He had tried marijuana once – 'one puff – one headache', – but
never anything stronger. He was a sexual compulsive (what
man wasn't?). He liked a glass of wine. But, by the sex, drugs
and rock-'n'-roll standards of the music business – at least as
far as drink and drugs were concerned – he was Mr Clean.

His normality was, kind of, abnormal. When he arrived
for a tour of Australia in the mid eighties the organizers
were struck by it. 'We were used to people who smashed
up hotel rooms, had orgies in the bathroom, took drugs and
treated minions like shit,' one of them recalls. 'Then along
came Julio and what were the worst things you could say
about the guy? He liked us to organize girls to sit with
him at dinner. Big deal. He was a bit troublesome on the
Ray Martin chat show. He didn't want to show the left
side of his face and he insisted on having all the furniture
moved around the studio. He wanted Ray Martin's desk
turned round and for Ray to sit on the side opposite the
one that he always sat on just so the camera would only
get his right-hand profile. It was a little weird, but we
were used to much worse. Mostly Julio was charming,
well-mannered, cultured and courteous. He wore a suit and

tie and liked to talk about fine wines. He wasn't exactly Sid Vicious.'

Indeed not. But if he was just a nice guy in a suit with lovely manners, how could that be interesting? Answer. It couldn't. So it was that Julio was constantly challenging himself to be more colourful, as it were. Often the interest arose from painting himself blue and sorrowful. That he had a natural predisposition to depression is certainly true. But, perhaps it was also true that he was not the type to go off and waste a good depression all on his own when he could use it to fuel first his music and secondly, his public image. There was talk, for example, of admittance to a psychiatric clinic in 1983, where he claimed to have spent several weeks being treated for depression. Then again in 1985 he confessed: 'I have just been through the worst six months of my life. Had I not pulled myself together with all my strength I'm sure I would have ended up in a psychiatric clinic.'

In May 1988, he was back on the theme again – this time telling the *Daily Mirror* that he had been to see a psychiatrist to help him stay faithful to his then girlfriend, Brazilian beauty queen Dayse Nuñes, and in June of that year he went still further by telling the *Daily Star* that some months earlier he had attempted suicide. He had, according to the report, held a gun to his head and was only prevented from pulling the trigger when his daughter Chaveli had walked in on him.

'We sat by the pool and talked for hours,' he said. 'She told me how much she enjoyed her time with me and I realized how ridiculous I had been for even contemplating ending it all.'

There were other stories which appeared later which also pointed to a suicide attempt in 1988. This time, however, the claims were that Julio had taken an overdose. Previously, he had seemed depressed by the realization that he had fought like a maniac to achieve world fame and in so doing had lost his sense of reality. Now there were other reasons given.

'Every magazine and newspaper I read at that time seemed to concentrate solely on the number of women I'd supposedly slept with,' Julio wailed, as though he himself had not set up the parameters for his image. 'I just couldn't stand it any longer. People thought I was just a brainless stud. Nobody ever mentioned my music or my voice. It seemed the whole world was only interested in my sex life.'

Alfredo Fraile certainly agrees that Julio could be an extremely sad man. His life experiences, he said, had left him with a legacy of sadness. But Fraile also accepts that the sadness was part of the legend created for Julio – the solitary singer, whispering sad songs in an echoey room. 'The people loved to see Julio in this way,' Fraile admits.

But where did the myth end and the reality begin? With Julio it was difficult to know. At the times when he seemed the happiest, he could, in fact, be at his most melancholy and vice versa. 'There are all sorts of people around who believe they know Julio very well,' says Fraile. 'But they know only what Julio has decided to show them – which isn't very much.'

They have witnessed the myth believing it is reality. They assume they have been confided in, whereas, in fact, they have been shut out. 'Julio can seem to be the most open person, but really he is defensive,' says Fraile. 'He doesn't open up, because he is afraid that people will hurt him.'

There is another important reason, according to Fraile, why Julio distances himself and keeps all inquirers at bay, and it is simply this: 'Julio knows that people need to believe in things – whether it's God, or their husbands or even a singer. They need to know something about the thing that they believe in, but maybe not too much, because if you let people in too close then you destroy the myth and this Julio knows. That's the reason, perhaps, that he puts this distance between himself and the people.'

The true Julio, the real man, then, remained shrouded –

even when the world's press assumed he was opening his heart to them.

In 1991, again in his interview with Kitty Bean Yancey, he summed it up himself. 'What I represent is a fantasy,' he said. 'The legend is stronger than the reality.' Could it have been that the reality was a lot less Herculean and a lot more human? According to his father, Julio has never attempted suicide. His son, he says, 'loves life too much.'

Depressions? 'Yes, the normal kind of thing. He was depressed when his marriage broke up, of course. He was not happy. And then again about three years ago he decided to have plastic surgery done on his right eye. He had a wrinkle that went from his eye to his cheek and he didn't like it. Then his friend Regine, the Paris nightclub owner, suggested a plastic surgeon to him who could sort the problem out and like a fool he went to this person.

'Anyway, in the end the operation was a disaster. Julio hated the result and for eighteen months he was in a real depression about it. Eventually, I found him one of the world's best plastic surgeons in Chicago and this person put him right again.' Julio was back on top form.

Not a god then, just a mortal, with all the frailties and vanities of anyone who senses they are no longer young. But this was one story that he did not shout from the rooftops. The myth makers would not have liked it.

Chapter Sixteen

It was late in 1981, in the lull between Christmas and New Year, that an event of such significance was to take place that it stripped Julio of all his myths and legends and left him raw, exposed and visibly bleeding. The event was to involve the man who continued to be the most influential person in Julio's life. His father.

It occurred on 29 December, a time when the streets of Madrid were strangely quiet and deserted. Dr Iglesias, who at sixty-six still headed the infertility unit of Madrid's biggest maternity hospital, La Maternidad de O'Donnell, had gone to his office hoping to take advantage of the holiday calm to catch up on paperwork. At around 3 p.m. he left the building heading for home. Outside, the street was empty and echoey. The light was fading fast. Dr Iglesias heard footsteps behind him and when he turned round he saw what appeared to be two members of a TV camera crew. They began calling his name.

He stopped and when they drew level, they told him that they were from a West German television company making a film about Julio. They asked the doctor if he would be interviewed and, being in a good and festive mood, he agreed to go to a nearby café with them. As they walked along the pavement, however, a car came towards them and screeched to a halt at their side. The two men then turned on the doctor, tied him up and bundled him blindfolded into the boot of the car. Dr Iglesias had been kidnapped by members of the Basque Separatist movement, ETA.

The doctor was drugged and taken first to a hideout in Burgos, some 200 miles north of Madrid. After several days he was again given sleeping pills and this time transported in the boot of a car to Trasmoz, a tiny village near Zaragoza.

During his twenty-day ordeal the doctor was kept in darkened rooms in solitary confinement. 'Nobody spoke a word to me,' he says. 'They would put food in front of me and that was all, but they never communicated or answered my questions. Perhaps they believed that if we began a conversation I would talk them round and they would have to release me.'

The effect on the doctor was profound. 'I went half crazy,' he admits. 'There is nobody who has been liberated from a kidnap who doesn't come out of it half mad. All the things that happened to me during the Civil War were chicken shit in comparison – I really can't think of a worse torture for any human being. To be kept in isolation. To have no one to communicate with at all. To believe at any moment that you are about to be killed. It is an unbearable experience.

'I kept myself sane by walking up and down the room liked a caged animal. Up and down. Up and down. I walked kilometres every day. I think perhaps that all of us in the Iglesias family, including Julio, have a guardian angel that protects us and I feel strongly that some force bigger than myself was helping me to get through what was happening to me.'

For Julio, too, it was a devastating experience. He learned of his father's kidnap on the very day that it took place from his ex-wife Isabel, who called him in Miami. ETA swiftly demanded a £1 million ransom. The kidnappers required half the ransom in used American notes and half in Spanish currency. Julio withdrew the equivalent of £500,000 from his bank and had it switched from Miami to Spain in preparation for the exchange. He also dispatched Carlos to Madrid to handle matters at that end while he himself waited by his Miami phone.

'During the twenty days he was missing I sat in my house in Miami on a chair next to the telephone,' he told journalist Noreen Taylor two months after his father's release. 'Julio, who cannot bear to be one hour in the same place, sat in that chair, waiting, hoping. There were the terrible [hoax] telephone calls to say he was dead and there were the wonderful letters, 200,000 of them. At night I tried to sleep – nothing but nightmares. I tell you that was the crossroads of my life.'

Certainly, it was one of them. 'One of the very big experiences in Julio's life,' says Alfredo Fraile, who remained close to Julio during the ordeal, even moving into the house at Indian Creek to be near his friend and protégé.

Back in Spain, Carlos dealt with the police and press while Julio remained shrouded from view, issuing statements via spokesmen. 'The two of them [Julio and the doctor] are more like close pals than father and son,' was one of them, published in the *Daily Mirror*. 'Julio cannot eat or sleep since it happened. He just paces up and down and jumps each time the phone rings. He's ready to do anything to get his father released safe and sound.'

This, according to rumour, which is supported by Julio's own father, even included contacting the Medellin cartel. 'Everybody had told Julio that the only person who could get me released was the Colombian drugs baron, Escobar, because he was in contact with ETA and would be able to negotiate on Julio's behalf,' the doctor says. 'Julio was willing to do anything and so he was put in contact with Escobar who said that he was willing to help, but for a price. Julio had to pay him money – though I don't know how much – and he gave Julio his assurance that he would liberate me.'

In the event, the doctor's liberation occurred before Escobar's rumoured intervention ever got a chance to take place and before any ransom money had been exchanged. At 3 a.m. on 18 January 1982, police and anti-terrorist troops – led by Joaquin Martorell, who bizarrely went on to become Julio's manager in the late eighties – launched an SAS-style raid on the tiny two storey house in Trasmoz. After commandos blasted their way in with explosives attached to the front and back doors, four people were arrested. They were Luis Goti, his daughter and her boyfriend and another man.

Strangely, the raid at Trasmoz had been set up to effect the release of another kidnap victim, José Lipperteide – an industrialist from Viscaya who had been featuring in the daily news bulletins alongside Dr Iglesias.

'The police were convinced they were about to free Lipperheide, that he was the one being held at Trasmoz,' recalls Alfredo Fraile. 'So it was a complete shock to all of us when it turned out to be Julio's father who was released. A shock and a relief.'

Among the first well wishers to call Julio were the Spanish Prime Minister, Leopoldo Calvo Sotelo and the Minister of the Interior, Juan Roson. Julio acknowledged their good wishes and those of the fans, and swore privately that such a thing would never happen to a member of his family again. Indeed, it was after the 1981 kidnap that stories of Julio's extreme paranoia – as far as his family security was concerned – began to emerge. In 1989, for example, it was reported that he had spent £2 million to ensure round-the-clock safety for his daughter Chaveli. This sum had included the employment of bodyguards and the purchase of top security luxury apartments in Rome and Barcelona where Chaveli was said to be pursuing a career as a model. In the same reports, it was also claimed that all his daughter's boyfriends were security vetted.

'Julio blamed himself for what happened to his father,' said his close (platonic) friend, Vivienne Ventura, who, along with Virginia Sipl and Alfredo Fraile, had been by his side in Miami when news of Dr Iglesias's release arrived.

'In the past he was so unconscious of security, but now he'll make pretty sure his family will never suffer like that again,' Ventura told the press.

In other words, Julio had become painfully aware that fame and fortune had a way of making the famous, fortunate one – and those close to him – sitting targets for lunatics, criminals, terrorists and opportunists. After all, it was almost exactly a year before his father's kidnap that John Lennon had been gunned down by a crazed 'fan' outside his New York apartment. It could have happened to anyone in the public eye. 'Being rich and famous does not get rid of your problems,' Julio reflected on this very topic in 1988. 'It just gives you new ones.'

In the euphoria that followed Dr Iglesias's release, however, Julio attempted to put these concerns on the back burner. There was, for example, the business of the press conference to attend to. At Julio's insistence, and much to the annoyance of the Spanish press, this was to be organized by Julio's people and to be held in Miami.

A pale and bewildered Dr Iglesias was flown directly to his son for a tearful reunion and then confronted by a barrage of microphones and cameras belonging to the world's press. Dr Iglesias punched the air triumphantly as he regaled the company with his tales of endurance, superhuman discipline and bravery. He was, indeed, the ultimate survivor – as his wife would doubtless have been able to testify had she not been notably absent from proceedings.

There was, however, one post-kidnap photograph taken of the entire Iglesias family, including Charo, which was circulated to the world's press. Pictured with Julio are his children, his niece and nephews, his brother, sister-in-law and father. Though Charo stands next to her husband there is no physical contact between them and they gaze in opposite directions. Where other women might have registered relief and love at the release of their husbands, Charo's expression remains distant and enigmatic. There were to be none of the 'husband and wife in joyful reunion' shots that normally follow such traumas. There again, it would have taken considerably more than a kidnap to have healed the rift between these two disparate and distant people.

It was just over two years later, in fact, in April 1983, that Dr Iglesias finally secured his divorce from Charo on the grounds that they had lived apart over several years and the marriage had broken down irretrievably. He claimed at the time that his kidnap had caused him to reappraise his life and that his marriage had been a casualty of his new outlook. In fact, as both he and Charo knew, the marriage had been over for a very long time before ETA took the good doctor captive. It had been over almost as soon as the marriage vows had been exchanged. It had been over for almost forty years.

In his interview with Noreen Taylor in March 1982, Julio spelled out the traumatic effect of his father's kidnap. 'You have to know that I am not the same man I was before the Basque Separatists kidnapped my father,' he said. This was, actually, to overstate the case. Certainly the kidnap had been profoundly troubling, but life continued just the same – both professionally and personally. At thirty-eight, after all, Julio was fully formed.

It is true, however, that having confronted the potential loss of his father, the two men grew even closer, if possible, than they had been before. Dr Iglesias became a frequent member of Julio's entourage, travelling to far-flung corners of the world so that they could have what precious time was left together. 'He's not so young anymore and I want to spend as much time with him as I possibly can,' Julio told Gabrielle Donnelly in 1985. 'But time is always a problem for me.'

Indeed it was – always had been and always would be. It was not for nothing that by the end of 1981 he had already sold 70 million albums worldwide, and had made some 400 TV appearances in 50 different countries. The same year of his father's kidnap he had made his British breakthrough and performed in Egypt, Israel, Australia, Europe and Latin America. Princess Grace of Monaco had invited Julio to perform at the Red Cross ball in Monte Carlo and he had given a show in front of Nancy Reagan for the first but certainly not the last time, in Virginia, at the Wolf Trap Farm Park for the Performing Arts.

Though he had the seal of approval from the White House itself, however, Julio remained a virtual unknown to middle America. A fact that he was keenly aware of and was committed, along with the campaign generals, to changing. These now included the Italian singer-songwriter and actor Tony Renis, who was well known internationally for his own songs, such as the 1962 hit, 'Quando, Quando, Quando', and for those that he penned for others like Shirley Bassey's successful 'Never, Never, Never' and Perry Como's 'I Don't Know What He Told You.'

Renis and Julio had met in a Rome TV studio where they were working on different shows. 'He knew of me as an established singer and songwriter, while on my part I was already a big fan of his,' Renis told *Billboard* magazine in 1984. 'At the time he was . . . the most famous star in Italy. We decided to start a collaboration.'

The partnership was based, as was that with Arcusa, on mutual respect. Renis not only admired Julio as a performer but as a songwriter, believing that his talent in this area was largely overlooked. 'Unfortunately only a few people know how big a success he is as a songwriter,' claimed Renis. 'In 95 per cent of his hit songs he wrote the lyrics. He is not only a great singer but also an important writer in his language and should be considered a fully-fledged poet.'

The duo were to work together first on 'De Nina a Mujer' (the celebrated song that was written about Julio's wife and dedicated to his daughter) for which Renis put Julio's lyrics to music. The single was a phenomenal international success as was the album that bore the same title. In Brazil, for example, 2 million copies were sold, and in Japan over a million.

It was clearly a collaboration that worked. Julio and Renis worked on several other projects including 'Momentos', the smash single from the 1983 album of the same name. Most important of all, in 1984 the two men were to collaborate on what was for Julio the most important album of his recording career, *1100 Bel Air Place*. For this was the album with which Julio would finally conquer the hearts and minds of America.

Not that an album alone would have done it. To succeed in America you must become part of the star system – this Julio understood. To become part of that system you must retain the services of those who control it and those who control it are the mega bucks celebrity representation organizations. Without them you are dead in the water.

Up until the eighties, of course, Julio and his generals had more than proved their capabilities in terms of conquering the world market. But faced with the US challenge, even the acumen of a managerial genius like Fraile seemed insufficient to the task. It was time to bring in the big guns – and in show business terms they don't come any bigger than Rogers and Cowan, the international celebrity public relations company, and the William Morris organization, one of the world's most powerful and highly respected celebrity agencies. Together, these two would launch a two-pronged attack on the American market that would rocket Julio onto the Planet Success and go down in show business history as one of the most triumphant marketing campaigns of all time.

Julio had first come to the attention of the second of these organizations back in 1980 at the Viña del Mar Festival – a venue which, for him, had always been highly providential. He had won one of his first contests there in 1969 and played there later to large and jubilant audiences and met many of those who were to influence his destiny. One such, that year, was Dick Alen, vice president in charge of William Morris's international division. Among the music world luminaries already in his stable were Chuck Berry, Rod Stewart and Smokey Robinson. That year he was at the festival with some other clients, The Four Tops and K.C and the Sunshine Band.

'Julio was the star of the festival,' he recalled in a 1984 interview with *Billboard* magazine. 'I'd heard the name but never seen him and when I saw him perform I felt he could be an American star. I felt the public was ready for him and I spent the next year trying to convince him of that fact.'

It was almost as if Julio had wanted the big prize for so long that at the precise moment when it was in sight his courage failed him. He was scared to launch his attack at the wrong time or in the wrong way. Not for the first time in his life he was in a state of semi paralysis.

'Around about that time I used to call him Mr No because everything we suggested to him he used to say no to,' Fraile recalls.

But once the wheels started turning, Julio began to move with them and the engine of success became unstoppable.

Throughout 1981 and a large part of 1982, Dick Alen watched Julio's triumphs and waited. In Brazil, in 1982, for example, more than 80,000 people had attended Rio de Janeiro's Flamingo stadium to see Julio perform, and in the UK five Albert Hall dates had been sold out. He had received the Crystal Globe Award from CBS as its best-selling recording artist and seen the unveiling of a life-size statue in his likeness at the Grevin Museum in Paris.

The world loved Julio and there was no question in Dick Alen's mind that, with the right approach, America would fall too. With persistence, by mid 1982 he had managed to talk the singer round to his way of thinking, signing him to his stable of stars. Alen was to take over the responsibility of booking Julio's worldwide concerts – though the immediate emphasis was to be in America. In the meantime, Deborah Miller, who was another vice president of the company, this time in charge of the television variety department, became responsible for booking Julio's TV appearances – which were to prove so vital to the strategy.

The key to the William Morris approach was one of selectivity. Julio was not to sing just anywhere or to appear on just any old TV show. Each appearance would represent a new and worthwhile initiative in the drive to popularize Julio in America.

The choice of venues was crucial. 'We tried to pick places where the taste makers and community leaders, the people that make the American taste would come to see the show,' Dick Alen told *Billboard*. 'We wanted places where the American audience is comfortable when they see the artist, where they can sit back and enjoy it.' They were to forsake the big bucks potential of large venues for intimacy. They wanted America to get into bed with Julio, as it were, and it is difficult for even the biggest and most charismatic star to seduce when he appears to half the audience as a kind of Latin Lilliputian – a small suntanned speck on the stage.

On the question of Julio's essential Latin quality, this, Dick Alen reasoned, must be used but also controlled. 'We had to make sure that we didn't book him as a Latin artist,' he said. 'He doesn't forget his Latin heritage, but the idea was that he would become an American artist whom both Latin and other people would go see.'

Julio himself all but whistled 'Yankee Doodle Dandy' to fulfil the American artist illusion. 'I learned the buildings, the humour, the sounds, the tempo, the phrasing. I learned to understand what happens here,' he said of the American experience. 'I started to like being in America. I even started to like the food, like hamburgers and ketchup. I like the taste of tomatoes in Italy and Spain – ketchup to me is like marmalade with tomatoes, but now I like it. And the wine . . . I love it, and I've learned about it since I was fifteen. Now I've started to appreciate some California wines. I've come to enjoy things I never in my life imagined I could like.'

Julio was smart. He knew that to succeed in America he must meet the fans on their terms and in their language, rather than his own. 'When I came to America I was successful all over the world,' he said. 'But they don't care about that here. If it's not happening here, forget it. You can be number one in China. But forget it.'

He knew, too, that no other Hispanic or Mediterranean star had ever truly made it in the United States. There was Charles Aznavour and Maurice Chevalier – but their appeal had remained limited, to say the least. And why? Because they had remained resolutely true to their roots. They had remained foreigners. Julio understood that the key to success lay in preserving his Latin charm and using it when necessary, but also in immersing himself in America and becoming 'one of them'. This he was able to do with consummate ease, with, of course, a little help from his friends.

It was in October 1982 that Julio sat down with Warren Cowan of the Rogers and Cowan public relations organization to discuss his future in America. 'We went to the Westwood Marquis Hotel and were introduced to Julio. They showed us some tapes of his concerts in Egypt and Israel and Japan, and the moment one sees the attraction of this man on tape, you realize that he has star written all over him,' Cowan, ever the PR man, told *Billboard* magazine.

'We talked for an hour or two . . . I was particularly impressed by something he had said that day, that he wanted to succeed in the US not just for himself, but also for other European and foreign artists, very few of whom had ever made it in this country.'

Cowan's organization began to ponder on how they could help their new client to achieve this aim. By the beginning of 1983 they already had their game plan, which was to be a triumph of showbiz networking and media promotion. Julio would appear in all the right places and with all the right people. He would sing the right songs and say the right things to journalists. As ever, he was to be his usual charismatic self – to bowl the opposition over.

'We found that once we could bring Julio together with the journalists he was able to charm them and win them over just because of his ability to transmit and to relate to them and they to him,' observed Warren Cowan. 'He has a lovely humility,' he added. 'And he's always laughing at himself.'

What neither Julio nor Rogers and Cowan kidded themselves about, however, was the importance of the show business network. Thus, the public relations company who also numbered David Bowie, Paul McCartney and Duran Duran among its music industry clients, saw to it that Julio was introduced to the Hollywood firmament of glittering stars as though he had been a virginal debutante at court. It began on 8 January 1983 with Julio's 'surprise' appearance as the headline entertainer at the American Society of Technion's annual benefit – organized on behalf of the Israel Institute of Technology.

The aims of the benefit were to raise money for the Institute to aid its development of irrigation systems and other technological innovations. Or something like that. More importantly, it was a major Hollywood bash held at the Century Plaza and organized by Kirk Douglas. It was one of those affairs to which any star who was not invited might seriously consider committing Hari-Kiri.

Douglas gives a somewhat ingenuous account of how Julio came to headline at the benefit dinner. 'They [the society] wanted to have some entertainment and my wife Anne – who is pretty good at these things – said, "Look, why don't we have somebody different?" She's from Belgium and she said, "You know, there's a guy who is well known all over Europe but not very well known in the United States and I think it'd be interesting if he would do it." Julio Iglesias. So we asked him, he was gracious enough to come and he was a smash. They loved him.'

It's a nice story but infinitely more probable that Rogers and Cowan called in favours to secure the Technion benefit for their new signing. After all, Warren Cowan had been best man at Kirk and Anne's wedding He admits: 'We helped his appearance at Technion and we took pictures beforehand of Julio with Kirk and Anne Douglas, which were then released.' This is simply how Hollywood operates.

Whatever motivated the invitation, Julio seized the opportunity with both hands. Not only did he appear for free, he spent $60,000 of his own money to put on a full stage show with fifty backing musicians.

'It was a distinct turning point in the Americanization of Julio,' says Larry Vallon, who was then director of the Los Angeles Universal Amphitheatre, a venue at which Julio would consolidate his success with a series of concerts two months later. 'The [Technion] show was great and from that show on he became the darling of Beverly Hills society. He was on the society pages and every woman at the Technion benefit fell in love with the guy. A lot of people at the show were studio heads and record company executives and really big opinion makers and it all filtered down. Our sales for the

March 1983 Amphitheatre shows just went crazy after that dinner.'

A 'friendship' ensued between Kirk and Anne Douglas and Julio. They had entertained him at their home before the Technion benefit and found him 'very charming, very interesting, very intelligent.' With some help from Rogers and Cowan, again, they went on to host a cocktail party at the celebrated Chasen's restaurant to welcome Julio to Los Angeles two days before his opening at the Universal Amphitheatre. 'We tried to find every important celebrity who knew him – jet setters who had travelled extensively and knew him from Europe – and we helped arrange the reception at Chasen's,' Warren Cowan confirms.

Old friends and new influential ones were all on the invite list to the party – among them Joan Collins, Charlton Heston, Gina Lollabrigida, Angie Dickinson, Morgan Fairchild and Priscilla Presley, who had, obviously decided to bury the hatchet. 'Almost 100 (press) stories came out of it,' recalls Warren Cowan. 'And it made him an instant name here in Los Angeles and around the country. It was on TV and all over the trade papers. Almost an instant overnight awareness of Julio Iglesias.'

It was all working brilliantly, as was the Julio Who? campaign which was another brainchild of the Rogers and Cowan organization. Its intention was to spark the curiosity of a largely Julio-ignorant population and then to supply them with the answer to the question Julio Who? in the flesh.

Julio's American TV debut was on Johnny Carson's highly influential *The Tonight Show* in February 1983 and it was here that Carson first introduced the Julio Who? joke which became a kind of leitmotif for the promotional campaign. It was quickly picked up by other prime time shows like *Today* and *Entertainment Tonight*. David Letterman, the doyen of chat show hosts, brought a telephone and an interpreter onto his show and began a global ring round in which he asked random telephone subscribers around the world if they'd ever heard of Julio Iglesias. Naturally, the answer tended in most cases to be yes.

It seemed suddenly that Julio was everywhere, but the campaign was infinitely more selective than it appeared to be. Thanks to Alen and Miller at William Morris. The offers of appearances and interviews began pouring in but each was carefully considered in terms of what it could do for the cause. There was never anything haphazard about the campaign.

In 1984, Deborah Miller spoke to *Billboard* magazine of this continuing philosophy. 'We try to have a reason for doing a specific television show,' she said. 'Because you can get so over-exposed on television and wear out your welcome and we don't want to do that. We always look at every decision from the long-term stand-point. So when we make a judgement as to whether we should do a television show it's with this guideline in mind. What is the reason we should do it? Because without a reason the appearance has no point, and if it has no point then it becomes superfluous.'

In 1983, for example, there were three more appearances on Johnny Carson's *The Tonight Show*, plus a date on the rival Merv Griffin show, and, in April 1984, there was an interview with Barbara Walters on *20–20*. 'Because it exposed him to an audience he might not otherwise have been exposed to,' said Miller. 'It became a news-based story, more journalistic.'

Other key appearances during the campaign were Bob Hope's eightieth birthday special in Washington D.C. in 1983 and the televized 'All Star Party' for Frank Sinatra in December. There was also, in that same month, *Christmas in Washington*, in which he appeared with the Reagans, Donna Summer and Andy Williams.

'To be honest,' Fraile says, 'Julio did not want to do this because he thought he might look ridiculous. I told him it was an important event to be part of and we fought about it. In the end he agreed to do it. And later he told me I was right.'

There were other contretemps during the American campaign between Julio and Fraile – notably over the much-celebrated recording of the Julio and Willie Nelson duet, 'To All the Girls I've loved Before', which was to be key in the capture of the American audience.

According to the mythology, the duet was the idea of Willie Nelson himself who was not just a well-known country singer but more an American institution. Nelson was said to have called Julio during his Albert Hall concerts in London in the summer of 1982. He had, apparently, heard Julio on the radio and decided that he had all the makings of a great country singer. Julio was said to be shocked and delighted at Nelson's suggestion that they should perform a duet. Perhaps the story is true – though it seems more likely that the collaboration was a marriage arranged by Julio's people in the knowledge that a duet with Nelson, who was more American than apple pie, would ensure the Americanization of Julio, too.

Whatever the case, Julio could see the benefits of the idea, though the choice of song was not as cut and dried as the publicity suggested. 'To All The Girls I've Loved Before' had been written by Albert Hammond and Hal David back in 1976 and was originally intended for Frank Sinatra – who never actually heard the song. Then in the summer of 1983 it was brought out of storage as a potential number for Julio and Nelson.

According to the hype, when Hammond came to Julio with the song, the singer instantly declared it ideal for the duet. According to Fraile, Julio had been offered the song as a solo venture by Hammond sometime earlier and had not liked it one bit. 'I had said to Julio even then, "This song is perfect for you." But being Mr No at that time he couldn't agree.'

It took some persuasion to convince Julio that the song could work for him and Nelson. 'Then when we made the recording it was a very big success and again Julio told me I had been right about it all along. But you know, it was becoming very tiring this constant battling with Julio. Really, I was becoming quite worn out by it.'

Already the cracks that would turn to a yawning chasm had begun to appear. In the meantime, Fraile remained at Julio's side, travelling with him to Austin, Texas, to record the duet, plus 'As Time Goes By' for Willie's album – at Nelson's own studio. It had taken the two men just one night to record the vocals, after which they were said to have had a lavish dinner washed down with two of Julio's infamously expensive bottles of Spanish wine. By 6 a.m. the next day, Julio and his team had flown out of Austin.

The single would be released in March 1984 and would rise to number one in the American country charts and number five on the general singles chart. In October 1983, however, the duo tested the water with a performance of the song at the Country Music Awards. 'Boy was he scared for that,' comments Deborah Miller. 'It was a tough audience, but the response was just fabulous.' It was, as Miller points out, one of the major turning points in America's acceptance of Julio. There were now newspaper diary stories that George Bush jogged to the record and that New York's Mayor, Ed Koch played it every morning while working out. America and Americans were falling in love with Julio.

It was a landmark record for Julio, also, in the sense that it had proved to him that he could marry his European sensibilities with the musical standards of the United States – that he could sing in English and succeed. It was, thus, an important precursor to the all important *1100 Bel Air Place* – which would finally be released in August 1984. In the meantime, growing Julio-awareness in America was capitalized on with a compilation album released in July 1983. It featured old faithfuls like 'Begin the Beguine' and was called simply, *Julio*. It sold in excess of 850,000 copies in the US. If there's one thing the man could do, it was sell records.

Chapter Seventeen

Cut to 23 September 1983. It is Julio's fortieth birthday – a milestone age, a watershed, a time to reflect on gain and loss, on the past and the future. A time to rejoice or to dismay. Depending.

On this occasion, however, rejoicing seems more the order of the day. After all, Julio's American success is already surpassing all expectations and his worldwide popularity goes from strength to strength. In Spain this year more than 100,000 people have attended concerts in Madrid and Barcelona and, as Spain's most famous export, he has been received by King Juan Carlos and Queen Sofia for the fourth time. In Japan 400,000 people have attended his 23-date concert tour and now – the icing on the birthday cake – he is in Paris to have a double award bestowed on him by the city's mayor, Jacques Chirac.

The first is the Medal of Paris and the second, and most important for the singing star, is the glittering Diamond Record Award, bestowed by the *Guinness Book of World Records* for having sold more than 100 million albums in six different languages, making him the highest-selling recording artist of all time. The only territory that has not yet surrendered to him is the moon. But at forty, who knows? There is still time.

Leaving the auditorium after triumphantly collecting the award, Julio is surrounded by baying women all wanting to touch their hero, to kiss him, to eat him alive. A TV journalist approaches Julio, waving his microphone.

'So what now, Julio?' he asks. 'What's left?'

'I still want more! Much more!' he replies.

'And after that?'·

'To sing on another planet . . .!'

Julio is a man still up in the sky, hoping to touch the moon and the stars. *La Vida Sigue Igual.* On his fortieth birthday he is borne aloft on wings of glory. CBS have flown in a celebrity crowd plus journalists and record distributors from around the world to Paris. The city has declared it 'Julio Iglesias day' and in the evening a 'select' 500 people will celebrate with Julio at the Pre Catalan restaurant on the Bois de Boulogne.

He is in the spotlight. His real home. While back in Miami, Virginia Sipl is still waiting for her man. But only just. In the last three years she has seen him linked with countless women in the press and read his revelations about most of them in his autobiography. She has put up with his myriad infidelities – some of them real, some of them simply conjured up for image purposes.

Often she has packed her bags, going back to her mother in Caracas, only to return to Indian Creek when Julio snapped his fingers or twanged the strings of her heart. 'Anyone who has ever truly been in love will understand it,' she says by way of explanation. And there is no question that she was indeed profoundly in love with Julio.

Julio, in his own way, loved her, too, but did little to disguise his betrayals of her – perhaps because he knew that this was one woman who, unlike Isabel, would forgive him almost anything. As early as 1980, for example, there was

Julio's affair with an American model referred to in Virginia's *Semana* magazine memoirs simply as Devy (though Debbie seems more likely). According to Sipl, the model had a face like a small Pekinese dog 'but this was not much of a consolation.'

Julio, it seemed, had become besotted by her and would sneak out on a bike like a love-sick teenager to phone her from a public call box.

'With time I realized that it was simply my love's nature to be unfaithful,' she says. 'You had to take him or leave him that way. But this was something different. This passion for the "little Pekinese" – although short lived – had hurt me badly. He had been devious. I felt more tricked than ever. Betrayed.'

It was to be one more occasion when she left – one more when she returned for more of the same treatment. Between 1981 and 1983 she had to suffer the indignity of seeing Julio linked with any number of mates. Not only had there been Sydne Rome and talk of an affair with Priscilla Presley but there was Phillipe Junot's old girlfriend, Giannina Facio. 'I feel good with her,' Julio told the reporters. 'She loves me for myself.'

During 1982 there were links in the press between Julio and page three girl Janine Andrews, and ex-Miss UK Caroline Seaward who always denied a liaison. Then, in March of that year, he was busy claiming to journalist Noreen Taylor that there was absolutely no woman in his life. Perhaps this was because Virginia had removed herself temporarily after one of their legendary bustups, or perhaps because he preferred to be secretive.

Life continued just the same with reports in February 1983 of a connection between Julio and Tahitian dancer Vaitiare Hirshon. He had met her while filming a TV special on the French Polynesian island. The producer had brought in a dozen exotic dancers to record a number with Julio and

Vaitiare was one of them. After the recording, Julio invited all the dancers to come and stay at Indian Creek. 'So the house was suddenly full of Polynesian smiles,' Sipl recalls. 'Indian Creek was no longer the paradise that it used to be. It had become Indian Creek Hotel. Journalists, colleagues, lifelong friends, new acquaintances . . . And as if that wasn't enough, then came the Tahitians.'

Virginia doesn't know why Julio chose Vaitiare above the others. But after the visit there were stories that her man had taken the young dancer on holiday to the South African game reserve at Mala Mala. 'I'm in love with her – and that's that,' he said. 'Her age is no handicap. I feel as young as she is.' Shortly afterwards there were reports of an impending marriage in July. Julio's reassurances, again, that it was all a question of publicity did little to soothe Virginia. Nor did the repetitive phone calls to Indian Creek from Vaitiare's mother after Julio had severed his relations with the young dancer. According to Julio, Vaitiare's mother was calling because her daughter was sad and spent the entire day crying in her room. Julio felt sorry for her, he said.

'Listen carefully,' Virginia claims to have said to him. 'I don't see why you have to feel sorry for her. You know as well as I do how many tears I have cried for you. My mother never once called to tell you about it.'

It was a rare moment of strength that she was to back up by moving out of Julio's house and into an apartment a stone's throw from Indian Creek. Even then, she claims, 'I loved Julio. I was trying to save our love. I don't know why, but I always believed he needed me. Probably because he never stopped telling me so. It might seem paradoxical, but it was for that reason that I went to live on my own . . . but still close to him.'

The relationship appeared to continue but was simply hobbling towards its ultimate demise. Julio continued to talk to her of love and of marriage and of the child that they would one day have – even buying a luxurious apartment for her in Caracas. Here, he insisted, she would be able to bring their child when visiting her mother. But in her heart Virginia knew that Julio was simply building castles in the air. He signed the papers for the purchase of the apartment, but never actually saw it. It is unlikely that he ever intended to share it with Virginia. It was bought more by way of a parting gift to a woman who, said Carlos, had already benefitted hugely from Julio's generosity. According to Sipl, Carlos claimed that 3 million dollars had been sunk in the Virginia fund. But Virginia herself maintains that money received was only ever spent on Julio, his children and his house.

Sipl had always regarded Carlos and, indeed Charo, as friends – though she was later to discover that this was, in fact, a dangerous assumption. A major rupture occurred between herself and Julio after Carlos reported to his brother that Virginia had been seen by a record company spy at an open air concert in Caracas with a new 'boyfriend'. The man in question was, in fact, an old school friend of Virginia's. During all the years that she lived with Julio she was never, she says, unfaithful to him and she was not about to start now. But this did not stop the wildly jealous Julio from taking his brother's words to heart. Madly, he convinced himself that Virginia was on the point of marrying this 'boyfriend' and left her high and dry in Caracas, refusing to speak to her for a month – and this, despite the fact that he too was again seeing Vaitiare. Once more, however, the rift between Julio and Virginia was patched up, though, in reality, with nothing stronger than Elastoplast. Virginia forgave the unforgivable again – returning against her better judgement to Miami. But as for relations between herself and Julio's family – who doubtless sensed that the affair was in its death throes and that Virginia was no longer important – this was another matter.

Neither Carlos nor Charo would speak to her after the event

– Julio claiming to her that, in fact, Carlos could not stand her. 'The person who should have been upset was me, because after having lived with them for so long, they condemned me without even giving me the benefit of the doubt,' Sipl says. 'The absolute truth was that this Venezuelan boyfriend of mine never existed. And more: while I was with Julio I was absolutely faithful to him.'

Most confusing of all to Virginia was Charo's reaction to her – Charo who, probably more than most women, should have understood the depths of Virginia's suffering. It was not, after all, so unlike her own with Julio's father. Instead, she took the view that Virginia was yesterday's woman and was not to be entertained. On several occasions Virginia tried to meet with her only to be confronted by rejection. 'I lament her incomprehensible attitude,' she says, 'because I always loved her. With what she did, she demonstrated to me that she had never really liked me at all. She had simply pretended to.' Again, this could be Isabel speaking.

The love affair with Julio limped on towards the summer of 1983. Virginia rented a new apartment at Bel Harbour – even closer to Indian Creek than her last bolt-hole – and stayed in Julio's bed whenever there was no one else there. She had become more a lady of the night where once she had been the lady of the house. On the eve of his Spanish tour Julio had visited Virginia at her apartment and they had a romantic dinner together before he flew off to his homeland. Days later his name was linked with Miss Switzerland in the press. 'I thought that Julio had completely lost his respect for me,' she says.

Despite this, in 1984 Sipl returned briefly to Indian Creek, but this time her stay was to last just three months. Destiny that had brought her together with Julio in the first place, now brought his 'nurse' Piti back across her path. Unwittingly she was to deliver the final death blow to the relationship by extinguishing the one hope that remained in Virginia's heart.

Throughout the relationship, Julio had not only been happy for her to look after his own children, with whom she had formed an unbreakable bond, but he had talked constantly of the child that they, too, would one day have together. Piti, who had also had an affair with Julio, confided that he had also promised her a child. 'He promises one to all his women,' she added. 'And I'm sure he means it from the heart.'

This, Virginia says, did not bother her. She had known the truth of it intuitively all along. But the statement that followed was like a body blow that wiped out what little love remained in her heart for Julio. According to Piti – who, being his nurse, should know – throughout the duration of his relationship with Virginia he had taken pills produced for him by a Chinese herbalist that would ensure that he would not father a child.

The only medication Virginia had ever known him to take were sleeping pills during the period when his father was kidnapped. But it was 'entirely logical' for Julio to have taken these pills which, she says, 'were doubtless fashionable at the time'. It was, she says, completely unforgivable. Far worse than any of his infidelities. So it was that the relationship ended – in silence, and without emotional scenes or arguments. 'I could no longer wait patiently for Julio to call down the moon,' she says. 'For all his promises, his castles in the air, to become reality.'

When Julio returned from Los Angeles, where he was entrenched in the recording of *1100 Bel Air Place*, Virginia had left and this time it was for ever.

She took up residence again in Caracas, where she became a TV presenter and had a daughter. The identity of the father was not revealed and though there was some speculation that it could have been Julio, Virginia utterly denies it and, indeed, it seems highly unlikely.

As in all relationships, there had been an internal logic to that of Virginia and Julio. She had seen the right side and the left side of his personality, and had been so deeply in love with the first that for years she thought she could live with the second.

He was, she says, 'cultivated and fantastic. He conquered me irredeemably and I gave him my freedom. I know and I feel that he loved me . . . in the only way that he is capable of loving . . . My love for him was stronger than his failings. And my capacity for forgiveness was as big as the love that blinded me.' Her sins, she says, were to have loved too completely and to have 'abandoned everything to fall in love with someone whose fame and success meant that he could never belong to me alone.'

She recalls the love affair without rancour and wishes him luck and love. In 1987, the old lovers bumped into one another once more in Caracas – they laughed and talked like old friends. 'He invited me to go to the Bahamas with him. Julio will never change!'

She concluded her memoirs with the words: 'The pleasure of having known Julio will never end.' But, of course, the pain of it meant that there could never be any going back.

The demise of the relationship between Julio and Virginia came at exactly the wrong time as far as Julio's children, Chaveli, Julio José and Enrique were concerned. They had formed a strong bond with the woman who came to occupy their father's life for over six years. So it was, to say the least, unsettling for them when they came to Miami to live with their father in 1984 and found her gone.

Distraught as they had been at the break-up of their parents' marriage – and they were indeed devastated by it – they could have hated Virginia Sipl, seeing her as competition to their mother. Instead she had captured them with her sunny nature and easy funloving ways. To the visiting Iglesias children, who would come to Miami each summer to be with their father, she was a breath of fresh air after the somewhat rigid and disciplined methods of their mother.

They adored her and she adored them right back. She would spend Julio's money on up-to-the-minute leisure wear for the children to supplement the rather more formal clothes they had brought with them. She would take them to fairgrounds and to the movies. She was popcorn, candy floss and Peter Pan's Wendy rolled into one. If Julio was touring during their visits – which was frequently the case – then her role became part nanny, part mother and part big sister. With Virginia and their cousins – Carlos's children – Chaveli, Julio José and Enrique would spend endless days by the pool, swimming, playing tag, having fun. Virginia treated them as she would have treated her own children and this was crucial to Julio, who could not have sustained a relationship with any woman his children did not approve of. The well being of his children mattered to him.

Julio never claimed to be a good father. 'Good fathers,' he said in 1994, 'are supposed to get up early in the morning to change nappies and are there to meet the children from school. I didn't do any of that. I was always on tour in different countries.' But, in his own way once again, he did love his children, and suffered immense despair, after the marriage break-up, at being separated from them.

In her memoirs, Virginia Sipl recounts tales of Julio breaking down in tears after talking to his children long distance on the telephone. And this acute sorrow can be understood by any parent. Less comprehensible, however, bearing in mind his self-confessed limitations as a father, was his request that the children should leave their mother's side and come to live with him in Miami. Particularly since they would not be living with him but with their grandmother, Charo – who, it could be said, might not be the ideal candidate to raise

'Isabel's children'. The two women, after all, had never been the best of friends.

More bizarre still was Isabel's decision not to oppose her ex-husband on this issue – especially given her own, to say the least, difficult relationship with Charo.

In September 1983, she gave an interview to José Antonio Olivar for the Spanish news agency EFE. She had recently returned from Miami where she had discussed the children's future with Julio and reached an agreement with him that from mid 1984 they should emigrate to America to be with Julio for an initial period of two years. In the end, the arrangement was made a permanent one.

Already married to the Marques de Grinon at the time, she now had another daughter, Tamara, who was said to be inseparable from the other children. Indeed, according to Isabel, in their infantile innocence they had even begged that Tamara should go with them to Miami.

She explained her reasons for allowing Julio custody. Both she and Julio, she said, were keen for their children to learn English. 'And on leaving Spain there's no better place to be than at their father's side.' She also added that she appreciated that Julio missed his children. 'And it would be selfish of me to stand in his way . . . In all that which concerns our children there have never been any problems between Julio and me.'

The idea of ownership of the children did not exist between them, she said. 'There is none of that "They're mine" or "Now it's my turn." For my part, I understand perfectly that it means a lot to Julio to have his children with him, just as I recognize that they also need to be with him,' she added munificently.

It was all very civilized. But these were *her children*. They were informed of their parents' decision by Julio himself who, according to Isabel, sat them down and said: 'You're going to come to Miami for a couple of years. You'll see

Mummy whenever you want to because she'll come to see you whenever you need her.' But the truth was that, for the most part, their mother would be thousands of miles away in another continent. Put bluntly, she was detaching herself from them.

In fairness, during the interview she informed José Antonio Olivar that she could hardly bear to think about the separation and that frankly, 'I am not happy without my children by my side.' And yet it seemed a curiously emotionless Isabel that had agreed to an arrangement that would not only distance her from her flesh and blood but place them in the care of a mother-in-law who she neither liked nor approved of.

The decision is rather unfathomable – but perhaps her split from Julio had somehow caused a rupture in her relationship with her children, too. She had believed for seven years in her fairy tale marriage to Julio and her children had been part of the story. When the idyll shattered and she saw the marriage for what it had really been, it was almost as though the children had become part of the disillusionment. Or something like that.

In the interview with Olivar, she pointed out that the precise length of time that the children would spend in Miami was flexible. 'If we see that they're not adjusting well, they'll come back earlier, if we see that they love it then they could stay longer. Everything will be done with the best interests of our children at heart.'

But though the children's stay with Julio was to become permanent, it was Alfredo Fraile's contention that they never seemed particularly happy with the arrangement.

'I remember that Julio's children used to come to our house to be with us and our children and it was almost like they were our children too. They saw that the life at our house – a wife, a husband and children – was stable and normal and they were attracted to that because it was not their experience and it was what they wanted so much. Everyone needs love and security – especially children. Julio tried hard to be with them in Miami and to spend time with them, but they needed more than that. They needed what all children need – a happy family life.'

It was not that they were unloved. Photographer Gerry Davis recalls a photo session with Julio and his children at Indian Creek in which, he says, the star was extraordinarily at ease with them, happy and relaxed with them 'and quite unbelievably tender towards them.'

It was rather that his career inexorably came first. Indeed, in 1988 he stated quite boldly to journalist Jane Oddy, 'My profession is the most important thing in my life. If I said that my family and my children were more important then I would be lying.' It was a tough truth, a hard reality for the children, but one which in time they came to accept. In 1993, Chaveli stated without too much emotion: 'He [my father] was always into his work. When he had time he was with us. But family was never a strong point.' It was simply the way it was.

On the plus side, of course, they never wanted for anything materially and it was, doubtless, an extraordinarily glamorous and interesting world to grow up in. They were the children of a man who by 1990 was ranked, by Forbes, among the top eleven highest-paid entertainers in America. But with it came fame and recognition and that was tough to deal with. At an English boarding school where she was billeted in the mid eighties, for example, Chaveli was constantly taunted by cruel jibes about her father and would, according to Virginia Sipl, shed bitter tears over her longing to be simply one of the other girls. And it was for this reason, too, that in 1981, to coincide with the release of 'De Niña a Mujer', Julio had to bribe his daughter with sweets to pose for publicity pictures. 'I hated the press,' she said in her *People* magazine interview.

Later, of course, along with her brothers she learned to use it – just as her father always had. Recently, Julio José and Enrique have independently gone in to the music world as singers themselves, and the pages of glossy magazines, like Spanish *Hola'*, have proved invaluable in promoting their new careers. At twenty-four, Chaveli, too, is something of a press veteran – commanding legendary fees for interviews and photo sessions. She earned her spurs not just on her father's knee for the 'De Niña a Mujer' promotion but also as a teenage model when she saw her face on billboards and magazine covers throughout Latin America. It was not what you'd call a very normal childhood.

She is now a chat show hostess on a twice monthly programme for Univision – the US Spanish-language television network, based in Miami. The programme is called simply *Chaveli.* Her guests have, naturally, included her father, which could have made for a very interesting discussion indeed – particularly if she had asked him the questions which still hung over from her childhood. Like: 'Why did you and my mother separate?' It was a question that had, apparently, troubled her for years.

She'd been asking it since she was a little girl going through the textbook traumas of any child watching the two people that she loves most in the world tearing themselves apart. She had experienced the usual self hatred, the feeling that she was to blame, the longing to bring her parents back together, the unspecific raging against life.

'The first reaction of any child is just to put the two parents together again,' Julio himself commented to journalist Barbara Young in 1988. 'She did everything she could to put mother and father together. She cried and cried and cried. Now she is very understanding. But to understand is not enough. She does not try to make me feel guilty. None of us understand why it happened.'

This last was not exactly true. The reason that she did not ask her father the inevitable question on her chat show was that, eventually, somewhere along the line she had already gained the answer. 'He's always been a womanizer. That's his life,' she said bluntly in her *People* magazine interview, adding: 'I've always said, "I'm not getting involved in his life." I always looked for a husband who is not like my father.'

For all this, her wedding to twenty-eight-year-old Catalan-born Ricardo Bofill Junior – the son of one of Europe's most famous architects – on 11 September 1993, ended in separation within the year. Before the split, the newlyweds were said to be planning a large family – with which Chaveli would, no doubt, rewrite her own history and mend the sense of abandonment that both parents had produced in her. When children arrived, she hinted, she would give up work. 'If you leave your kids alone, they don't feel important,' she said, rather tragically.

In the event, it wasn't to be and the marriage floundered before it had really begun. The consensus was that, at twenty-two, she had married too young and had been so intent on creating a different life for herself that she had inadvertently repeated the mistakes of her parents.

Prophetically, sometime before marriage was even in the cards, her father had commented that his daughter was a major source of woe and wonder. 'I've never been a good father,' he reiterated. 'I haven't had the time. But this girl is everything to me. She has grown up too quickly, but I can't oppose what she does. Besides, she wouldn't take any notice. We never listen to our parents until we've been married at least twice,' he added. And, of course, Chaveli is now just one marriage away from fulfilling her father's prophecy.

Ironically, it is perhaps too much listening, observing and living in the shadow of her parents' lives that has caused

Chaveli's problems in the first place. Family history has a horrible way of repeating itself. *La Vida Sigue Igual* – for Chaveli, too, unfortunately.

Chapter Eighteen

'1100 Bel Air Place' was not just the title of the album that sealed Julio's American success, it was also the exclusive Los Angeles address at which Julio and his team were to billet themselves for more than a year while the album was being recorded.

For Julio, always a perfectionist, the making of the album was to be an obsessive quest to prove that he could merge his Latin style with that of contemporary America. It had taken five years of planning and would take a further sixteen months to record. Ultimately, it was to be more than just an album; it was a scrupulously executed labour of love. It seems unlikely that any other album in recording history was ever more pontificated over, fussed with or fretted about. Around eighty songs were considered for inclusion – half of them being rejected outright. Forty tracks were actually recorded before the final selection of ten was made. These included the Diana Ross duet, 'All Of You', 'The Air That I Breathe' with The Beach Boys and the Willie Nelson duet, 'To All the Girls I've Loved Before'.

Richard Perry, who had produced Julio and Willie's single,

was also to co-produce the album with Ramon Arcusa. Fifteen of the songs were cut with Perry as producer while Arcusa oversaw production of the other twenty-five.

Brought in on the advice of CBS, Perry had also worked with other major stars like Carly Simon and Diana Ross. He was the quintessential American producer and his main aim was to bridge the gap between Julio's usual style and one that would lend itself to the ears of a modern US audience.

'I think the key was being able to plant the seeds to show him that he could sound commercial in America and make records here with American musicians and writers,' said Perry, while being interviewed for a special *Billboard* magazine fifty-page supplement on Julio in 1984. 'Everything was crafted very carefully so that he could have the room to flourish and grow in this new environment. I think I proved to him that he could stay true to his style while sounding more contemporary.'

The writers Perry mentions were to include Albert Hammond, once more, who had co-written 'To All the Girls I've Loved Before' and now revamped 'Air That I Breathe' – originally penned by him and Mike Hazelwood for The Hollies. He also co-wrote 'Moonlight Lady' with Carole Bayer Sager and contributed English lyrics to 'Me Va Me Va' and 'Bambu'. Hammond – who had known Julio from the seventies, having met and performed with him at the Viña del Mar Festival – had been raised in Gibraltar and was, therefore, bilingual. He, too, was to be an associate producer on the album.

'I brought Albert into the production because of his musical abilities and because I felt his rapport with Julio and his ability to speak both languages were unique assets,' says Perry. Umberto Gattica, one of the best sound engineers in town, was also brought in, as was Tony Renis and many of the best session musicians in Los Angeles. On the 'When I Fall In Love' track, the legendary saxophonist, Stan Getz, applied his genius.

The album, which was recorded mostly at Sunset Sound studios, was initially due to be released in the spring of 1984, but as Arma Andon, the record company executive who was overseeing the fraught launch, explains: 'We were minutes away from going to press with about a million records when Julio called me at home and said, "I want to change the mix." We had to accommodate him.'

In the end, the long-awaited record was not released until August 1984. Within five days, a million copies had been sold in the US – a number which was to swell to 4 million copies making *1100 Bel Air Place* a quadruple platinum success. Julio was triumphant but declared the album 'the most difficult thing I ever did in my life.'

'My singing is different in many ways,' he added. 'Feelings, accents, moods, phrasing. I may not cut another English album for two or three years. It was too painful.'

Most painful of all – in practical terms – had been mastery of the language itself. During Julio's brief stay in England, back in the sixties, he had concentrated on the language of love with Gwendoline and neglected the language of the country. 'When I first met Julio in 1983, his English was extremely limited to put in nicely,' says Julie Adams, who became a speech coach in residence. It apparently took Adams six months to teach Julio to sing 'To All the Girls I've Loved Before' rather than to 'All The Gulls'. At one point she resorted to using a Kermit the Frog puppet to show him how much his mouth needed to open to form certain sound. 'I knew if he started singing about love on the 'bitch' there'd be problems.'

Now forty, the linguistic habits of his own native language were deeply entrenched – the phrasing of sentences, the breathing techniques, the emphasis on certain syllables and the method of forming words. Furthermore, most of his intimates were Spaniards or 'Cubans' as Priscilla Presley referred to them. The house at Indian Creek was something of a Latin colony, where English was rarely used. Adams attempted to remedy the above with endless months of mind-numbing language lessons that often took place for twelve hours a day, seven days a week, in Miami, Los Angeles and the Bahamas. Her job was not simply to convey the pronunciation of words but the way that certain emotions in English lyrics should be expressed.

'There were dark days when we were hanging on by a thread,' she told *Vanity Fair* in January 1990. 'But Julio's English did improve immeasurably.'

'Now I understand the news and jokes on *Saturday Night Live*,' Julio informed the *Vanity Fair* interviewer, Maureen Orth. 'Before, you have to 'splain everything to me.'

There were, however, other areas of pain during the recording of *1100 Bel Air Place*. Notably, in the relationship between Julio and Fraile. Until the American breakthrough, Fraile had been the ultimate right-hand man, the most important general of the conquering army. But, suddenly, in an unspoken fashion, he found himself demoted to the ranks. The William Morris organization was handling the bookings, Carlos was handling the money, and Rogers and Cowan were handling the image, the public relations and the marketing. So what exactly was there left for Alfredo to do?

Though he continued at Julio's side, his role had become uncertain, perhaps even redundant – everything, it seemed, was running along very nicely and would have been with or without him. It was as though, having dedicated the best part of fifteen years to Julio's career, it had now been taken out of his hands. The monstrous success that he had helped to create now had a life of its own and was essentially the property of others.

On 2 May 1984, for example, work on the album was interrupted for Julio to attend a press conference, broadcast by satellite to ninety different countries, in which he signed a three-year sponsorship agreement with Coca Cola. The deal, reputed to be worth in the range of $20 million to Julio, had been set up by the LA-based Vail Music Marketing Group in conjunction with Coca Cola – a deal in which Fraile, for once, had not been the main mover. It would make Coca Cola official sponsors of all Julio's worldwide tours during the following thirty-six months. Julio, in return, would promote Coca Cola and Diet Coke worldwide in print, TV and radio media. He would also – adopted son of America that he now was – participate on behalf of Coca Cola in the Ellis Island Project to refurbish the Statue of Liberty.

The company hoped to trade not just on Julio's new-found US success, but on his long-established global appeal. He had exactly the style and class that they were looking for, they said, and they promised not to exploit it. Julio's work for them would include state of the art commercials that would be, they said, 'works of art in themselves.' Not for Julio the usual inane humming of Coca Cola jingles. They would, instead, 'present his art for the enjoyment of the public.'

'Other advertisers might want to squeeze everything they can out of a sponsorship deal,' commented Jim Vail, president of the Vail Group. 'With Coca Cola, it's as if they're putting a Ming Dynasty vase on display.'

It was an appropriate image as far as Fraile was concerned. As Julio's success grew he looked on with increasing dismay, not just at the erosion of his own role, but at the mincing, kid glove treatment that Julio was beginning to expect as a God-given right. He watched the fawning deification of a man whose human failings he knew perhaps more than anyone else on earth – a man whom he loved despite them. And he did not like it.

'The problem is that Julio, like all artists, *needed* criticism – although the more successful that anyone becomes the more they want to hear the beautiful things. I was always on Julio's side. I spent fifteen years fighting on his behalf. But, at the end, I was also the only one who was prepared to tell him the truth.'

Fraile had become a voice in the wilderness, viewed by Julio as a prophet of doom and dissent. Meanwhile, the saccharin approach to Julio began to nauseate Fraile. 'We began touring in the States and everyone around him would always say, "Ah, Julio, this is perfect. This is just perfect." But no one is perfect all the time and Julio and I used to fight bitterly about this.'

The year-long sojourn in Los Angeles exacerbated the problems between the two men. They had spent years living in each other's pockets. But now they became mutually irritated by one another's presence in the classic way of all failing relationships. Fraile began to feel not just dispossessed of his job, but emotionally and geographically displaced, too. He was homesick – which for a man who had done nothing but travel for more than a decade, was a bizarrely unfamiliar and uncomfortable sensation. It was, thus, in Los Angeles that he began to calculate what he calls 'the equation of my life'.

'Julio had the success and all the material things that he wanted – and that was enough for him. But I didn't have any of the fame or the glory and I certainly didn't have the same amount of money, either. I had six children and I had never seen even one of them being born. I made a balance sheet of everything that I had lost and everything that I had gained and it seemed to me that I had lost too much and not gained enough.'

Despite his growing unease, however, Fraile remained at Julio's side for the much vaunted 1984 world tour which was to kick off in Denver in June and then take in a wide sweep of both American and Canadian cities. Between 16 and 18 August, there were to be three Canadian appearances in Toronto, Montreal and Ottawa. But it was on the second date in Montreal, on 17 August, that the relationship between

Julio and the man who had been not just his manager but a brother in arms – one of the strongest and most loyal of all his allies – was to come to an end.

His relationship with Fraile had always been volatile – sometimes even verging on violent. But despite this, it ended, rather like the other important relationships in Julio's life, quietly and sadly, without tears or traumas or recriminations.

Fraile recounts that Julio, who was obsessed with the success of the all-important tour, had been behaving unbearably. He was snappy, impatient, and found fault with every aspect of the tour arrangements. He would pull his usual stunt, which was to allow others to slavishly set each concert up then arrive at the last minute with his 'I don't like this and I don't like that' complaints. 'On that tour he was constantly difficult and it was a very unhappy experience,' Fraile says. 'We fought a great deal.'

This was normal, however. Fighting between the two men was common currency. Generally, they shouted, squared up to one another, went off and sulked and then made up again. But the atmosphere had somehow changed between them. Fraile recalls that on the night of the Montreal appearance, the usual rituals were observed. Julio came offstage, Fraile wrapped him in a shawl and the two men went together to the dressing room – where Julio again did what he had been doing for the last fifteen years. He asked Fraile what he had thought of the show.

The tradition was cast in stone. 'He always used to ask me what I thought about the concert and I always used to give him my honest opinion. And if it wasn't positive then he would argue, for sure, because nobody likes criticism. He would say, "Alfredo, you don't understand – you know nothing." And I would say, "Yes, Julio, I do understand, for one very good reason. I understand because I am the public." And when Julio was singing I'd be down there with the public and I'd listen to what people were saying. So I knew what I was talking about and Julio accepted this in his heart.'

But on this evening the conversation was not to end in the usual joshing and amicable embrace.

'Julio asked me what I'd felt about the Montreal show and I replied to him that it had been perfect, great and the encores had proved how much the audience had liked it.' Fraile added that it had certainly been a much better success than the show the night before in Toronto.

'Uh-huh,' said Julio, 'and why is that?'

Fraile began his explanation. '"Well, yesterday the sound wasn't so good so you weren't so comfortable and maybe you didn't sing as well as usual. So that meant that the communication between you and the audience wasn't so good." I also added that it was his job to communicate with the audience – that it was the thing he did best and that if he wasn't communicating then it was, basically, his fault.'

Julio was silent for a few moments and then with ice-cold rage asked Fraile: 'Why is it, Alfredo, that you always answer all my questions with so much logic?'

Fraile replied: 'Because, Julio, I am a logical man.' And, indeed, had it not been for the brilliant logic that he had applied to Julio's early campaigns the singer might not have been where he is today.

Nonetheless, Julio replied: 'Well, I'm sick and tired of your logic, Alfredo.' To which Alfredo countered that he, too, was sick and tired of Julio's irrational outbursts – and of his lack of logic.

'Close your eyes, Julio,' he said. 'And when you open them I'll be gone. I will disappear from your life and you need never see me again.'

Fraile left Julio's dressing room, and two minutes later, as he was waiting at the stage door for a car to take him back to the hotel, the road manager, Fernando Echevarria – who was a good friend of them both – approached him. He had been sent by a mortified Julio with the message that Fraile was the person that he loved most in the world. 'He had told Fernando to tell me not to be stupid and to come back. But I knew in my heart at that moment that the really stupid thing to have done would be to go back because, really, it was completely finished between us.

'I said, "Look, Fernando. This is a decision I have come to over a long time and I think it's better that I go like this than to go in another way in a worse moment."'

Fraile returned to the hotel where, again at Julio's insistence, he was approached by Fernando. 'This time I said to him, "Fernando, who do you care most about – Julio or Alfredo?" And, tactfully, he said. "You, Alfredo." So I said, "Well, today, Fernando, Alfredo is free – he doesn't want to live like this anymore. He needs to be free. So don't ask me to go back anymore."

'Fernando and I had dinner together and the next morning, without seeing Julio, I caught the plane home to Miami. When I got back I took my wife and my six children on holiday to Cape Canaveral which, during seven years of living in Miami, I'd never even seen.'

During the following ten years he was to attempt to, as he puts it, 'make it up to my wife and to my children for all the years that I had not been with them.'

On returning from Cape Canaveral, he wrote a letter to Julio, in which he explained his position. 'I told him simply that the equation of my life no longer seemed to be adding up and that I needed to make a different kind of existence for myself.' He sent the letter not just to Julio but to all those members of the 'family' who had toured and worked with them. 'I did it for the simple reason that I knew that this was the only way to really cut the tie. Many times before, we'd row, I'd catch the plane home, he'd call me, we'd make up and I'd go back to him. But this time I wanted it to be finished for good.'

Julio never replied to the letter and it was to be fourteen months before the two men saw each other again. The legendary, and by then 80-year-old Mexican singer, Pedro Vargas, was giving a concert in aid of the victims of the Mexican earthquake and Julio was performing a number with him. Vargas had invited Fraile and his wife and knowing that Julio would be there, they accepted.

In the time that had elapsed there had been rumours that Fraile was bad-mouthing Julio – which seems highly unlikely. 'People offered me lots of money to talk and I never accepted their offers,' he says. 'Also, when people came to me they thought if they spoke badly of Julio they were doing me some kind of favour – but I never felt that way. To my mind, something of Julio belongs to me and something of me belongs to Julio. So I simply don't allow that kind of thing.'

Fraile was disturbed by the false accounts from those who now had Julio's ear and wanted to clear the air. 'Also, to be honest,' he admits, 'I wanted to see him again and to embrace him.'

He arrived at Julio's hotel and and went up in the lift to the singer's suite. Julio was walking down the corridor. 'I was nervous,' Fraile recalls. 'It had been a while since I'd seen him and I didn't know how he would react. But he reacted well – with affection.

'He was nervous, too,' Fraile adds. 'He said I looked well – but fatter. He asked me what I was doing there and I said I'd come to speak to him. I passed my arm through his and we went into his room. We talked and sorted it out. It was cathartic and good for both of us. We met with love and friendship and happiness. But I also saw, once and for all, that our relationship was broken.'

The two men parted as they had lived – as friends. 'I told him that if he ever really needed me he could call me and I would go to him,' Fraile says. But Julio has never taken him up on the offer.

The singer remains godfather to one of Fraile's daughters and during their Mexico meeting Julio said that he wanted to make her a gift. 'He asked me what he should buy for her and I said, "Send her a letter or call her – she'll appreciate that a lot more than a present." Maybe Julio and I were both guilty of this – we always thought we could make amends with material things. But over the years I learned a different way.'

There is no legacy of bitterness as far as Fraile is concerned. 'I wish Julio nothing but happiness and success,' he concludes. 'But the one thing I also know is that I could never go back to Julio's life again. This I know with all my heart.'

Chapter Nineteen

In material terms, at least, the eighties were to be for Julio what they had been for so many – the years of plenty. Only in Julio's case even more so. From the time of his American breakthrough onwards, no article or interview about him ever appeared without the journalist panting at the singer's wealth – describing his assets, real and sometimes imagined, in salivating terms.

He was said to own mansions in Tahiti, Hollywood, the Bahamas and Spain – though, in fact, Julio had ceased to own a property in his own country since the annulment of his marriage with Isabel. In addition, there was a house in Venezuela – presumably the one he had bequeathed to Virginia Sipl – and a ranch in Madariaga, near the Argentine coastal resort of Mar de Plata. Its size was somewhere between 200 and 4,500 acres, depending on which report you read.

At the ranch, named 'Momentos' after Julio's 1983 hit, he was said to be building the world's largest swimming pool, a 320-foot monstrosity, though the estate already had a 600-acre lake. There were also plans for two polo fields and a polo clinic that Prince Charles was, reputedly, invited to open. An offer which he apparently declined.

Back in Miami, the reporters waxed lyrical about Julio's fleet of cars – if lined up, it was said, they would plunge America's whole North-East road network into gridlock. Pride of the fleet were two Rolls Royces which, rather famously, combusted one summer when one of Julio's staff had left jump leads attached from the battery of one to the other. Julio was said to have kept the number plates of the two ruined cars to remind himself that, like King Canute, he could not control everything.

There were limos and, of course, a red Ferrari Testarossa, the ultimate phallic symbol – though the truth was that Julio, who hated driving anyway, tried it only once and declared it too difficult to get in and out of for a man with his back problems. It was mostly left to adorn the driveway. An icon of virility that could growl and throb into life at the turn of a key.

Mostly, anyway, Julio preferred to fly. His Gulf Stream jet was priced at anything between four and eleven million dollars. It sat in a state of constant readiness on a private nearby airfield, while, in the meantime, there were tales of Julio's two helicopters, their propellers perpetually flapping like epileptic windmills on the lawn. It was the kind of thing a satirical writer could have a field day with – and, indeed, one did. In 1986, Spanish writer Maruja Torres wrote a hilarious romantic fantasy, *Oh Es El* (Oh It's Him) in which she lampooned the multi-million-dollar lifestyle of Spain's most famous export.

There was, after all, endless ammunition for Torres. There were stories about Julio's domestic arrangements which included the employment of anything between twelve and forty staff – depending on which report you believed. Then there were the tour staff – numbering somewhere between fifty and 120 and including one woman who was said to be in Julio's employ simply to wash and massage his feet after shows.

Generous to a fault, he was said to insist that all employees not travelling on his private plane should travel first class on other airlines. By 1987, it was claimed that his total staff bill topped the million pound a year mark.

He was said to be a good employer, and the lower down you were in the organization the nicer he was to you. 'Julio was always big with the little people,' then press chief Fernan Martinez recalls. And this applied not just to employees, but to fans.

'In Las Vegas, a waiter asked if he could bring his daughter to meet Julio,' recalls Martinez. 'Outside the casino there was this very wealthy Brazilian who was waiting to give Julio a lift in a Rolls Royce. The waiter was in a Chevette with his daughter and Julio got in with them. The Rolls had to follow behind.'

It was endearing – Julio displaying that irresistible right side of his nature once more. But never let anyone forget that Julio was King and that Indian Creek – or wherever he happend to be at any given moment – was where he held court.

As one British journalist, Ian Parker, observed while interviewing Julio during a gig at Atlantic City in 1995, his style could be overbearingly imperious. 'When he asked for something for the first time, he used a tone that was not rude, but suggested that he had already asked several times; his tone incorporated slight irritation that his need had not already been attended to, telepathically. People fetched and carried and tried to anticipate. Most pop stars know two or three years of this and then look back at it all with a shake of the head. Julio has been getting what he wants for thirty years. When he needed the air conditioning turned down, he said, "Frio" and it was done.'

It had been this way for years. In the eighties, American

journalist Guy Martin, who had been allowed into the inner circle, drew parallels between Julio's world and that of a real king. 'He lives offstage in high mediaeval style with an actual court that performs every single one of a court's functions. He has valets, pages, consorts, liege lords, court musicians, composers, ministers of the exchequer, ladies in waiting.'

At 'court', Julio was at his most comfortable, usually eschewing the invitations of others, preferring to entertain at home. 'He is the perfect host,' Fernan Martinez asserts, 'but a lousy guest because in someone else's territory he becomes shy and displaced. He doesn't like to ask if he can go to the bathroom. At Indian Creek, though, it's another matter. If you call at Julio's and he's eating, he'll offer you half of what's on his plate. In this he's very Spanish.'

It was at Indian Creek, too, that Julio preferred to woo the women. After the demise of his relationship with Victoria Sipl, they arrived and departed in quick succession as though through the revolving door of a plush hotel – which was, basically, what Indian Creek had become. The paramours came and went, interspersed by one or two more serious relationships. Notably, in the mid-eighties there were tales of a deep love interest between Julio and an American, Mary Matthews. (And to prove it, neither her name nor picture ever appeared in a single newspaper article at the time, connecting her with Julio.) On top of this, there was also, according to the man himself, a serious liaison with an unnamed Yugoslavian journalist – but neither relationship was to last.

Mostly, however, the women were no more than weekend visitors who would ensconce themselves in the King's private rooms, making love and playing Pac Man with Julio – who had a passion for the said computer game and kept one in his bedroom. When they had left there would be the usual shower of flowers from Julio, whose annual florist bill was purported to be in the region of $50,000.

On some levels, at least, he certainly knew how to treat a lady and he was willing to share his extensive knowledge and experience on the subject. He would perch cross-legged on one of his large Sultan-style sofas like the Bhagwan Shree Rajneesh addressing students in search of the meaning of life, and propound his theories on successful scoring to visiting journalists.

'Ladies' eyes will tell you everything you must know . . . but, of course, from the toes to the eyes, all is important.

'On a first date, ask the lady where she wishes to dine, then don't go there. If she's known there, you become nothing.

'Never attend a party without a goodlooking woman, even if she's your sister or you have to borrow her for the evening.

'At a party, don't head for the girl who's a "10", because she expects it. Pick a "6". Numbers "1" through "5" will then compete for you, because they'll feel it's easy to overcome a "6". And numbers "7" through "10" will always notice you because they'll wonder why you picked the "6" in the first place.

'When making a conquest, if the lady is a dentist, talk to her about teeth. Don't bring her into your world. Enter hers.

'I never give my shoulder to a woman, meaning I never turn my back to go to sleep. And I never turn my back before I go to sleep either.'

He had talked about his songs, he had talked about the women, now onto the wine, which, by the 1980s, had become a kind of religion for Julio. He was said to keep private wine cellars in Miami, New York, Madrid, Paris and California. The latter, indeed, was said to hold 25,000 bottles of wine worth something in the region of £7 million.

'I have often spent £8,000 on a single bottle,' he told journalist Robin Eggar. 'But when you want the best you have to pay for it. I don't think that's too much to pay for a wine. Many of the wines I drink are thirty years old – to wine connoisseurs they are like precious antiques. When you open a bottle of wine that old it is like asking it to give you its life – and that deserves some respect.'

Journalist Feliciano Fidalgo, whose close friendship with Julio is largely based on their mutual love and appreciation of wine, also recounts tales of telephone calls from Julio, in far-flung places, often in the middle of the night. 'Julio would call me from New York or Buenes Aires, or wherever he was, and say, for example, "Feliciano, if you could just taste a little sip from this bottle of Château Mouton Rothschild that I'm drinking you'd fall down dead."

'Once he called me in the early hours from Australia and when I picked up the receiver I heard him say, "Oy, Feliciano, have you got any idea how phenomenal the wines in Australia are?"

'Then, in Ibiza, we were having a conversation, about how the best Spanish wines often fail to have the quality of the best French, and I told him about this new Spanish wine that I'd found. We went to the restaurant where I had tried it and I ordered the wine – it was a bottle of El Pesquera 1982 – and when Julio tried it his eyes widened and he said: "Dear God, this is something else, Feliciano!" He called his secretary and had her call the vineyard. Then he bought up every single bottle of that vintage – making the vineyard famous in the process.

'You have to understand that for Julio wine is an even more important method of communication than music. Not drinking it to get drunk – because he never does this. In fact, he rarely drinks more than a small glass. Instead, he savours it like an aesthete and it is almost a religious experience. He likes to open the bottle himself, to decant it, to smell it and to serve it to people with his own hands. It is part of a complete experience. A sacrament.'

Wine, Julio also said, was the one thing that improved with age. Unless, of course, you took into consideration his ever-flourishing sales figures which, each year, grew to newly staggering heights.

Along with the discussions of wealth, no article in this period ever appeared without the recitation of mind-numbing statistics about just how many albums and singles Julio had sold at any particular point in his career. Indeed, it seemed that a statistician must be permanently employed by Julio to spit out figures like the F.T. index on amphetamines.

Julio had, each journalist informed their readers, outsold his friends, Frank Sinatra, Barbra Streisand and Michael Jackson. A fact swiftly followed by a chunk of black type of the 'Julio has sold 100 million albums, given 2,214 live concerts, gained 680 gold and 221 platinum records, performed in 150 countries and so on' variety.

The statistics would be printed in the full knowledge that by the time the article appeared – even if it were the next day – the figures would already be out of date. But then who, apart from Julio and Julio's record company, was really counting?

The figures were included in publications for effect – but, lest they should make readers glassy-eyed, another interesting nugget of information was inserted. It was that 'every thirty seconds, somewhere in the world a Julio song is sung or played' – though no one ever bothered to question how this rather daft and incalculable statistic was ever arrived at.

At the same time and roughly every thirty seconds, Julio himself was busy making calculations of a different kind. These were pretty much along the same lines as those which Fraile, too, had made. He was making, as his old friend would say, 'the equation of his life.'

He had achieved all that he had set out to do. He had conquered the globe and even America now lay at his feet. He was as rich as Croesus, ruler of his own kingdom, he had erected his own flag on the Planet Success. So why, exactly, did it seem to Julio, as it had seemed to Fraile, that he too had lost more than he had gained? Why exactly was it that the eighties, which should have been the happiest and most triumphant of his life were, in fact, the bleakest?

On 7 February 1985, Julio received what was for him the ultimate recognition of his success – the planting of his star in the paving stones of Hollywood's Boulevard of Fame. No star ever shined brighter or was more hard earned than this one. Henceforth, his American fan club were said to set aside the first Saturday of each month to visit the glowing brass symbol of Julio's success like a shrine and polish it with a formula that was 1 per cent ammonia and 99 per cent love.

On the day the star was planted in the paving stones, the said fans were there in force. Los Angeles police had to halt traffic and contain the enthusiasm of a delirious crowd. Julio, displaying his usual love of symbolism, wore entirely new clothes from shoes and underpants to shirt, tie and jacket. The occasion, after all, marked, for him, another moment of rebirth – a new beginning. The city's mayor, Tom Bradley, declared it 'Julio Iglesias Day'. Julio, in the meantime, declared it the 'happiest day of my life.'

At this particular juncture, however, happiness was not the singer's strong suit. He was in the grip of a depression that was to occupy much of the latter half of the 1980s – a period where he travelled from one psychiatrist to another to seek the source of his pain, as he had once travelled to physicians to explain the agony in his spine.

He was suffering from the left hand, right hand madness that had been a leitmotif in his life but which now became the main song rather than the chorus. He had an acute and dreadful sense of himself as the man with everything and nothing. He had lucre, but he lacked love. He had fame, but he had few genuine friends. He had his children with him in Miami, yet he was barely able to spend a minute with them. He had the world at his feet, but in his head, he felt unworthy. He had success in his hands, but how to stop it slipping through his fingers? He had climbed the mountain of fame, but lived in daily terror of tumbling from its summit.

With the departure of Fraile in August 1984, he had lost the man who grounded and centred him. He had also lost one of the few genuine friends who knew who he was and who loved him for himself.

In emotional terms, too, the departure of Virginia Sipl had been devastating – for she had been infinitely more than his lover. She had cherished him like a small child, washing his hair, applying suntan lotion to his over-weathered face, imploring him not to bite his nails and to give up smoking. She had been his salvation and he knew it.

After she left there were the usual stream of women – that, unlike the wines, seemed to get younger and younger. Having already been linked with the Misses UK, Switzerland, and Universe, in October 1984 it was the 18-year-old Swedish beauty queen, Cecilia Horberg, who held his attention. But fleetingly.

In December 1985, he declared to the British press: 'I don't even have a woman in my life anymore. If you don't feel well in yourself it's impossible to love somebody else.'

Julio was clearly suffering from severe depression. 'I fought like a maniac to achieve world fame and in doing that I lost my sense of reality. I suddenly found I was empty. I didn't feel anything anymore. I had given all I had. I suddenly didn't want anything anymore. I was disgusted with everything.'

Earlier in the year his depression had come to a head in Frankfurt.

'It was my first performance in Germany in nine years,' Julio explained some months after the event to Cindy Adams, interviewing him for *Ladies Home Journal*. 'There was a lot of pressure on me. The first fifteen minutes of the concert were to be broadcast live on television. It was important to me. I could feel myself getting nervous.

'The lights went down, and I had no time to get my concentration together. In that second I couldn't sing a note. I coyld barely speak. I walked offstage. The doctor who travels with me tried everything. Everyone tried. "Julio, take tea, take bread...whiskey." But nothing would come from my throat. Finally I went back onstage and said, "Ladies and gentlemen, excuse me. This has never happened before. The management will give you back your money."'

It was his body's way of telling him that he was close to a nervous breakdown brought on by unhappiness and overwork. 'In this last tour I have slept in 170 different beds,' he lamented. 'And who could possibly put up with that? In Frankfurt, I realized that I was playing Russian roulette and that I had already fired five of the six bullets – the next one would be fatal.' His conclusion was that he had been 'completely drunk on success.'

Wisely, the doctors suggested rest. But, as ever, Julio's remedy for depression was to disappear deeper into his addiction – to toil all the more, to find more success. He retreated, in July 1985, to a peach stucco mansion he had bought in the Bahamas and, though he had declared *1100 Bel Air Place* an experience he would not care to repeat in a hurry, he hurriedly began work on what was to be his second English language album, *Non Stop*. It was the fifty-eighth album of his career and a fitting title for his life.

This time, seventy-five numbers were considered for inclusion into what was to be a ten-track album. Each was selected by Julio, again in collaboration with Ramon Arcusa, with the usual mind-boggling fanaticism.

'We live with a song,' Arcusa told journalist Holly Miller when she visited the retreat. 'We listen to it a hundred, a thousand times. If we don't get tired of it, it's a good song.

A keeper. Sometimes we pull a song from an album at the last minute.'

Plagued by anxieties and depression, as Julio was at this time, the album was to be an agonizing three years in the making. The simplicity of *1100 Bel Air Place*, with its catchy and rather naive songs and its famously familiar collaborators, had worked brilliantly for Julio.

'I thought, God . . . this is not so complicated,' he reflected on the success of *1100 Bel Air Place* in 1992, in America's *Interview* magazine. 'So I said, "Okay let's do another one."'

But *Non Stop* became a much more complicated and vexed process. 'I went to the studio looking for songs. Suddenly, with the band, I started to get more and more confused, to the point where I spent two and a half years in the studio because I was so insecure. I thought everything I was doing was completely wrong.'

The album was released in June 1988. But despite featuring a much vaunted duet with Stevie Wonder, 'My Love', sales somehow reflected the rather negative and depressed spirit in which the album had been made.

'I put the album out and it sold a million and a half, which is good, but it's not 10 million albums, like the first [*1100 Bel Air Place*],' Julio said. 'You know, when you make a big album and the record company is used to selling your albums like crazy and then you have a bad album – a *frustrated* album – the company gets a little . . . They say that was a miracle, the first album.'

The album was frustrated but then so, too, was its creator, on too many levels to number. During the making of *Non Stop* he had released another four albums with relative ease – relative, that is, to the heartache of producing *Non Stop*. One of them, *Sentimental*, had been in French, the other three were in his native Spanish.

The most successful of these had been *Un Hombre Solo* (A Man Alone), which was released in November 1987 and earned Julio a Grammy the following March in the Latin pop category.

'But, then, the irony is that Julio is always at his best when he is singing in his own language about sentiments that relate to his own culture,' reflects Gabriel Gonzalez. 'And I told him this quite recently, after he released his fourth English language album, *Crazy*, in 1994. Julio said he thought it was the best album that he had ever made and I told him that I disagreed. But this is something that Julio does not want to hear.'

For Julio, the success of *Un Hombre Solo* was annihilated by the failure of *Non Stop* and he plummeted still deeper into depression. It was around this time that the suicide attempt stories began to emerge in the press and though Julio later denied them, claiming that his depressions did not take the form of suicidal fantasies, he was, nonetheless, clearly not a happy man at this time.

In England, he gave a series of rather tragic interviews that demonstrated that, though he had more money in his bank than he could begin to count, in terms of his personal stock he was at bankruptcy level.

'I'm shit,' he told journalist Cathy Gubin from *Woman's Journal* magazine. 'I'm not handsome and I have skinny legs. And don't think that the public's impression of me is anything like my private life offstage. Sometimes I just go to my room alone when I've had enough of all the fans; it's then that I have one of my low periods, when it's easy to feel I have nothing.'

The lamenting had already started in America in the months preceding the album's release. 'I'm full of complexes. I'm full of psychiatrists,' he admitted to journalists. He was plagued once more with the psychosomatic problems that so often characterized his depressions. 'It's [as if] you develop a cancer in your brain and you go from doctor to doctor thinking you have a cancer.'

What Julio was suffering from, however, was not cancer at all. It was, rather, a kind of terminal sadness.

Though he had made an album called *Un Hombre Solo*, he was, of course, never alone for very long. During the making of *Non Stop* there had been the usual succession of disposable affairs, but in fairness none were serious contenders for the vacant role of *La Nova Mas*. Then in September 1987, while visiting Rio to promote the album, *Por una Mujer* (For a Woman), he met 19-year-old beauty queen Dayse Nuñes – the first black Miss Brazil. And Julio was, once again, smitten.

By the beginning of 1988, Julio and Dayse had gone public, a fact which seemed to undermine notions that she was ever a real love interest. Still, Julio posed with the beauty for the cameras, announcing, 'I've fallen in love with her.' And for a time they did seem inseparable.

Then in May 1988, just prior to the release of *Non Stop* and in the thick of his depression, Julio confessed that he was seeing a psychiatrist to help him stay faithful to Dayse. 'Blondes excite me,' Julio confessed. 'I find it hard to resist them.'

It was to end badly. By July 1988, Julio was claiming once more that he was celibate. Dayse, in the meantime, who clearly did not have the staying power of certain of the other women in Julio's life, had hightailed it back to her former boyfriend.

'One day I'll fall in love again,' said Julio. 'But when two people love each other they are both in jail. And when I perform I'm so free.'

By August he had dismissed his previous claims of celibacy as 'absurd' – he needed sex like others needed water. Now he was linked with the impossibly pretty – and very blonde – German model, 24-year-old Pitt Kippenhein. Rumours of a Christmas wedding between Julio and Pitt abounded, but they were only ever believed by those who also accepted the existence of Santa Claus.

Why, after all, would Julio marry, when so much of his success was based on the idea of him as a restless lonely man forever seeking the woman in which he could find solace? If he had found her then, surely, the audience would stop buying his records and desert him in droves. It could never be worth the risk.

By the beginning of 1989 it seemed that Pitt was already yesterday's news – just another telephone number on Julio's cluttered Roladex which was said to bear the joyful names of thousands upon thousands of women.

Chapter Twenty

As the sun began to rise on a new decade, so it seemed that the clouds began to lift from Julio's troubled psyche. He appeared happier, more at ease in his own skin, more accepting of his life, despite all its apparent contradictions.

Perhaps it had been the numerous psychiatrists that had helped the tormented singer to find solace or perhaps Julio had been his own physician. If so, then this time he had helped himself with a therapy that seemed to consist of helping others. Julio had become a philanthropist.

It was in the late eighties that Julio, who had always been generous to those around him, now began to see the wider implications of the word charity. Let it begin at home. Why not? But let it also extend to society in general. Then there could be new meaning and purpose to so much wealth and success. The idea became a life raft.

Thus it was that in a short space of time Julio raised money for the victims of Colombia's Nevada del Ruiz volcano disaster and for a South American charity set up to save abandoned children. He became the figurehead of an anti-drugs campaign in France and honorary president of the American Muscular Dystrophy Association.

In much the same vein, March 1989 saw his appointment as special envoy in the entertainment field for UNICEF. He initially committed to thirty concerts, over a period of five years, in aid of the United Nations children's fund. The first two were planned for Madrid and Paris and a third would take place in Moscow.

Posing with beautifully wide-eyed, brown-skinned children in far-flung places was, of course, as good for a singer's publicity as it was for a politician. Yet there seemed something genuine in Julio's attempts to give back some of what life had given to him – something noble and belonging to the right- rather than to the left-hand side of his personality.

'When I became involved I didn't realize how bad things were,' he told British journalist Victoria Freedman. 'You see kids and play with them for a couple of hours, then you leave in your nice car. You feel bad that you can't take them with you. The only thing that can save these kids is governments spending money on them instead of on bombs. But I can give them as much as I can from my concerts and I'll do that until the day I die. It cleans my life, it helps my conscience.'

His conscience about what? About having earned too much? Loved too little? About having devoted his life to the fans who did not know him, at the expense of the people who did and loved him anyway?

He doesn't say. But by 1990, there is new buoyancy in his conversation – put him in the sea, he says, and he will swim and swim until he reaches the shore. He is sounding like a survivor.

Naturally, there are still the daily traumas that are common currency to the rich and famous. Late in 1989, his brother Carlos came up from under to resign his post of chancellor of the exchequer in his brother's crazy kingdom. After nine years at Julio's side, he was sick of all the stress, he said. Sick, too, of the people who surrounded Julio. These, he said, were no good to man nor beast and did nothing but feed his brother's insecurities.

It was doubtless true. But Julio wasn't listening to them anymore. He lent an ear only to his psychiatrist and to his own conscience. He began to use the language of the boxer. He had been down, but never out. He would fight till the day he dies. They would have to carry him from the ring in a box.

The body blows – many of them below the belt – continued. But the brickbats no longer seemed to have the ability to KO Julio.

There were tales once more in the press that Julio's people employ beautiful young models as a photographic prop for Julio. Tell us something we didn't know.

Then, in 1991, Julio found himself named in a Mafia trial by mob supersnitch 'Crazy' Phil Leonetti, who claimed that Julio was cozy with crime boss 'Big' Paul Castellano. He, they alleged, was gunned down on the orders of Godfather John Gotti. Now Julio was said to be in cahoots with the deadly don himself. Just as if.

'Get real,' says Julio. 'Absurd,' says Julio's dad. 'So, Mafia bosses come to my son's concerts and sit in the front row. What can he do if the Mafia like his music?'

What, indeed, for the whole world continued to love it – as the figures proved. Between 1989 and 1990, Julio was said to have earned some $44 million and by 1992 his record sales topped the 160 million mark. He'd made around 70 albums and had 80 hit singles. His sellout concerts were said to net in the region of £6 million a year.

Then, of course, there was the money from all the merchandising – which stopped just short of suntanned Julio dolls, but included sunglasses, ties and watches, plus a women's perfume, 'Only', launched by Julio at a press conference in April 1989. The sweet, sweet smell of success.

At the end of 1992, the statistics churned out regularly by Julio's people read as follows: 400 platinum discs; 1,050 gold; 1 diamond; 3,000 concerts given; 900 TV appearances; 75 countries visited.

Julio continued his endless orbiting of the globe – taking in the last bastion, the People's Republic of China, in 1993. The dragon ceded to him like a lamb and by the beginning of 1996 he was hailed as the country's most popular foreign artist and given China's Golden Record Award to prove it.

Just what he needed – another award. Over the years he had garnered hundreds of them. By 1996, they jostled helplessly for position on the walls of Julio's Miami office, with hundreds of gold and platinum discs.

These – like the record sales, which topped 200 million by 1996 – had been increasing with reassuring regularity in the years after the doomed release of *Non Stop*. Significantly, after the failure of this album Julio returned to the studio to undo its wrongs with another meticulously produced English language album – *Starry Night*. This time Julio was back on top form, doing what he does so brilliantly – caressing the listener with his tonsils. The album, featuring breathless ballads like Albert Hammond's '99 Miles from LA' and Don MacLean's 'Vincent', was an instant hit with the fans and re-established Julio back at the top of the music industry pile.

The album had taken over two years to produce – a period during which Julio was able to release eight albums in his own language, admittedly including some compilations. But there was to be nothing hurried about the English language albums. They were too important and Julio remained obsessed with success in this market. 'To have success everywhere but in America is like a painter without the colour red,' he told American journalist, Edna Gundersen.

Starry Night was released on the Sony label, the company having not only bought CBS out, but signed all its major artists, with Julio number one on the list in the early 'nineties. It was his first effort on their behalf. Rocketing sales figures ensured that they were not disappointed.

Almost immediately, Julio and Arcusa began making plans for their fourth assault on the Anglo-Saxon market. This time it was to be, largely, an album of duets, featuring American icons like Dolly Parton and Art Garfunkel. Sting was also recruited to accompany Julio on the British singer's own song, 'Fragile'.

The effect was rather as it had been when Julio sung 'Summer Wind' with Frank Sinatra on the latter's first album of duets in 1993. It gave Julio enormous credibility. When *Crazy* was released in May 1994, it was suddenly cool to have it in your record collection. The album sold 15 million copies in the US and went platinum in England, too. Despite the usual critical rumblings in Spain's music industry, the whispered accusations that Julio had betrayed his roots once more and sold out, the record too sold out and became number one in the Spanish album charts on the day of its release.

'I felt my music was becoming too obvious and I wanted to try something different,' Julio told British journalist, Jane Moore, during a 1994 interview for the *Daily Mirror*. 'I was very nervous about this album. But it's the most successful one I've ever made.'

By 1994 he was trying something different, it seemed, not just musically but in his life. From 1990 onwards he began making moves to drop the old Latin Lover label – it had ceased to amuse, or to be fashionable. He admitted now with horror rather than pride, that he had made love in seventy-one countries. He had done the sensible thing and submitted to an AIDS test that showed him to be completely free of the disease. As Julio's father always said, there's a guardian angel watching over Julio.

All those years of bed-hopping he regretted as having been 'complete bullshit'. Yet women still intrigued and fascinated him. In 1989 he was said to be besotted with Brooke Shields after she starred with him in a video to accompany his Spanish album *Raices* (Roots). He was also said to have asked her mother for Brooke's hand in marriage. Before long, however, he was back in the arms of old flame Vaitiare Hirshon.

Amusingly, with the stunningly exotic Vaitiare still by his side, early in 1990 he began to talk about deficiencies below the belt. 'I can still do it,' he smiled. 'But not very well. It takes me much longer and I have to really concentrate mentally.'

The self-loathing had turned into something lighter – an endearing form of self-deprecation. He was pretty funny. To prove it, he appeared on the *Golden Girls* in 1992 as Sophia's date and on Dame Edna's show in 1993. He had, he said, been trying to break down the Aussie megastar housewife's door the whole night to make love to her. On past form, it was not out of the question.

But Julio was doing his best to change and the reason for it, he said, was love. Early in 1991 he had met the beautiful 26-year-old Dutch model, Miranda Rynsburger, as he was waiting to board his private jet in Jakarta.

'As soon as I saw her I just melted at her beauty,' Julio said in 1994. 'And the more I got to know her, the more I realized she's beautiful inside and out. She's such a wonderful woman and she's changed me forever.'

Miranda had become that rare thing – someone Julio romanced both publicly and privately. That she had arrived in Julio's life during an era when monogamy was back in style, and at a time when Julio was attempting to lose his Lothario label, may well have been fortuitous. But Julio continues to insist that he loves her deeply and genuinely. She is, he says, the girl who makes his heart beat faster.

She lives with him at Indian Creek, wisely travelling with him, too. They have posed together lovingly in every corner of the world. 'She's very smart, Miranda,' Dr Iglesias affirms. 'Much smarter than the rest.'

Julio has talked to her of children – nothing new in this. But he has also discussed it with members of the press, which is definitely a departure. 'I could perhaps be a father again,' he has said. 'I never even thought I'd hear myself saying that at this stage of my life.'

This time, recreated as he is, almost in the shape of a nineties New Man, he could do it all differently. Change nappies, push prams, pace the marble corridors of his Miami mansion with his crying offspring over his shoulder. Or perhaps not. After all, has Julio really changed that much?

Some of the old ways at least die hard. Recently, for example, at Indian Creek, a hapless TV crew, about to commit the eighth deadly sin of shooting Julio from the left, found themselves sabotaged by the singer's press aide. He leapt across the lawn directly into their field of vision, arms flaying like one of Julio's helicopters. 'Wrong side,' he yelled. 'Wrong side!!'

Later, Julio himself explained to his journalistic guests, 'Darling, I would have to be completely drunk to allow you to shoot me from the left.' Or dead, of course.

Death is a fate which he hopes will befall him at the age of 120 while singing 'To All The Girls I've Loved Before'. Onstage. But that's a long way off. In the meantime, he says, he will never give up. Performing is his life.

What then of the dreams of domesticity. Miranda, Julio and baby – all cosy-cosy at home. Could they ever become reality? 'It would be like opening his veins and letting the blood flow. It would kill him,' says his current production manager, John Searle.

Perhaps Miranda can content herself with the idea that

Julio is finally, at least, faithful to her. Though to be honest, on this subject he is – well – a little vague.

'So are you faithful now, Julio?' he was recently asked by a visiting journalist.

'Yes . . . yeah. But what's faithful? It's not a general word that you can say exactly what it means to everybody. I'm faithful to myself, very much,' he added.

For real straight talking we must head back to Spain. Back to the land of his birth and to the father who created Julio as surely as Geppetto ever fashioned Pinocchio.

At eighty-one he sits beneath the parasol of a Madrid pavement café – wiry, dapper, still playing to win, still playing the field. With eyes magnified behind huge glasses, he gazes at the beautiful young 'girlfriend' at his side. It could be Julio himself in crazy fast-forward.

'Is Julio faithful to Miranda?' he muses and his laughter hangs in the air, like the dying bars of one of Julio's own famous melodies.

'Is Julio faithful to Miranda?' he repeats, just to be sure that he's heard you absolutely right . . . 'Now you're really talking Chinese.'

In the words once more of the song that catapulted Julio to fame. *La Vida Sigue Igual*. Life Goes on The Same.

Index

135, 137–9, 154–5, 158, 163,
177, 188
staff 276
Trasmoz 230, 232
TV
  appearances 81, 235, 238, 243, 292
  Costa Rica, magnate 74
  debut 242
  Festivals 104
  journalist 248
  presenter, Sipl, Virginia 253
  Rome studio 235

UK, Miss 283
Un Canto a Galicia 5, 136
Un Hombre Solo 285–7
Un Truhan 214
uncles 86
UNICEF 290
United Nations 9
  children's fund concerts 290
United States 88, 174, 187, *see
  also* Hollywood; Las Vegas; Los
  Angeles; Miami; New York;
  Texas; Washington
  audience 264
  challenge 236
  English 87
  record companies 175–6
  success 239–45, 267
  tours 138–9, 163
Univision (US Spanish-language
  television network) 259
USA Today 214
Vail, Jim 267
Vail Music Marketing Group 267
Valencia 48, 143
  Mestella Football Stadium 143

Vallon, Larry 241
Valls, Fernando 27–8
Vanity Fair 266
Vargas, Manuela 112
Vargas, Pedro 53, 272
Variety 176
Venezuela
  Caracas 173, 188–9
  Sipl, Virginia 195, 248, 251–4, 275
  tours 133
Ventura, Vivienne 233
Vete Ya 103
Vienna, festival 93
Viña del Mar Festival, Chile 53,
  91–2, 178, 208, 223, 237, 264
Virginia, Wolf, Trapp Theatre 235
Visigothic architecture 118
Vogue photographer 147
von Pfeifer, Baroness 188
Walter, Barbara 243
Washington, White House 235
West Germany, television company
  129
wheelchairs 43
When I Fall In Love 262
William Morris organization 236–8,
  243, 266
Williams, Andy 243
wines 239, 245, 279–80
  private cellars 279
Woman's Journal magazine 286
women 158, 221, 226, 248, 260,
  278–9, 283, *see also* sexual
  encounters
Wonder, Stevie, duet *My Love* 285
work ethic 105
world
  fame 134–5, 236, 268